The Story of
AXMOUTH HARBOUR

Nigel Daniel

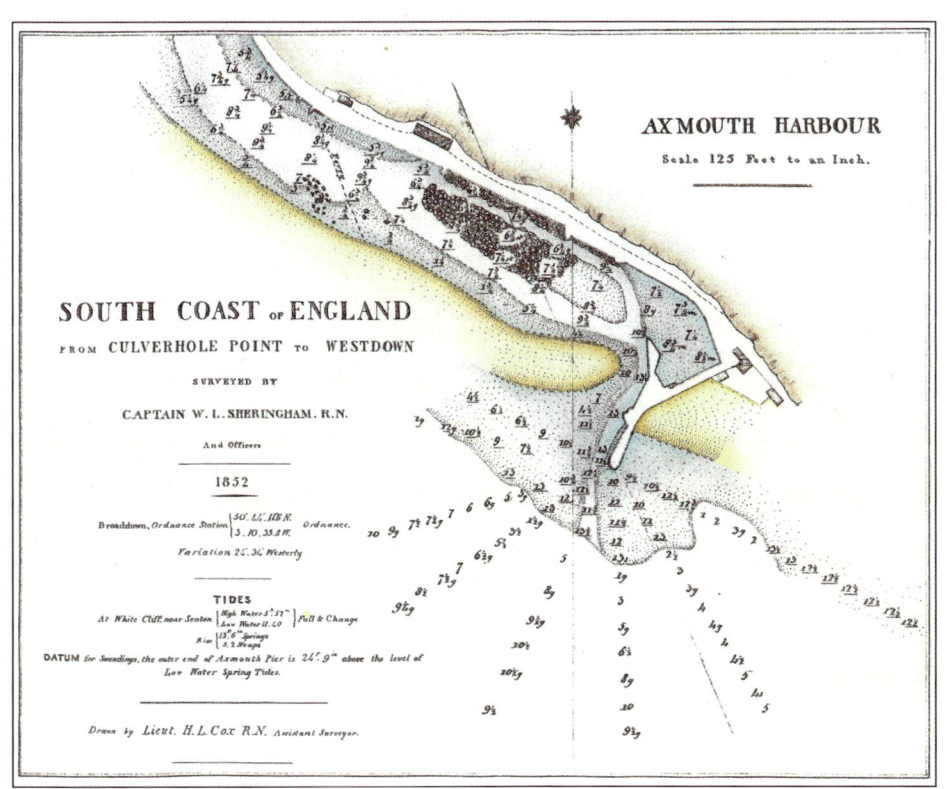

HALSGROVE

Published in 2024

Copyright © 2024 Nigel Daniel

All rights reserved. Apart from any fair dealing for the purpose of private study, research, criticism or review, as permitted under the Copyright, Designs and Patents Act, 1988, no part of this publication may be reproduced, stored in a retrieval system, or transmitted in any form or by any means, electronic, electrical, chemical, mechanical, optical, photocopying, recording or otherwise, without the prior written permission of the copyright owner. Enquiries should be addressed to the Publishers.

Every attempt has been made by the author and publisher to secure the appropriate permissions for materials reproduced in this book. If there has been any oversight we will be happy to rectify the situation in future editions.

A CIP catalogue record for this book is available from the British Library.

ISBN: 978 0 85704 364 1

Halsgrove
Halsgrove House,
Ryelands Business Park,
Bagley Road, Wellington,
Somerset TA21 9PZ
Tel: 01823 653777
Fax: 01823 216796
email: sales@halsgrove.com

Part of the Halsgrove group of companies
Information on all Halsgrove titles is available at: www.halsgrove.com

Printed and bound in India by Parksons Graphics

Contents

The Haven's Evolution — 6
Axmouth Harbour — 6
Brief geological explanation — 7
The once broad haven — 9
The estuary's navigable limits — 12
The entrance to the once broad estuary — 14
First mention of the shingle bank — 16
Early users of the haven — 19
Roman influence — 20

The Medieval Period — 22
The Montebourg connection — 23
Medieval shipping in the haven — 25

Post Medieval Activity — 30
Leland's description of the haven — 30
The first recorded intervention to stem
  the shingle encroachment — 31
Indications of Axmouth's prosperity — 34
Axmouth passes from Royal ownership — 35
Seventeeth century survey of the haven
  activity — 37
The great 'fish' — 40
Reclamation of Seaton Marsh — 40
Continued efforts to reclaim the haven — 43
The Pharos — 46

Nineteenth Century Revival of the Harbour — 49
Construction of Hallett's Harbour — 54
The restored harbour opens — 54
Axmouth Harbour Act — 57
Navigation and pilotage — 61
The 1824 storm — 67
Development and operation of the harbour — 68
Harbour layout – the holding basin — 69
The main quay — 70
The coal wharf — 71
Squire's Lane quay — 71
Village foreshore berths — 73
'Vicarage' quay — 74
Axmouth vessels — 75
Arrivals and departures — 75
Tidal survey — 78
Local cartography — 79
Return of a seafaring village — 80
Axmouth Coastguard — 81
Axmouth Ferry — 83
Axmouth village ford — 84
Axmouth Harbour ford — 85
Reports of storm damage — 86

Commercial Decline — 88
The harbour slips back into obscurity — 88
The English & Bristol Channels Canal — 92
Axmouth Bridge — 92
Trading ceases — 94
Churchyard mooring rings — 96
The wreck of the Berar — 97
Beach trading continues — 99
A period of quiet inactivity — 101
The Halletts last connection with
  the harbour — 103
Waterside Road — 103
Further cliff falls — 103
Several fishery in tidal waters — 105

Change in Emphasis — 107
The first signs of change in harbour usage — 107
World War Two. — 107
Post Second World War — 109
Local fishing fleet — 117
Some notable vessels — 118
The harbour is sold to the local authority — 119
Small signs of improvement — 121
Fishing Rights sold — 123
Swell without storm — 124
Recognition of the harbour's renewed
  importance — 126
Wrecking? — 126
New Axmouth Bridge — 128
Bronze Age sword in Axe — 128
Medieval wreck – the Axe Boat — 128

The Present-day Harbour — 130
Retaining the harbour's natural character — 130
Factors affecting the viability of the estuary — 133
Silting — 133
Flood defences — 135
The harbour and entrance today — 138
Present day activity — 141
Fishing — 142
Leisure activities — 142
Axmouth boat building — 144
Harbour improvements continue — 145
The harbour's future — 145
To conclude — 149

Appendices — 150

Appendix i
Axmouth Harbour – historical time line — 150

Appendix ii — 154
Tidal Notes — 154

Appendix iii — 156
Present day pilotage

Glossary of terms & References — 159

Acknowledgements

Ron Harwood – Local historic pictures and photos.
Graham Myers – Local Axmouth historian – access to extensive research from 19c. *Pulman's Weekly News* and local museums.
Ted Gosling – Local historic photographs.
Paul and Alex Mears – H.J. Mears & Son, Axmouth Boat Builders.
Michael Clement – Local Axmouth historian – Axmouth village history.
Dr Craig Lambert, Southampton University – important information relating to local 14c shipping.
Christies Ltd – Image of Axmouth Harbour by E.W. Cooke, 1861.
Dee Byrne-Jones – Local historic photographs.
Eric Gordon – Axmouth Harbour management & development.
Bryan Davis – Assistance in LiDAR mapping reproduction.
Morag Steven, Eileen Mather, Di Taylor, June Daniel and Sarah Fowles for their support and advice throughout.

Dedication

In writing this book I would like to thank Eric Gordon for his unstinting encouragement. Eric possesses a great depth of knowledge, particularly his understanding of navigation and general seamanship, which is remarkable. He has accumulated a life time of maritime knowledge, stretching back to before his days as a wartime Junior Naval Reserve Officer. Eric's first impression of the haven was many years ago, from the sea during a voyage up Channel. Little did he know that one day, it would become his home port. Like the author, Eric also embraces a passion for local history, particularly that of Axmouth Harbour. Many times, a certain topic concerning the haven's past has been discussed, analysed and put into context, lending further substance to this story. I am most grateful for his support throughout the process of writing this book.

Axmouth Harbour, 1860.

The Haven's Evolution

Axmouth Harbour

Axmouth Harbour lies on Devon's south coast, tucked into the south-east corner of the county. Today's small tidal harbour shows little evidence of its once former historical importance. The history of the harbour naturally encompasses the Axe estuary which historically was of much greater proportions. The natural haven provided sheltered waters for the ports of Axmouth and Seaton to develop within its confines. From earliest known sources, trading was conducted from the estuary at varying levels, which continued throughout its history into the late nineteenth century. The early British tribes traded from the haven; the Roman occupation certainly saw the estuary as a significant trading base. There is evidence to suggest that the Fosse Way, or at least a spur of the important Roman road, terminated on the eastern shore of the estuary. With time, the estuary silted and diminished in size, trade was concentrated towards the deeper water of the mouth and ultimately within the boundaries of today's Axmouth Harbour. Finally trading ceased altogether and, after a period of quiet inactivity, the harbour has gradually taken on a new role, that of providing a base for marine leisure and fishing activities.

Generally, the history of Axmouth Harbour can only be obtained from assorted references contained within other historical records. No one definitive document exists that portrays the history of this once significant port. The more well-known references have come from various sources such as Pulman's *Book of the Axe*, a wealth of local history. The Devonshire Association has published within its *Transactions* two notable essays, Ramsden's *Axmouth Haven* and Margaret Parkinson's detailed *Axe Estuary & Marshes*. Earlier references come from the itineraries of Risdon, Stukely and Camden, but one that stands out is Leland's itinerary written in the 1500s. His account provides one of the earliest descriptions of the harbour, the estuary and its surroundings. And finally, some of the earliest references to Axmouth are recorded in the Domesday survey of 1086. The accounts of those early commentators cannot be verified with any degree of accuracy. However, the picture formulated over the years has resulted in a common theme that prevails throughout the harbour's history. From earliest records, the harbour's viability has struggled against the forces of nature. These physical changes have been brought about by the interaction of coastal erosion, siltation and prevailing climatic conditions. Local traditions have perpetuated the considerable importance attached to the haven. In turn throughout history, they have been endorsed by various antiquarians. Finding such evidence to substantiate the claims is more difficult. Whilst undoubtedly the estuary has provided a base for commerce over the centuries, its overall importance may have been slightly less than traditionally thought. Equally, the demise of the medieval haven has long been attributed to a single catastrophic cliff fall, which in reality is pure speculation, but over time has become the accepted downfall of the haven.

The aim of this book is to draw together those historical accounts, discuss their merits and place them in chronological order. In addition, with use of local knowledge and recently discovered information, to try to fill in some of the gaps to produce a cohesive history of Axmouth Harbour.

This has fulfilled a lifelong ambition. As a youngster interested in local history, there was little detailed information available regarding the haven's past. The very first study of the school library's *Book of the Axe* provided that initial insight. Pulman's references to the harbour offered tantalizing glimpses, hitherto unknown; which in effect inspired the whole process of searching out long forgotten accounts and bringing them back to life. Each thread of information, combined together weaves an interesting passage through time – the story of Axmouth Harbour.

Brief geological explanation

The local geology has influenced the way in which the harbour has transformed from a large open haven to the present day small tidal estuary and harbour. A brief understanding of the surrounding geological processes that have evolved assists in understanding the changes that have occurred. A good visual interpretation of the River Axe Valley geology can be gained from viewing the nearby range of coastal cliffs through which the river and estuary pass. The cliffs clearly reveal the various sedimentary strata bordering the estuary. The unseen geology below the estuary has generally been assumed to conform with the surroundings. More recently, exploratory test drilling into the estuary bed has provided a much more detailed picture of the geological processes that have occurred, chiefly those of erosion and deposition.

Mercia mudstone (formerly known as marl and now categorised specifically as Branscombe mudstone) forms the base to the range of hills bordering either side of the estuary. To the east, Haven Cliff's marl rises approximately 50 metres above sea level. The remaining 50 metres to the summit, comprises Upper Greensand with overlying chalk, ultimately topped with a thin layer of what is referred to as 'Clay with Flint'. To the west, Seaton's West Cliff has less height and is therefore almost entirely composed of marl with a thin upper layer of clay with flint above. The taller cliffs a little further west – White Cliff and Beer Cliffs – are separated from West Cliff by a notable fault and are composed of Upper Greensand with a prominent east facing range of chalk cliffs, containing considerable quantities of flint. West Cliff and Haven Cliff are connected beneath the estuary by the underlying strata of marl. This lies at some depth

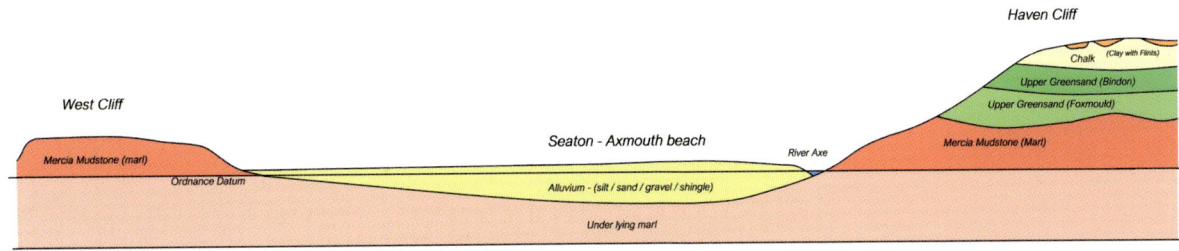

Geological cross section of lower Axe Valley. (Nigel Daniel).

below a significant layer of alluvium, deposited over the millennia and now forming the present valley flood plain.

The Axe Valley was created by ice sheet meltwater eroding the East Devon plateau some 10,000 years ago. This was at a time when sea levels were much lower than at present. The English Channel formed a low lying plain, containing the confluence of the major river tributaries flowing westwards into the Atlantic. A theory has been put forward as to why the Axe Valley appears unusually wide, this in comparison to the size of the River Axe. It is suggested that this may have occurred during the Ice Age, such that a temporary dam was formed across the Bristol Channel by the ice sheet pushing south from the Welsh mountains towards Exmoor. Melt water meeting this barrier, rose and overflowed the ridge just east of the Blackdown Hills, close to Chard. This large volume of water flowing into the Axe Valley caused enhanced erosion, which may explain its excessive width.

Post Ice Age, the melting ice sheet caused substantial rises in sea level and in turn flooded the many river valleys of the south west. The indented coastline produced many examples of drowned river valleys or rias of which the Axe was one. Additionally, the southern part of the UK has slowly sunk as a result of glacial rebound, termed 'isostatic adjustment'. As the ice sheet covering northern Britain melted it released downward compression, resulting in up-thrust of the land mass. This was countered by a rebound effect, causing southern Britain to subside. The process continues to re-align the land mass today, in effect causing a slow apparent rise in sea level irrespective of climatic changes and the minor fluctuations in sea level.

Throughout the Holocene period the area has experienced a considerable rise in sea levels, during which time vast quantities of silt have accumulated in the base of the Axe Valley. This has resulted in an alluvial flood plain and shallow estuary. In conjunction, wave action has caused coastal erosion, forming sea cliffs at the termination of the flanking hills and finally a substantial shingle bank has formed across the entrance.

Silting of the estuary has been the result of three major factors. The first two can be attributed to natural causes; but the third, a comparatively recent event can be attributed to man's intervention. The natural run off and erosion of the hinterland has been the key process of silt accumulation within the estuary.

The River Axe, rises just south of Cheddington in Dorset, some 22 miles from its mouth. Along with its tributaries it has transported vast quantities of silt into the lower reaches. This has formed an alluvial flood plain made up of meadows, salt marshes and mud flats. To a much lesser degree the coastal tidal stream has contributed to silting. Erosion at the base of the cliffs immediately to the west of the estuary has brought sediment into the estuary. During periods of rough weather, wave action has agitated the eroded silt which in turn has been transported eastwards into the estuary on the flood tide. Similarly, the unprotected base of Haven Cliff prior to the harbour wall construction allowed erosion of the soft marl, supplying additional silt, carried into the estuary during each flood tide.

Subsequently the progression of shingle accumulation slowly narrowed the entrance. The build-up may have partly resulted from silt deposited within the estuary. Both elements working together, such that the shingle spit permeated with silt provided a firm base for its continued encroachment eastwards.

Then, finally the effects of human intervention. Reclamation in the seventeenth century, by artificially enclosing the bordering salt marshes (Seaton Marsh) to create pasture land, represented a substantial reduction the size of the tidal estuary, one which had immediate effect.

All these factors have collectively and successively reduced the crucial volume of tidal water entering and leaving the estuary (tidal prism). That volume of water is directly proportional to the size of the entrance channel. The diurnal flood and ebb of the tide ensures the entrance remains scoured. Any reduction in volume caused by silting creates a diminished force; this has inevitably led to the present narrow entrance through which the Axe flows seaward.

The process of silting continues today. Run off from the valley fields, (a considerable watershed) constantly deposits silt into the lower reaches. A large proportion of this silt in spate conditions passes through the estuary and is deposited into the coastal shallows. However, a lesser quantity settles within the estuary, a process that continues imperceptibly year on year.

The growth of the shingle bank slowly limited navigation and hence the harbour's ultimate decline from its early prominence. Many attempts were made to control the adverse effects of shingle encroachment, or at least slow the process by constructing various forms of training walls (piers) at the entrance. Some had limited success, but none was successful in maintaining the early significance of the haven. Today the haven is much reduced in scale and continues to be reliant upon the training effect of the pier, without which shingle encroachment would soon bar the entrance.

The once broad haven

Over the last two thousand years the physical size of the estuary has substantially reduced. Various historians have attempted to define the boundaries, many of which are based on conjecture and speculation. There is sufficient evidence to suggest that during the Roman occupation, the tidal influence extended approximately 3 miles inland. An impression of its extent can be gained by tracing the path of the 5-metre contour on present day ordnance survey maps. The area enclosed by the contour lies generally close to the intersection of the flat alluvial plain with that of the rising gradient of the surrounding hillsides. Using this as an indication the actual head of the estuary would have terminated a little less than a mile north of today's Axe Bridge (A3052).

In detail, by following the 5m contour inland from below Haven Cliff, skirting the east side of the estuary, the contour extends northward through to the village of Axmouth where there is a noticeable indentation. This suggests that a creek extended eastwards just north of the settlement, possibly named *Uxelis* but later known as *Alsemude*, *Axmuda* and then of course Axmouth. This can

Map of upper reaches of tidal Axe. (© The British Library Board Maps OSD 45 Part 4).

be identified today by the low-lying field used for the camp site, immediately north of the Harbour Inn and the church. It would have provided a sheltered inlet within the estuary, an ideal location from which to conduct trade and having the protection of Hawkesdown hillfort immediately above.

Continuing northwards, just past Stedcombe, the River Axe previously flowed close to the eastern side of the valley, providing some credence to the supposed translation of Stedcombe meaning a medieval landing. North of Axe Bridge, the contour diverges slightly to the east, away from the River Axe. This may be the remnants of a shallow creek lying in the direction of Bruckland. The contour then tracks back out into the main body of the Axe Valley to its most northerly extent half a mile south of Nunsford.

One would suggest this was probably the limit of tidal influence – terminating in shallow mudflats and saltmarshes. This also ties in with the river crossing at Nunsford, the old direct route between Colyton and Musbury and on to Axminster. This may well have been the original passage across the river at its tidal limit before Axe Bridge evolved as a lower crossing point. Today the tidal influence during large spring tides still extends approximately half a mile north of Axe Bridge.

The 5-metre contour then returns south and west, but before reaching Axe Bridge it branches briefly north west in the direction of the River Coly. Again, this probably represents a shallow tidal creek extending up to Colyford Bridge.

The contour continues south once more along the old estuary's western shore, with inlets leading off to the west at Cold Lake, Stafford Brook (Red Mead) and the area once known as White Cross; coinciding with the location of the early medieval port of *Fleote* (Fleet). Finally, the contour continues south below Seaton's St Gregory's church, passing Merchant's Roads and eventually terminating at the coast below Castle Hill. Adjacent to this point and some two hundred metres to the east lies the *Barrow*. Some local historians maintain this is a natural marl mound, suggesting it would have formed an island in the estuary's early development. Later, it will be seen that a seventeenth-century document contradicts this, indicating that the Barrow was man made, formed as a defensive position to protect the haven.

The foregoing is speculative, but provides an impression of the estuary's extent from say the third century when the Roman occupation was well established.

A more accurate reflection of the estuary's true extent was recently defined by means of geological survey. In 2008 Winchester University was commissioned by East Devon District Council to carry out a *geoarchaeological study, both to inform the authority on the potential buried archaeological resource in the area proposed for Higher Level Environmental Stewardship, but also to provide information on past environments of the Axe estuary*. The study, Axe Estuary Wetlands – Geoarchaeological Survey – Report No. 0708-14, (AEWGS) was authorised in order to assess the geological make-up and archaeological features within the wetlands. This was deemed necessary prior to greater development of the wetland's nature reserve, including the formation of the Black Hole lagoon.

The study concentrated its work to the west of the Willoughby embankment (the seventeeth-century reclamation bank utilised in the ninteenth century by the railway and presently by Seaton Trams) and the area west of the River Axe above Blackhole Marsh. Starting in the southern-most part of Seaton Marsh, the survey extended northwards through the Blackhole lagoon and finally terminated in an area spanning the lower reach of the Coly. Admittedly, this does not include any part of today's tidal estuary east of the embankment, except for small areas where the tides reach has access.

A series of five survey transects orientated on an east/west axis were laid out across Seaton Marsh, stepped successively from south to north. Each transect had between five and eight bore holes, the first set (T1) were located just north of the new infill development at the southern end of Seaton Marsh. The most northerly one (T5) formed a dog's leg to the east of Colyford Common, spanning the lower reach of the Coly, across the banks of the Axe.

The survey has revealed some interesting results and questions some long-held beliefs as to the extent of the tidal influence extending inland.

As expected, the southern part of the marshes comprised a network of saltmarshes intersected by silted up tidal creeks, bordering mudflats. The results from both Transects 1 and 2 comprise of a considerable amount of marine sand down to a depth of -3.0m OD, the lower stratigraphy suggesting this area was once subtidal.

This changes on reaching Transect 3, north of the Willoughby embankment (now within the Blackhole lagoon), there is no evidence of marine sand, but changes more to estuarine silts and clays. Transect 4, was sited a little further north, near to Stafford Brook at the southern end of Colyford Common, an area outside and to the north of past reclamation activity. Indications show this has remained in the upper saltmarsh zone throughout its history of sedimentation and therefore little changed. Transect 5 represents the zone where intertidal sedimentation has given way to deposition in alluvial sedimentary environments, an indication to the extent of the estuary.

This would imply that the River Axe north-east of Colyford Common was a meandering freshwater river, much as it is today. Floodplain deposition in this area seems to have been on a relatively minor scale at a time pre-dating the Romano-British period. In other words, the lack of intertidal sediments indicates that the tidal influence and therefore the extent of the estuary, appears to be limited to this area.

Thoughts that the estuary extended much further inland would appear to be much less likely. No doubt the Axe was under tidal influence further north but the physical inland size of the estuary would have been much less than originally thought. Equally the same applies to the Coly in that the tidal influence probably extended little further than today's Colyford Bridge (A3052).

With the continuing rise in sea level, the process of 'marine embayment' occurred. This led to the formation of the haven in the

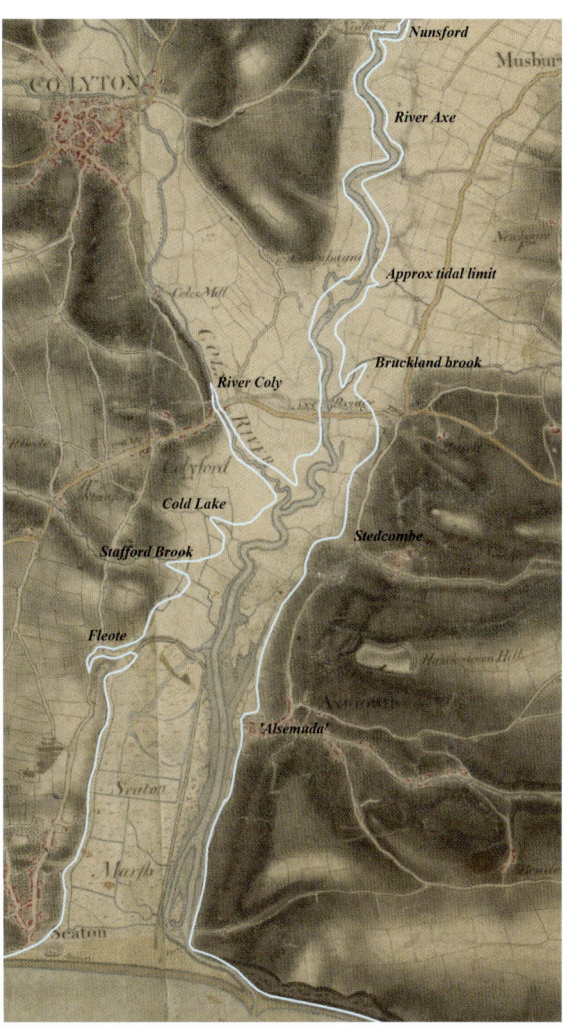

The extent of the early haven. (© The British Library Board Maps OSD 45 Part 4).

lower estuary. Relatively deep water would have formed a useable harbour. Historically this corresponds to the Romano-British and early medieval period.

Moving on in time, the survey geology indicates a relative fall in sea level, where there is a return to saltmarsh from intertidal sediments and mudflats. This comparative lowering may be a result of the shingle spit starting to take effect. Its growing formation would have constricted the tidal flow, reducing the volume of marine water entering the estuary. The reduced flow through a narrower entrance provided shelter for the establishment of salt marsh where once mudflats existed in the southern part of the estuary. This is reflected in the earliest accounts of the haven during the fourteenth century, when the shingle spit encroachment began to affect navigation.

The survey also included some LiDAR mapping which provides detailed topographical features. It clearly shows the system of old tidal creeks within the reclaimed Seaton Marsh. This provides interesting evidence when interpretating historical accounts of the estuary. Unfortunately, recent infill of the southern portion of the marshes now makes it impossible to interpret any topographical features in the area adjoining the back slope of the beach. It is generally understood that the southern part of the marsh was at a lower level being closest to the estuary entrance. Following reclamation, drainage of this area presented many ongoing issues.

The estuary's navigable limits

There are no accurate means of determining the depth of the estuary in those early days. An indication of its navigable depth relates directly to the size of vessels utilising the estuary. Trade was undoubtedly carried out in Roman times, with seagoing vessels capable of voyages beyond the near continent; probably the first such sizeable vessels to use the haven. Roman trading ships typically had a draught averaging around 2 metres, some larger vessels a little more.

The Mediterranean designs tended to be round-bilged in shape and less likely to take the ground, preferring to remain afloat at low water. Roman trading vessels of north west Europe were modified into a more flat-bottom design (Gallo-Romano, Celtic influence) enabling them to cope with tidal waters. To gain shelter within the haven it would have required navigating a reasonable distance inland, clear of the exposed waters in the entrance. Local trading vessels may have evolved further to take advantage of the shallower tidal creeks. The actual limit of navigation is very much open to conjecture – but probably extended no further than 2 miles inland, in reality accessing no further than the medieval ports of Fleote and Aslemuda.

Stukeley, writing in his 'Itinerarium Curiosum', published in 1724, quotes :- *'More inwards, towards the land beyond the great bank of beach, is a marsh which the sea has made, landing its self up when its free flux was hindered. This is full of salt pans, into which they take the sea water at high tides. When they dig these places, they find innumerable keels and pieces of vessels, with nails, pitch and anchors, six or eight foot deep, because it was formerly part of the haven. Anchors have been found as high as Axminster, and beyond it, tho' now there is no navigation at all.'*

Stukely's comment regarding fragments of vessels being found in Seaton Marsh would indicate that a water depth of at least 2 metres existed in the areas where the salt pans were later constructed. Some of these areas can be identified today especially with aid of LiDAR mapping showing the remains of shallow embankments enclosing the rectangular pans. Two specific areas existed, one in the southern area of marsh formerly known as Salt Plot and the other below White Cross at the northern end of the marsh. Importantly the latter is close to the area identified as Flueta, Fleote or Fleet, the early medieval port, pre-dating present day Seaton.

The quote regarding anchors having been found as far inland as Axminster is an embellishment of the estuary's legendary importance. The River Axe at Axminster is some 20 metres above present day mean sea level. Additionally, if one takes into account that sea levels have actually risen and not fallen over the last 2000 years, it makes it even less plausible. Discovery of anchors thought to be left by a vessel would seem unrealistic, although one cannot rule out that they may have arrived there by some other means, a local foundry perhaps?

Pulman quotes in his *Book of the Axe*:- *'The remains of a vessel of about seventy tons were found in the bed of the river a long distance from its mouth. The vessel was of massive build and doubtless of a far anterior date to that of Leland's fisschar boat.'* Similarly, another nineteenth century commentator notes, *'Yet as far north as Musbury archaeologists have found anchors, tree-nails and the keels of pre-Norman ships—one of them over seventy tons.'*

Again, one would suggest this elaborates the haven's importance. Later it will be seen that quotes of this nature have been embellished beyond any archaeological record which exists today. The only confirmed identification of an ancient wreck within the estuary is the 'Axe Boat' (see p.129). This vessel was originally identified in the 1830s and its discovery probably led to a number of misleading quotes such as those above.

The navigable depths within the lower reaches of the estuary are equally difficult to determine. Depths may have been in the order of 3 to 4 metres at low water (Chart Datum) within the main channel. The borders of the estuary would have shallowed into mud banks and mud flats terminating in creeks, with salt marshes reaching inland to the tidal limits. The deeper channels leading to the shore would have provided creeks with suitable shelter that may have allowed access for commerce. Little evidence exists of those early trading locations. Quays and wharfs would have been of timber construction, leaving us with little or no indication today, although archaeological discoveries in the nearby vicinity provide potential clues.

Some indication of the estuary's original depth can be gained by taking a cross section of the valley near to the present-day entrance. If one projects the valley gradient downwards from either side, one could gain an impression of the depth at the intersection located nearer to the eastern side of the valley floor. This point now lies buried beneath overlying shingle and silt. Admittedly, this is a crude estimation of the underlying depth; however, this has been substantiated by more accurate means. A series of test bore holes were conducted by the Axe Yacht Club in 1999. The exploratory drilling was conducted in order to assess the options for retaining works around the perimeter of the AYC mooring basin. Three bore holes were drilled along the western edge of the mooring basin – to the west of the present course of the River Axe. Their location marks historically where the estuary once flowed more centrally in the valley towards the sea.

Each of the core results was very similar, the most seaward borehole was made in a position approximately 100 metres south of Axmouth Bridge, adjacent to the south-west corner of the mooring basin (50°42.207'N 003°03.577'W). The underlying marl bed-rock was detected at a depth of 11.4 metres below Ordnance Datum (OD), or approximately 9 metres below today's low water (LAT). This accurately demonstrates the accumulation of deposition within the original drowned valley. Similarly, the AEWGS Report confirms this, where the marl bed-rock was located 4.0m below OD in Transect 1, only 60 metres out from the original raised shoreline.

The core data recorded from the top of the present-day beach level (6.0m above OD) to the underlying marl (11.4m below OD) composed of the following geological features. Unsurprisingly the upper layers consisted of rounded gravel (shingle), predominantly flint and chert with fine silt and broken shells. This continued down to a depth of 7.4 metres below OD, at which point the gravel became more angular. This demonstrates the depth of accumulated shingle – some 13.4m. Beneath the angular gravel a layer of denser silty clay was identified, separated by a layer of sand before reaching the marl (Mercia mudstone). This forms the original eroded base of the valley floor at a depth of 11.4 metres below OD. The composition would suggest that a sandy sea bed existed over the marl followed by a later gravel deposition. It would appear that the movement and establishment of the shingle bank as it progressed across the estuary mouth, formed over the underlying sand. The presence of more angular gravel at 5 metres below OD may indicate less weathered shingle consistent with a local coastal erosion. Rounded gravel and shingle form the upper layers, visible today as Seaton and Axmouth Beaches. Overall, the depth of accumulated material from present day beach level to the underlying marl is some 17.4 metres.

Clearly the accumulation of such a vast amount of material has occurred over many thousands of years. The shingle movement as described in the mid 1400s was probably the early visible result of a process that had been underway for a much greater period of time. The core samples demonstrate that the eroded depth of the estuary was once much deeper, before the deposition of sand, silt, gravel and shingle. However, the period in which man has had an interest in the estuary's navigation is comparatively short, suggesting that the navigable depth during the period under consideration within this document has never been particularly deep.

Geological cross section showing bore hole data. (Axe Yacht Club).

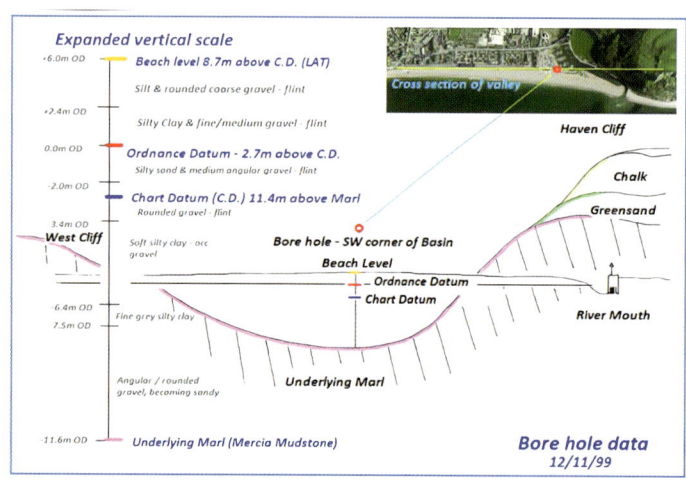

The entrance to the once broad estuary

Assumptions can be made regarding the estuary size and depth but very little can be deduced as to the form of the estuary entrance. Coastal erosion has seen the flanking cliffs recede inland, but the rate at which this occurred can only be estimated. The local coastline is prone to land slipping whereby on the rare occasion large portions of coastal terrain have slipped in one movement over a very short period of time. Whilst during the longer periods between slips the erosion has been much less noticeable; nevertheless, erosion has continued unabated. Undoubtedly one can assume that the estuary extended further seaward than its present termination, but by how much is guess work.

Geologists using Ordnance Survey map data, have calculated the rate of cliff base recession for ten sections between Haven Cliffs and East Pinhay, during the period 1904 to 1958. Recession was greatest in the west, at approximately 0.9m per year, and lowest in the east, adjacent to Monmouth Beach, at 0.1m per year. Clearly this is a rough calculation. Purely by local observations over the last fifty years, there has been nothing like 45 metres of coastal recession! In isolation the more recent Haven Cliff slips of 1877, 1915 and 1931 might have skewed the figures, since the debris of green sand/chalk/marl temporarily extended a considerable distance seaward. The debris eroded away comparatively quickly returning to the original coastline backed by the marl cliff. In reality, by comparing the present base of Haven Cliff with photographs taken one hundred and fifty years ago there has been little recession.

Haven Cliff 1931 – seaward extent of cliff fall debris.

Devon historian J.W.R. Coxhead writing in *Devon & Cornwall – Notes & Queries* (1974) published a brief account titled, *Axmouth Haven – East Devon's Lost Harbour*. His account quotes from Lieut. Col. J. V. Ramsden the geologist who wrote in the *Transactions of the Devon Association* 'Axmouth Haven' (No.77-1945) '*Climatic conditions were very severe during the 14th century. Its heavy storms must have cut away large blocks of the Haven Cliff at Axmouth which had previously acted as an eastern flanking wall to the haven.*'

Coxhead follows this quote with – '*Historical documents tell us that the neighboring port of Lyme Regis was totally destroyed by a terrible storm in the year 1377. It was probably the same storm that carried away a great part of the Haven cliff at the mouth of the Axe*'.

The above sweeping statements have over time become the immortalised cause of the demise of the haven. In fact, there is no evidence that a large cliff-fall to the east of the haven precipitated its decline over such a short period of time or on such a grand scale. The statement somewhat rashly links a nearby single event with a series of differing processes that had been underway for a much longer period. The storms that destroyed the Cobb were down to wave action. Major coastal land slips in the vicinity have usually been triggered by long periods of wet weather causing erosion of sub strata within the land mass. Although the fourteenth century was a period of significant storms, erosion of Haven Cliff to this degree seems improbable.

In fact, it was more likely that the process of longshore drift from the west set in motion the silting of the haven. To suggest that one storm would have carried away the eastern flank of the estuary implies coastal erosion on a colossal scale, even compared with more recent large landslips. Haven Cliff would appear to be eroding consistently in line with the cliffs and coastline to the east. Even the reasonably large slips between 1877 and 1931 had no effect on the river entrance, the debris being eroded and dispersed eastwards by longshore drift.

Ramsden supports his theory suggesting that the 10-fathom contour (18m) has been pushed almost a mile further offshore than

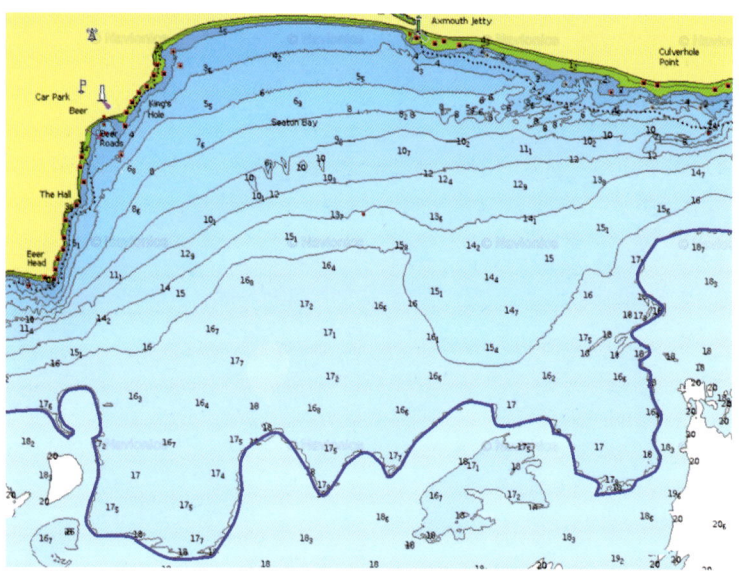

Present day bathymetric survey showing 10fm contour. (Navionics - not for navigation).

elsewhere along the East Devon coast. In reality when viewing the 18m contour on contemporary nautical charts the contour extends seaward across the full extent of Seaton Bay. This suggests the shallowing is as much through the deposition of silt from the estuary, as from a specific isolated rock fall.

Alternatively, if indeed Haven Cliff had extended further seaward, it could be argued that the cliff would have acted more as a barrier to longshore drift. The passage of shingle to the east would have been obstructed by such a prominence, possibly resulting in greater accumulation within the entrance.

Coastal erosion may have had less of an effect than is generally believed; comments of lost Roman towns to seaward of Seaton would seem hypothetical. Ultimately, we are left with no historical accounts of the entrance to the estuary in early medieval times. It would seem logical that although the Axe estuary may have been described as a broad haven, the entrance may have been encumbered with some form of shingle bar from a very early date. It may have been of insufficient size to restrict medieval navigation and equally beneficial in providing a measure of shelter once within. Lack of erosion within the estuary tends to confirm this; the eastern shore shows very little erosion at its base, although its appearance is now considerably changed since the construction of the riverside road (*Waterside*). The western shore shows signs of low degraded river cliffs, especially in the area from Seaton church northwards to White Cross Lane. This may indicate that the river originally flowed more to the west side of the haven (the area of *Merchants Roads*) before being diverted to the east by the shingle spit. Alternatively, the low cliffs could have been a result of sustained easterly weather during the period when the estuary was more open to the elements.

First mention of the shingle bank

Development of the shingle bank was first recorded in the mid-1400s. Already, by this time remedial works were being proposed to counter the effects of the encroaching shingle. It is generally thought that through the process of longshore drift, shingle progressively extended eastwards from the base of West Cliff/Castle Hill, gradually stretching across the entrance of the haven. A long-held belief suggests that shingle first linked up with the Barrow, an island feature on the west side of the entrance. However, evidence now suggests that the Barrow was a man-made feature constructed in the seventeenth century. Notwithstanding, the shingle spit had progressed sufficiently to restrict navigation, with the associated impact on local commerce.

The effect of local longshore drift assumes the lateral movement of shingle from west to east, resulting from the prevailing south westerly winds. The wind generated wave action hits the coastline obliquely, producing an easterly drift of shingle. In the case of the

Axe estuary, one would assume this to be correct since according to most commentators shingle has progressed from west to east since earliest times.

A study of Seaton Bay by civil engineers Lewis Duvivier in 1974 questioned the degree of longshore drift, theorising that shingle within the confines of the bay acted as a closed cell. The study suggested that shingle movement is driven both east and west but overall remains within the physical constraints of the bay. Weighed against this, over the last thirty years there has been a marked reduction in shingle between Seaton Hole eastwards through to the Chine. Coincidentally the reduction has corresponded with the construction of a short concrete groyne at East Ebb rocks in Beer (1990). The groyne was constructed to protect the cliff base and encourage beach accumulation within the cove. It has exceeded all expectations. Beer Beach has more than doubled in width, possibly at the expense of Seaton's western beach, which became much depleted, the groyne effectively cutting off the supply. However, over the last few years shingle has spilled over the groyne and is once again moving eastwards. But strangely it is also accumulating in considerable quantities beneath the cliffs between Beer and Seaton Hole where only rocks and boulders had previously formed the foreshore. Similarly, shingle is accumulating beneath the cliffs from Beer Head in towards Beer Beach; this appears to be a new trend, unrelated to the groyne construction.

It is also noticeable that the orientation of Seaton Beach has changed, such that there is greater accumulation to the east in the area of Axmouth Beach. Fifty years ago, the combined stretch of beach from Seaton Hole to the river mouth formed a crescent shape of almost equal width bordering Seaton Bay. With the reduction of shingle, the underlying marl is more often exposed west of the Chine following stormy weather, leaving the cliffs unprotected. Subsequently rock armouring has been placed beneath the cliff to substitute the protective beach. Similar events were recorded in the 1930s, but after each exposure the beach naturally re-established itself. A more recent study by civil engineers Posford Duvivier suggests that a severe gale in December 1989 transported between eight and nine thousand cubic metres of shingle away from Seaton Hole, distributing it eastwards along Seaton beach. This mass migration of shingle has not returned west to Seaton Hole, although the recent movement from Beer Beach is slowly replenishing it.

Nineteenth century commentators reasoned with the same effect of longshore drift. Peter Orlando Hutchinson (the nineteenth century Sidmouth diarist and artist) is quoted in Pulman's *Book of The Axe*:-
'It will be remembered that all the rivers in this neighbourhood, to the distance of some miles, disembogue in the same manner—that is, that they are bounded on their right banks by a low flat tract, and on their left by the rising cliff. As witness the Otter at Budleigh Salterton, the right bank of which is bounded by a flat expanse like the Marsh at Sidmouth,—the Exe, the right bank of which is occupied by the Warren,—and at Seaton, the Axe, where a great extent of meadow called, also, "The Marsh," or "The Salt Marsh" lies along its margin in the same way.

'Whilst they are all bounded on their left banks by high land and rising hills. This fact is accounted for by the prevalence on this coast of the westerly winds, which are ever driving the breakers on the beach in a slanting direction instead of point blank or at right angles to its range.

And thus the sand and shingle, being obliquely wafted, tend to accumulate on the western side of these deltas, forcing the rivers to the hills on the east, where they escape by narrow channels into the sea. Doubtless, much change has taken place in the littoral features of south-eastern Devonshire. And so great is the power of these apparently impotent streams to produce remarkable changes, that they will sometimes bring about considerable geological alterations, either by the transfer of drift-matter from the inland districts where they take their rise, down to the sea, or by the formation of bars and shoals at their mouths, composed of such drift matter, often vegetable, together with sand, pebbles, silt, shells, or other materials, being, on the other hand, of marine production.' Hutchinson was clearly an advocate of longshore drift, but through whatever reason in the early 1400s the shingle beach started to form such that it eventually created a barrier across the mouth of the estuary, leaving just a narrow entrance beneath Haven Cliff.

The period over which it took place is difficult to determine. It may be such that shingle beaches along this section of Lyme Bay coastline were less extensive during the early medieval period. Perhaps through a result of climatic changes, an extended period of storms and relative stabilisation in sea levels, the right conditions were created for greater accumulation of foreshore shingle. The evolution of Chesil Beach may provide an insight. It was initially formed from predominantly sandy deposits, this during the period of rapid sea level rise at the end of the last Ice Age – 20,000 to 14,000 years ago. The eroded sand and gravel were driven ashore to form a barrier beach completed 5000 years ago. Following this, the relict cliffs of East Devon left stranded by the Ice Age, were re-activated with the relative stabilisation of sea levels. A combination of re-working extensive subtidal debris aprons and erosion of existing cliffs yielded large quantities of gravel. Through longshore drift, the material provided consolidation for Chesil Beach. Similar conditions prevailed locally, resulting in the formation of the shingle spit across the haven entrance.

With the establishment of the protective shingle spit, the estuary would have been less prone to erosion from wave action. The sheltered waters within would create the ideal conditions for greater silting. As the estuary shallowed it would have provided increased stabilisation for further growth of the shingle spit, each effect enhancing the other until we are left with today's much diminished estuary. The effect of shingle overlaying a firmer sandy seabed is still very much evident today. One has only to wade into the sea off Seaton Beach at low water springs to note that within a couple of metres the shingle comes to an abrupt stop, the seabed then continues seaward made up of fine sand.

The present shingle beach is largely composed of flint, chert and some Budleigh pebbles – of which flint makes up the greater proportion. The material is consistent with the flint beds that lie within Beer Head's chalk cliffs and that of the clay and flint layers capping the cliffs further westwards.

In conclusion, rather than Coxhead's suggested single calamitous cliff fall to the east, a slow process, similar to the formation of Chesil Beach, resulted in the formation of the shingle spit. This was a combined process of changes in sea level, coastal erosion and longshore drift. The result was graphically described by Leland in 1542 as a *'mighty ridge'*. The process, first recorded in 1450 was one that had been evolving over a much greater period. It was only when navigation was affected and therefore commerce, that concerns were raised.

Early users of the haven

During the Neolithic period (c.4000 to c.2000 BC) there is evidence of trading throughout the South West. Pottery known to have been produced on the Lizard peninsula during this period has been found in the near locality, suggesting carriage by sea for such delicate items to survive transport. Another theory suggests that the clay was transported to the locality and the pottery made locally. In either case it is highly likely that the goods were transported by sea rather than by land. In return, it is known that flint was traded westwards from the Axe (sourced from Beer cliffs). The type of craft being used at this time would have been primitive small vessels of hollowed log construction, primarily for use in sheltered waters. These subsequently developed into wooden framed craft with hide skins, capable of sea going passages. Planked vessels had yet to fully evolve, although there is evidence of early sewn planked vessels in use during the early Bronze Age (2000BC). Such examples have been discovered in the Humber and Severn estuaries. They would have been used for short coastal passages, propelled by paddle, eventually evolving primitive sails to assist them off the wind. During the Iron Age north west European craft truly developed into the sea going vessels. These vessels were initially of hide construction, such as the curraghs, and ultimately developed into wooden plank construction.

The ancient British tribes of the Dumnonii to the west of the Axe and the Durotriges to the east were probably the first people to make use of the estuary for basic trading. A string of Iron Age hillforts run north from the mouth of the Axe. The first two forts occupy commanding vantage points overlooking the estuary above its eastern shore, Hawkesdown (Hochsdun) fort above Axmouth and Musbury Castle a little further inland. Blackberry and Membury Castles lie to the west and north. A recent find at Hawkesdown discovered seven small lead sling bullets (*glandis*) of mid-first century AD, of a type suggesting an early Roman attack. In addition, the northern end of Seaton Down Hill has traces of early defensive ditches. One would expect that communication, trade and skirmishes would have brought the differing tribes into contact; crossing the estuary would have provided the most direct means for east/west traffic in the lower valley.

It is during this period that the early ridgeways were established connecting established communities, trade centres and ports across southern England. In Edith Brill's *Ancient Trackways of Wessex*, she traces many ridgeways and suggests the Great Ridgeway stretched from East Anglia to Devon. It took the route across Salisbury Plain, through Dorset until it reached the Devon border west of Lambert's Castle. From there it headed south crossing Trinity Hill to Charton Cross, then with an abrupt change to the west it headed along Stepps Lane before either diverging along Barn Close Lane and finally down Squire's Lane to reach the haven or continued down Stepps Lane into Axmouth and thus reaching the upper stretches of the haven.

The Phoenicians are thought to have traded with the South West, especially in the export of tin and copper mined from Cornwall and West Devon. Locally, various sources mention that the Phoenicians had a trading station on the Axe, possibly at the site of Fleote (Fleet) on the west bank. There is little evidence to back this up. One could assume that an open estuary would be attractive to such activities but the Phoenician traders were more interested in the base metals available further west. The Axe whilst offering good shelter, would have been at a disadvantage, being some distance east of the mining activities. Transporting ore by land eastwards to the Axe and bypassing the more western deep-water estuaries of Cornwall and Devon would seem improbable.

Roman influence

One could suggest that prehistory changed to history with the coming of the Roman influence. Archaeology provides definitive evidence of the Roman occupation in the locality, but there also exists contemporary written evidence of their invasion and occupation. The Romans asserted their authority over the local Dumnonii inhabitants and established a period of order and calm. Trade naturally developed in order to service the invaders with all manner of commodities. A natural harbour providing shelter and relatively deep water would have been held in high regard, the Axe estuary was able to offer that facility and provide a base for further expansion westwards.

Significant archaeological remains were discovered in the nineteenth century, consisting of a Roman villa and bathhouse at Honey Ditches. Built on the western shore of the estuary, below Seaton Down Hill, the villa had a commanding view seaward. The site is known to have been occupied previously by Iron Age people with evidence of round houses. The Romans occupied the site in the second and third centuries and constructed a settlement including a villa incorporating a small bath house and a range of barns; the majority of which were surrounded by an enclosure. Much later activity has been recorded from the medieval period, no doubt utilising the benefits of the site and recycling the building material left by the Romans. The Honey Ditches site now lies covered over for preservation and has been scheduled as an Ancient Monument, awaiting further investigation.

A potential Roman landing point on the western shore may well have pre-dated the later medieval settlement of Fleote (discussed later). Located approximately 1 mile inland, a natural creek led into an area known as White Cross. Today the head of the creek lies close to the south of Seaton's new cemetery with little trace following the reclamation of 1660, but LiDAR surveys show vestiges of the old inlet. The advantages of a creek leading off the main estuary on the more sheltered western shore fits well with Honey Ditches, situated close by on the hillside to the west.

Interestingly, the marshes to the south of Fleote, below St Gregory's church are commonly known as *Merchant's Roads*. But in reality, it is the land north of Seaton church adjacent to the marsh that correctly holds the title as shown in the 1840 tithe map. This seems at odds with its nautical associations. The term *'Roads'* infers a roadstead, a safe anchorage, which prior to silting up the marsh would have represented. Perhaps over the years the title became associated with the adjacent plot of land, its true origins lost in time.

A few miles to the east of the estuary further Roman remains have been identified in the form of another villa at Higher Holcombe Farm, just west of Uplyme. Although not directly connected with the estuary it demonstrates the level of Roman activity in the close vicinity.

Then of course there is the Fosse Way, leading south from Ilchester. Uncertainty exists as to whether the great Roman road terminated within the lower reaches of the Axe valley. Fosse Way or not, sections of Roman road lead south from Axminster following the eastern side of the River Axe towards the shore of the old estuary. The most recent evidence of a Roman road was unearthed during the construction of Axminster's southern bypass, just north of Abbey Gate in 1990. It is believed to be the intersection between the Fosse Way and the Dorchester to Exeter Road. A section of incredibly well-preserved paving and drainage channels identified a well-developed road running east west. The road measured 15 metres in width and was thought to have been constructed late in the first century; it may have also been associated with a Roman fort.

Just south of this discovery the present-day OS map identifies a section of the Fosse Way adjacent to Balls Farm, now forming the A358. Similarly, remains were found in the nineteenth century near the gateway leading to Stedcombe House. Again in 1923, during road repairs, a stretch of Roman paved road was discovered opposite the entrance of the old Axmouth vicarage. This all indicates the importance of Axmouth and Seaton during Roman times, significant enough to warrant a direct line of transport from other well-established centres of Roman commerce. Some historical writers have suggested that Axmouth was the Roman station 'Uxelis'. Clearly there is evidence to indicate Axmouth may have Roman connections, yet no further discoveries have been found within the village. Foundations of earlier buildings have been located close to Stepps House, a well-preserved medieval property. Perhaps future research will reveal earlier habitation? In any event, the combined data supports the theory that a Roman road extended south from Axminster terminating at Axmouth.

Pulman quotes of other Roman activity in the area, '*A coin was found in November, 1865, by the workmen who dug the foundations of Bridgwater Place, Seaton, close to the road turning out of the main street to Axmouth Harbour (todays Harbour Road). It was much corroded, but appeared to be a coin of Valens, emperor of the East, who was the son of Gratian and became colleague in the government of the empire of his brother Valentinian in A.D. 364. All of the above is conclusive evidence that the Romans were much involved in the area.*'

The above statement palls into insignificance when compared with a more recent find, the Seaton Hoard. Over 22,000 Roman coins were found in the vicinity of Seaton Down during November 2013 by an amateur metal detectorist. The coins dated from approximately 260AD through to 348AD; they represent the third largest hoard to be found in Britain and the largest fourth century find anywhere in the Roman empire. Conservators continue to work on preserving the coins at Exeter's Royal Albert Memorial Museum.

There have been suggestions that lead mined in the Mendips may have been exported by the Romans from Axmouth. It would have offered the nearest natural harbour on the south coast, if one was to avoid navigating the less than friendly Bristol Channel. The Fosse Way would have provided a viable link between the two for export of this commodity.

The Medieval Period

As the Roman influence ebbed away the power struggles became more localized, developing into conflict between the old established tribes mixed with the rising ambitions of insurgents invading from the continent. The Saxon King Cyneglis of Wessex is thought to have expanded his aims further westward by taking advantage of the decline in influence of the Dumnonii. In 614 a battle was fought at Bindon between the Saxon invading force led by Cyneglis and the Dumnonii led by Clemen. The Saxons took advantage of the recent death of Bledric, leaving his inexperienced son Clemen to defend the Dumnonia lands.

With an overwhelming force, the Saxons soundly beat the Dumnonii at the Battle of Beandun (Bindon), forcing Clemen to retreat back to Exeter. During the late 600s the kings of Wessex pressed home their advantage and conquered the remainder of Somerset. Dorset was naturally over-run, culminating in the formation of an overall Saxon power base within the South West.

An extract from J.W.R. Coxhead's *Axmouth Haven – East Devon's lost Harbour*; written in 1974, *'With the coming of the Saxons the haven would have become even more important, because the manor of Axmouth was one of the estates belonging to the Kings of Wessex. In his Will (made about the year 881) King Alfred bequeathed Axmouth to his younger son, Ethelweard. In the Will the name of the manor is spelt Axanmuthan. In Saxon times Seaton, on the western side of the Axe, was called "aet Fleote" or Fleote (Fleet) meaning a creek or inlet of the sea filled with water at high tide.'*

This would indicate that even in Saxon times the existence of deep-water access to the shore was limited to shallow tidal creeks. The Seaton Tithe Map of 1840 makes reference to a plot of land named Fleet Hill; this appears to be the only clue as to Fleet's (Fleote/Flueta) location. The meadow numbered 616 is located on the small rise of land just to the north of Seaton's new cemetery. Today there is no visible sign of Fleote's existence, however future expansion of the cemetery may reveal some evidence! This promontory is bordered to the south by the now completely silted inlet leading to White Cross with Stafford Brook to the north, adjacent to today's Gravel Lane. The inlet would have provided significant shelter and is the most likely location of the original port of Fleote.

James Davidson (1885) refers to a deed of 1005, probably one of the earliest documents that indirectly relate to the estuary. The deed given by King Ethelred to a thegn named Eadsig, traces the northern boundary of *'aet Fleote'*. Interestingly, it describes a strip of mature saltmarsh bounded by the River Coly and 'Cold Lake' (assumed to be the inlet north of Stafford Brook) extending eastwards towards the estuary. The deed implies that the process of pioneer saltmarsh was well established for it to be included as valuable pasture, even if still affected by the tides. It clearly demonstrates that silting of the estuary and the process of saltmarsh development had already begun along the western shore, even at this early stage. The

Map of Fleet Creek. (© The British Library Board Maps OSD 45 Part 4).

progression from tidal mudflats to sufficiently stabilised saltmarsh was a sign of things to come.

Coxhead continues, *'It is significant that a tradition in the district states that the Danes, led by Anlaf, were able to sail their ships up the estuary as far as Axmouth before landing their army in 937. They were defeated with heavy loss by Athelstan, King of Wessex, at a great battle fought near Axminster.'* Some claim this was the *Battle of Brunanburh*. Both Axminster and Warlake have been the suggested sites of the battle, although contemporary thought now places the battle site much further away at Bromborough on the Wirral.

During the mid eleventh century Godwin, Earl of Wessex was one of the most powerful and influential magnates under the king. In 1046 his son Sweyn *'had done a shameful deed by the Abbess of Leominster'*, and as a consequence of his crime he was outlawed from the country and his lands confiscated. These were given over to his brother Harold (later king) and nephews Bjorn and Asbjorn. Sweyn sought help from his cousin King Sweyn of Denmark, but the king was in no position to assist. To seek vengeance on those who had taken his lands, Sweyn gathered a force at Bruges in 1049. The outlaw then crossed from Flanders to Bosham to 'treat' for the removal of his outlawry and the return of his lands. Neither Harold or Bjorn were willing to accept his demands. Four days of peace were given to the process where Bjorn offered to at least assist in the removal of his outlaw status by going with Sweyn to Sandwich to seek King Edward's pardon. No sooner had Bjorn reached Sweyn's ships than he was seized and dragged aboard, where upon the vessels sailed west to 'Axemouth'. On reaching the haven Sweyn slew Bjorn and buried him 'deep on the shore'. On hearing of this deed Harold retrieved the body of Bjorn and transported it to Winchester where it was buried beside his uncle, King Cnut in the old minster.

The Montebourg connection

Coxhead continues, *'King Edward the Confessor held the manor of Axmouth at the time of his death on 5th January 1066. In the Domesday Survey of 1086, the estate is called Alsemude and formed part of the extensive property held by William the Conqueror. The Domesday survey records:-"It is not known how many hides are there, nor for how much they gelded. In desmesne is half a carucate, and four servants, and eight villains, and twelve cottagers, with six ploughs." The King eventually granted the manor to Richard de Redvers a nobleman of Normandy, who gave it to the Benedictine Abbey of St Mary Montebourg in the diocese of Coutances in Normandy.'* It is more likely that Henry I granted the manor to Richard de Redvers, who in turn founded the abbey and granted the manor to its control. The abbey, ruined and rebuilt exists to this day. Montebourg lies on the east side of the Cherbourg peninsula, coincidently located close by a small shallow creek leading into the Channel.

The Domesday Book completed in 1086 provides extensive records of landholders, tenants, the area of land they owned, how many people occupied the land (villagers, smallholders, free men, servants, etc.), along with agricultural land, woodlands and livestock. The Domesday Book does not provide an accurate indication of the population since it lists only the heads of households, neither does it include clergy or religious houses. This apart it does allow certain comparisons to be made in gauging of the size of local settlements.

The head of Fleet Creek – looking east towards Seaton Marsh, Hawkesdown in the distance.

Chart of the English Channel showing Montebourg. (www.antique-maps-online.co.uk).

Those recorded in the locality surrounding the haven's shores were Axmouth (Alsemude), Stedcombe (Stetcomb) and Seaton (Fleote); each may have been regarded as a port within the haven. Both Axmouth and Seaton are deemed as being fairly large settlements, but Stedcombe was much smaller:

   Alsemuda (Axmouth): 24 households, 8 villagers, 12 smallholders and 4 servants
   Fleote (Seaton): 27 households, 6 villagers, 19 smallholders and 2 servants
   Stetcomb (Stedcombe): 5 households, 2 villagers, 3 servants

The survey gave no indication of maritime commerce, only the land-based taxable income for assessing the geld payment. Irrespective, one can make comparisons within the locality of other known maritime centres, and in doing so one quickly appreciates that both Seaton and Axmouth were of lesser importance. Otterton to the west, recorded 103 households, 16 villagers, 20 smallholders and 33 salt workers, although this also encompassed Sidmouth. Lyme recorded 43 households, 9 villagers, 6 smallholders and 13 salt workers. Strangely there is no mention of salt workers at Seaton although 11 salt houses are listed, a local industry that continued intermittently through to the nineteenth century.

The Rev. O. J. Reichel, in his *Hundreds of Devon*, states: - *'Richard de Redver's charter was confirmed by his son Baldwin, earl of Exeter, between 1142 and 1155 and also his gift of Lodres Priory (just east of Bridport) to Montebourg. In 1207 the men of Axmouth accounted for 20 shillings for having tanneries there. As in the case of the other alien priories (alien priories had their mother house abroad) Axmouth was granted in fee farm to the daughter house of Lodres. In 1285 the abbot of Montebourg was returned as its lord; followed in 1316 by the prior of Lodres. During the wars between England and France, Richard II gave Axmouth to the priory of St. Ann near Coventry, but Henry IV restored it to Lodres. On the suppression of alien priories, Henry V gave it to Sion Abbey in Middlesex'* (now re-built as Syon Park House, the ancestral London home of the Duke of Northumberland). At no time during this period is there any mention of Axmouth haven or revenues derived from it?

Incidentally, around this time according to Rev. George Oliver's *Devon Monasteries*, Axmouth was recorded as being the first location in Devon to produce cider, in the year 1286. No doubt this was brought about by the monks of Montebourg, who having a resident cell in Axmouth would have encouraged the harvesting of apples and the making of cider. It was an important commodity both in terms of a substitute to ale and as a means of payment for farm labourers.

Axmouth farms continued to produce cider until the late 1940s, but interest waned in favour of the readily available modern drinks and the old presses fell into disuse. However, in the late 1970s Axmouth thatcher David Trezise with the help and advice of some of the old estate farm hands rescued a nineteenth-century cider press and a hand operated mill which lay abandoned in a hedge. The restoration of the press and mill has allowed Axmouth to continue its tradition of producing cider, a village activity that still provides much interest amongst the locals today!

The Domesday Book as part of its assessment makes many references to quantities of livestock, such as sheep and cattle at each settlement. Sheep farming featured highly in the district and wool continued to be an important commodity right through the middle- ages. Newenham Abbey had been founded in the year 1246 by Reginald de Mohun, Earl of Somerset. The Cistercian abbey was established just south of Axminster on the eastern bank of the River Axe, not far from the old Roman road. The abbey would have provided a leading stimulus to commerce in the area, especially the emerging wool trade. The advantages of a safe haven close down stream would have been beneficial in the export route to the continent, especially the Low Countries. Significantly in 1315 Newenham, Torre and Buckfast Abbeys were listed as the chief exporters of wool to Florence from the West Country.

Medieval shipping in the haven

Some of the earliest references to maritime trading within the haven can be gained from customs documents termed *rolls*. These ancient sheep skin parchments (sewn together and rolled up, hence the term pipe rolls) record details of trading vessels in order to levy customs for the crown; they also list vessels requisitioned by the crown. The customs rolls specifically catalogue vessel names, type, tonnage, the name of the master and the number of crew. Through a chance enquiry, Dr Craig Lambert of Southampton University has provided a fascinating insight into the haven's medieval shipping, hitherto unknown. It was in 1320 that the Seaton (Seton) ship named *George* was recorded at Exeter engaged in general trading. This is the first mention of an identifiable vessel with its home port within the haven. We are particularly fortunate that Exeter is one of the very few ports that has detailed surviving customs records dating back to the thirteenth and fourteenth centuries.

From the early 1300s the Exeter customs rolls reveal various trading activities, identifying local ships, masters and crew. In September 1330 the Seaton ship *Nicholas* was engaged in the Bordeaux wine trade. Only the name of vessel's master (Cley) is recorded, and at the time she was trading between the English province of Aquitaine and Southampton. During this period there were a number of local vessels engaged in the wine trade, the customs rolls showing that the *George, Nicholas, Blithe* and *Michel* were all trading across the Bay of Biscay. In 1342 the *Nicholas* was recorded as engaged in Royal Service, a means of requisitioning ships to serve the king, usually in foreign expeditions. Vessels in Royal Service were either requisitioned by royal agents or by civic officials under royal command. In either event merchants and ship owners were expected to assist in the provision of ships and mariners to prosecute wars or defend the kingdom. That same year the Seaton ship *George* (transport), Hugh Guilliam master, was arrested along with his crew for withdrawing from Royal Service without authorization whilst in the port of Vannes, Brittany. Earlier in 1311 the *'bailiffs, goodmen and commonality of Seton'* addressed Edward ll to inform him that they were unable to provide a ship as required. Apparently, this was not uncommon in an effort to avoid the loss of revenue from losing a ship into Royal Service; presumably the charter rates dictated were less profitable than the more lucrative cargoes such as wine from Bordeaux.

The next mention of the haven concerns Edward III's expedition, the Siege of Calais in 1346 during the early stages of the Hundred Years war with France. Fortunately, there are accurate records of the number of *'shippes and maryners'* that each Devon port sent to this famous siege, enabling us to compare their comparative strengths and importance. The port of Seaton supplied two ships and twenty-five men, Sidmouth supplied three ships and sixty-two men, whilst Ottermouth is strangely not mentioned (indicating a combination of both ports). Unsurprisingly Dartmouth tops the league with 31 ships and seven hundred and fifty-seven men. One could draw from this information that whilst the haven's importance as a medieval port was less in terms of ships and men supplied, it belied the fact that it was already supplying vessels for Royal Service prior to the event, and had been since the early 1300s. The names of the vessels sent to Calais have yet to be identified, although the Seaton ships *George* and the *Nicholas* were in Royal Service around this period.

Following on from the Siege of Calais, detailed documentation continues to show Seaton vessels were actively involved in Royal Service. In 1371 the ship *Michel*, master John Trying with a crew of 28, was requisitioned by Humphrey, Earl of Hereford, who at the time was ambassador to the Duke of Brittany. It seems the vessel took part in the capture of 25 Flemish ships. In 1375 the Seaton vessels *Michel*, master William Chapeleyn, the *Katerine* and the *George* (each of 30 tons) were requisitioned under the leadership of

A late medieval ship, lying at anchor – Merchant's Roads. (Nigel Daniel).

Sir Philip Courtenay, the Earl of Devon; who became Admiral of the West primarily defending the coast from pirates. The earl also led a number of convoys to Gascony, the dates of which coincide with the requisitioning of these three Seaton vessels. The voyages were noted for fighting off attacks from both marauding pirates and the Spanish.

In 1378 the *Michel* of 50 tons was one of the largest Seaton vessels to date to be requisitioned. She was involved in a raid on Brittany led by Hugh de Calveley, governor of Calais; the vessel's master was John Robelet with a crew of 13 mariners and one boy. In 1396 the cog *Saint Marie* of Seaton was one of the ships involved in transporting Richard II to Calais. This requisition was very brief, lasting just four days; perhaps the vessel happened to be in the right (or wrong) place at the time.

Marie Ann Kowaleski's research published in the *Devon Maritime History* records that between 1390 to 1399 Axmouth was the home port to at least 10 vessels, of which at least one was involved with the Bordeaux wine trade. It is interesting that Axmouth is recorded as their home port rather than Seaton. There are a number of possible reasons for this. Both Axmouth and Seaton may have operated as independent ports within the haven. Equally the reference of Seaton or Axmouth may have referred to the haven in general.

Pew end – East Budleigh church – showing medieval ship.

On the other hand, towards the end of the fourteenth century Seaton may have started to feel the effects of silting within the estuary, whilst Axmouth prospered at its expense. At this time the boundary between the two parishes would have been in mid estuary. As the silt accumulated, pioneer saltmarsh gradually spread eastward from the western bank, eventually leaving only drainage creeks where the streams and brooks entered the estuary. This would have left Fleet literally high and dry along with the boundary forming the west bank of the estuary.

The inlet north of Axmouth's church would have remained close to the main channel of the estuary continuing to provide navigable access. As Axmouth grew in stature, the village clustered around the site of St Michael's church. The building dates back to before the Norman conquest, with its fine twelfth-century zig-zag decoration around the north entrance doorway. Interestingly an early wall painting in the south aisle of church has recently been attributed to the martyrdom of St Erasmus, the patron saint of Mediterranean sailors. (Fergus Cannan).

Kowaleski's research shows that the average tonnage of these vessels, when combined with Sidmouth and Ottermouth was some 32 tons. In comparison, a vessel of 40 tons and over was considered reasonably large. The three ports had nine vessels in Royal Service, six having their home port in Axmouth; these were larger vessels averaging 77 tons. When compared with the likes of Dartmouth which supplied 80 vessels, averaging 109 tons and Plymouth supplying 60 vessels, averaging 99 tons; Axmouth's vessels are understandably less but still larger than the average size vessel of the day. The term ton was loosely based upon the capacity of wine barrels – or tuns – estimated at 252 gallons. From this standard size barrel, the carrying capacity of a vessel was determined, though it was not unknown for vessels to carry more than their specified tonnage to reduce port dues, long before the days of regulation initiated by Samuel Plimsoll.

The size of vessel thus demonstrates that trade was still prospering and the haven had the ability to supply larger vessels for Royal Service. The type of vessels using the haven at this time were typically cogs, the workhorses of the period. They originated in northern European waters, trading with those countries bordering both the North and Baltic Seas. They were not particularly large, being in the range 50 to 80 feet in length and were single masted with just one large square sail. The hulls were double ended and constructed with flat bottoms. This allowed them to dry out, a requirement of many small drying ports, allowing cargo to be loaded and discharged into carts drawn up alongside the vessel. The bottom planking was of carvel construction (edge on edge) and with a tight turn of bilge the planking changed to clinker (lapped) for the vessels' top sides. Both the stem and stern posts were straight, the stem being raked well forward, the stern post raked slightly aft, which supported the rudder. Whilst primarily used for trade, the cog was easily adapted for Royal Service. The fitting of fighting platforms fore and aft gave rise to the term fore-castle (fo'c'sle) and aft-castle. This terminology has persisted throughout history; the fo'c'sle remains the forward stowage area aboard merchant ships and even aboard modern cable layers the working deck is still referred to as the centre castle, its medieval relevance long forgotten. The photograph opposite shows an early representation of a trading vessel, probably a cog; the medieval wall painting can be seen nearby in the nave of Combpyne church.

Smaller vessels known as balingers of clinker construction, were double ended, with the ability to both row and sail, providing transport for small cargo consignments. These single square sail vessels were handy to sail and being of shallow draught were ideal for short coastal trade passages, linking ports within shallow estuaries.

Towards the close of the fourteenth century the Exeter customs rolls detail two Seaton vessels engaged in Royal Service. In 1381 the *Gracedieu*, Bartholomew Cary master, and the *Margrete*, John Deker master, were both requisitioned by the king's agent Sir Thomas de Felton. The vessels were comparatively small at 26 tons each and were engaged in assisting landings in Brittany. Lastly a group of Seaton vessels engaged in the wine trade appear in the rolls of 1392, the *Trinite, Alisote, Barnebe, Welfare* and the *Barge of Seton* are listed. The names of the masters reoccur from earlier records, presumably having completed commissions aboard differing vessels, where the master was not the owner.

The last mention of local vessels being pressed into Royal Service was in 1513 during Henry VIII's war with France. Many ships from the West Country were requisitioned and among the ports mentioned in State Papers was 'Coleton,' Devon. We will come across this opportunistic re-naming of the haven a little later. One suspects it had something to do with the influential families of the Courtenays and Poles residing at Colcombe Castle and Shute.

As an aside, in 1345 Sir Hugh de Courtenay of Colcombe used his influence to restrict fishing on the Axe by obstructing the right of Peter de Brewes of Whitford to sit on the court leet as an elected water bailiff. Sir Hugh had raised a weir so that salmon and other fish could no longer pass upstream. The section of Axe fishery was quoted between *'le Flete de Seton'* and *'le Werpol Super le hull'*. The fishery was common to both the manors of Whitford and Colcombe

Combpyne church – wall painting of a medieval ship.

and would seem to refer to the section of river roughly upstream from the tidal limit to Whitford. *Le Flete de Seton*, indicates the northern boundary of Seaton (Stafford Brook). *'The Werpol on the hull'* presumably refers to a point nearer to Whitford. The tidal fishery below this section was anciently held by the manor of Axmouth and was jealously guarded, a right pre-dating the signing of the Magna Carta.

As a result of the Hundred Years War, Henry V conferred Axmouth upon the newly founded Abbey of Sion in Middlesex in 1415. Ownership of Axmouth thus reverted to an English monastery finally losing its ties with the alien priory of Mountebourg, Normandy also removing any local control from Loders priory under the auspices of Montebourg.

In the 1950 journal *Devon & Cornwall, Notes Queries*, J.W. Ramsden poses a question regarding an unsubstantiated report of the remains of a Tudor ship. The vessel was supposedly found when excavating the foundations for the new iron Axe Bridge in 1837 (replacing the ancient medieval stone bridge and itself now replaced by a very uninspiring concrete span for the A3052).

There appeared to be no information following his query and it is unsure where he gained this report. Such a discovery goes against the results of the Winchester geoarchaeological survey, which concludes that the tidal reaches in this area during Tudor times was at its extreme range with little depth for the navigation of ships.

Post Medieval Activity

Leland's description of the haven

Next follows one of the earliest and most descriptive accounts of the haven as seen through the eyes of Leland writing of his West Country itinerary of 1542, during the reign of Henry VIII.

He says:- *'From Colington to Seton, now a mean fisschar town, scant two mile. I passed over Cole water again at Coliford, I cam to Seton. There hath been a very notable haven at Seton. But now there lyieth between the two pointes of the old haven a mighty ridge and bar of pebble stones in the very mouth of it, and the river Ax is driven to the very east point of the haven, called White Cliff* [Haven Cliff] *and there, at a very small gut, goeth into the sea; and there come in small fisschar boats for soccur. The town of Seton is now but a mean thing, inhabited with fisschar men.*

'It hath been far larger when the haven was good. The abbot of Shirburne was lord and patron of it. The men of Seton began of late days to stake and to make a main wall within the haven, to have diverted the course of the Ax river, and there, almost in the middle of the old haven, to have trenched through the chisille [old English for 'gravel' or 'shingle'], *and to have let out the Ax and received in the main sea. But this purpose came not to effect. Me thought that nature most wrought* [shaped] *to trench the chisille hard by Seton town, and there to let in the sea.'*

To analyse his comments, it would appear that the estuary had already shrunk substantially over the intervening two hundred years since the Siege of Calais. The comment of a *'very small gut'* would not be inappropriate today! However, we do not know what he was comparing the entrance with; if it was some of the larger rivers further west, then it would indeed appear comparatively small.

At the same time Seaton Marshes had yet to be enclosed. The substantial area of salt marsh and network of creeks represented a considerable additional volume of tidal water when compared with today. This especially during spring tides, when at high water the tidal level would have flooded across the marshes towards Seaton church. To accommodate the tidal flow, one could surmise that perhaps the *'small gut'* was somewhat larger than the present-day entrance and of sufficient size to allow more than *'small fisschar boats'* to enter. Although it would have taken skill to enter and leave under sail, oar or kedge, working the tides would have been essential. The tidal stream in the entrance would have no doubt run as strongly as it does today, but with increased breadth, the entrance would have been less hazardous and more workable to larger vessels.

Leland makes no mention of larger vessels or any trade within the haven, although over a century later it was recorded that coastal barges were using the haven. Records are sparse with regard to trade during this period, with little or no evidence of revenue or taxes and the tonnage of vessels was slowly diminishing.

The first recorded intervention to stem the shingle encroachment

In 1450 Bishop Lacy of Exeter, granted forty days indulgence to true penitents who should contribute to the works *'in novo portu in litterore maris apud Seton.'* – the repair of the haven. No indication is provided as to the works resulting from his patronage. Leland's description *'of late days'* would indicate that the intervention occurred within a matter of a few years prior to his visit (c.1542), but equally the comments may be referring to Lacy's works of 1450.

Leland records *'The men of Seton began of late days to stake and to make a main wall within the haven'* and *'trench'* through the beach. This first (or second) attempt would have required extraordinary effort to re-direct the channel by excavating through the shingle bank. It would have been fraught with difficulties working against a combination of environmental elements. The work would have been seasonal, tidal flow and wave action even under benign conditions would have been a challenge (much as it would today). Add to this, floods and the occasional storm and one starts to appreciate what was achieved.

In this particular case the line of the pier probably utilized the marl ledge extending seaward from beneath the western extremity of Haven Cliff. Leland says *'almost in the middle of the old haven'*, so one could surmise that even during this period the haven mouth would have been diverted to the eastern side of the estuary, only forced seaward by the ledge beneath Haven Cliff. The ledge would have provided a firm base, upon which to establish the pier; construction further to the west would have had no firm foundation, since the marl slopes deeply into the old sunken river valley. During construction, excavation of the overlaying shingle must have been a continual problem to drive wooden piles or *baulks* into the underlying marl to gain a firm footing. There must have been many setbacks working against the effects of tide and wave action.

Sketch of haven entrance with impression of 1450 works. (Nigel Daniel).

Sketch from the Cobb map from 1539 showing early construction method. (Nigel Daniel).

The pier functioned as a training wall to concentrate the outflow of the estuary. The accelerated ebb flow scoured the entrance and stabilised the channel. Later attempts describe similar types of work, utilizing local resources, using rocks from the foreshore known as cow stones (typically rounded and weathered boulders of local Bindon limestone). The wooden piles were sourced locally using alder, recognised for its resistance to rot and a resource that grew abundantly along the river courses of the Axe and Coly.

The *main wall* would have been constructed using two parallel lines of wooden piles. These would have been infilled with rocks and boulders to form the pier. It would have resulted in a somewhat flexible structure, able to withstand the force of wave action without the rigidity of a permanent stone pier, the technology of the time allowed for little else. A Tudor map of 1539 shows Henry VIII's coastal defenses, and pictorially illustrates a similar construction method used for the Cobb at Lyme.

Leland's final comment is interesting in that he suggests perhaps the channel should have been *'trenched'* through the beach hard by Seaton town. At the time, the Willoughby embankment had yet to be constructed (discussed later). The estuary would have presented a broader expanse and it may have seemed less daunting to divert the entrance more to the west since the marshes would have yet to colonise the western bank. Today such a project would seem utterly implausible now that the lower marshes have been infilled and developed with housing, car parks and supermarkets.

There is another possible explanation for Leland's comment. Examination of the LiDAR surveys shows a network of creeks and channels within the marsh before reclamation (1660). A noticeable channel flowed through the saltmarsh close to the western shore of the old haven. This channel would have provided access to Fleote and if projected further south would have rejoined the main flow of the Axe towards the entrance, effectively leaving a large mid-stream island. From Leland's perspective, it would have made perfect sense to continue this channel along the western shore *hard by Seaton town*.

Post Medieval Activity

Importantly, Leland's comments refer to the earliest physical interventions in maintaining the haven. From the 1450s onwards, the harbour's viability has relied on various forms of training walls and piers to harness the tidal scour in maintaining the entrance free of shingle; some with more success than others. There are references that the Otter was *'clean barred'* with shingle in the 1400s, although a map drawn in c.1579 shows a pictorial representation with a wooden-piled entrance and ships lying within. The Otter was no doubt experiencing the same difficulties as the Axe, whilst Sidmouth had all but closed being a much smaller river outlet.

There is no record of how long the original pier lasted except for Leland's comment of *'late days'*, perhaps a matter of a few years. Presumably the lack of firm foundations, environmental effects and the extremely exposed position rendered it short lived. The structure would have been relentlessly pounded, requiring continual maintenance and with the added effect of winter floods it is not difficult to understand how vulnerable the pier would have been. The similarly-constructed Cobb was under continual repair, except it was erected on a firm limestone ledge and did not have to contend with the added effects of strong tidal streams. In 1481 it was reported that the Cobb had been destroyed; this same period of storms may well have caused the demise of Axmouth's first pier.

Incidentally, another quote from Leland describes how three years prior to his visit, a storm had washed away a pier at Beer. There would appear to be no other records of its existence, although the author came upon the remains of a pier whilst prawning some years ago at Seaton Hole. The low spring tide revealed a distinct line of rounded boulders forming the foundations of a pier, extending some 50 metres eastwards from the base of White Cliff.

The boulders are set on their ends and appear to be bound together with a form of mortar. The construction is too regular to be a natural feature and typically reflects the medieval method of placing the stones on end. This allowed the structure to absorb the surge effect from wave action where stones placed horizontally tended to be lifted by their impact. This form of construction can be seen today at the Cobb, on the outer face of the landing quay. The photograph (right) taken from the top of White Cliff shows the foundation line, with a seaward turn to the north, adding greater protection to the small harbour. There are obvious difficulties in dating this construction, but being close to Beer and theoretically just within the parish boundary, perhaps this was the pier referred to by Leland in the mid 1500s?

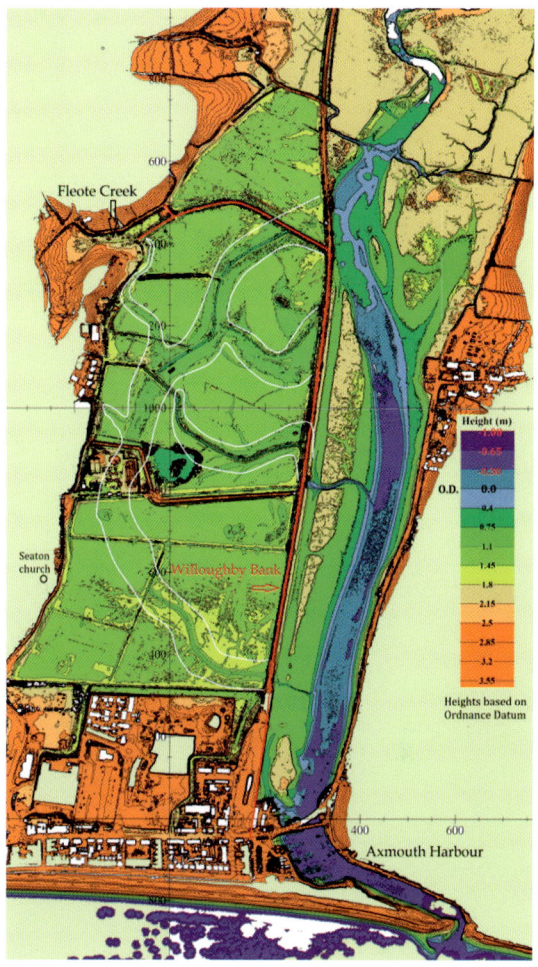

2018 LiDAR map illustrating early creek layout. (Defra).

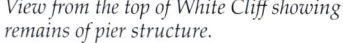

View from the top of White Cliff showing remains of pier structure.

Photo of a large spring tide (4.4m) looking across a flooded Axe Marsh. March 2020 (unexceptional conditions).

Within the estuary Leland describes Axe Bridge and its crossing, demonstrating the extent of silting in the upper reaches of the estuary:- *'The Axe runneth through Axe Bridge of two arches of stone, this bridge servith not to pass over at high tides, otherwise it doth.'* This indicates that the salt marshes on the approach to Axe Bridge were still susceptible to flooding on spring tides. Today during exceptional high tides with no influence from either storm surge or rain, the fields south of Axe Bridge occasionally flood, but not generally as far upstream as the bridge itself. More commonly flooding occurs with heavy rain or high tides coinciding with storm conditions (or a combination of all) which then provides an impression of what the broad haven must have looked like in those early medieval times.

Indications of Axmouths' prosperity

Around this time a number of properties within the village of Axmouth went through a form of gentrification, indicating a certain amount of wealth in the village due to the trading activities of local merchants. Pulman notes:- *'Upon a chimney of an ancient house at the end of the village towards Axminster, is cut a merchant's mark with the initials A.G. and E.W.G, below the line "God giveth all" with the date 1570.'* The faint outline of this mark can still be seen today, high upon the lateral chimney stack of Rustic Cottage, adjoining Corner House on Pound Hill. The initials are believed to belong to Anthony and Elizabeth Giffard a merchant family. Elizabeth was a daughter of the Wykes, an established merchant family who for a time lived at Bindon. On the south facing aspect of the chimney a sundial has been carved into the Beer stone masonry with the hour marks radiating out from the central point. A similar sundial once existed in the central chimney of Combe Farm, but this has long disappeared now that the chimneys have been replaced.

Rustic Cottage.

Combe Farm sundial.

Stepps House, a wonderfully preserved medieval open hall house, similarly underwent gentrification around this period under the ownership of the Mallocks. They had many connections with both local and foreign commerce. It was one of their descendants who invested in the venture to reclaim Seaton Marsh, a scheme that had long lasting and detrimental effects on the haven's viability. Interestingly Stepps House still possesses a carved Elizabethan figure in the parlour thought to represent one of the earlier Mallock merchant venturers.

During this time, the often-quoted tale originated stating that Axmouth possessed 14 hotels! This may seem implausible today but the village is known to have been of larger proportions and the interpretation of *hotel* may have been stretched to include hostelries of a lesser nature, such as cider and ale houses.

Leland described Axmouth:- *'I passed from Seaton at the ebb over the salt marshes and the River Axe to Axmouth – an old and big fisher town on the east side of the Haven.'*

Those few words would suggest that Axmouth was still regarded as a seafaring port of some size, larger perhaps than neighbouring Seaton across the estuary. He does not specify whether he passed over the salt marshes adjacent to the village, or further downstream at the point of the ancient passage. It would seem probable he used the ferry having first traversed along the back slope of the *'mighty ridge of pebbles'*, using the lane which led from Seaton to the estuary. Throughout history the lane has undergone various name changes, with earliest sources referring to it as the *Causeway*. This suggests it was bordered by water on both sides, the sea to the south and tidal salt marshes to the north. As the shingle spit extended eastwards, the lane became more established. Subsequently it was named *Passage Lane*, suggesting a strong connection with the ferry passage – many West Country crossings were known as *'passages'*. With the coming of the railway, unsurprisingly the name was changed to Station Road, although ultimately it has returned to its nautical heritage following Dr Beeching's cuts; in the late 1970s it was renamed Harbour Road.

Axmouth passes from Royal ownership

In 1539 Henry VIII granted the manor of Axmouth to Catherine, his last wife and on her death, it was ceded to Edward VI. Finally, on the 11th of July 1552 the manor ceased to be a royal possession, it was granted by Edward to Walter Erle of Bindon, a groom of the Privy Chamber. This was later confirmed by Queen Mary on her ascending the throne in 1553. Walter Erle in turn left it to his son Thomas who, as will be seen, carried out substantial works to repair the haven. On the death of Thomas Erle, Axmouth passed to the next descendant, Sir Walter Erle who continued with his father's efforts to improve the haven entrance and for a time had a measure of success. Eventually Axmouth and its harbour passed out of the Erles' ownership, when the diarist, Sir Walter Yonge purchased the manor in 1679. His ownership was brief since in 1691 it was sold to Richard Hallett of Lyme Regis, and remained in the Halletts' ownership for the following two hundred years.

Between the years 1575 and 1583 collections were made in churches across the country to assist in the costs of repairing the haven at the mouth of the Axe. Parochial records throughout the land detail the collections. Interestingly the harbour is referred to as *'Colliton haven'* or *'Collyngton haven.'* Some commentators interpret this as showing that vessels had once been able to navigate their way to Colyton. Clearly this was not feasible since the old Colyford Bridge (a chantry bridge accompanied by St Edmund's chapel) was built c.1245! The meandering Coly would have flowed through water meadows much as it does today. At best the Coly may have been navigable as far as Colyford Bridge (today's A3052), below which it would have opened out to a tidal creek, a branch off the main haven; the word *'ford'* is perhaps indicative. 'Colliton Haven' may

Carved Tudor figure in Stepps.

have been a more prominent term to promote interest, utilising the town's reputable commercial interests and market. The project was backed by some local leading gentry such as Sir Humphrey Gilbert, the early pioneer of colonial acquisitions in the New World. Letters patent were obtained and a royal proclamation enabled them to gain contributions beyond the county. Under this mechanism materials such as timber and stone could be impressed as well as labour.

Details still exist of those collections, extracts follow from two such parishes, Eltham, Kent:- *'1575 – paid for making the books of the collections toward the making of Coliton haven and for carrying the said books, two several days to London.'* Culworth, Northamptonshire:- *'1576. It paid for the carriage of the money for Collyngton haven to Northampton, it for a letter that was brought from Collyngtone haven. 1583, It received of ye collection money of Colliton haven.'*

In 1588 a licence was issued to eight West Country merchants one of whom resided in Colyton. It was for a ten-year period of exclusive trading rights on the West African coast between Senegal and the Gambia. It is thought this was chiefly formed to exploit ivory and gold, prior to the formation of the trans-Atlantic slave trade. The involvement of local merchants in such distant enterprises shows the level of activity in the area, associated with the determination to reinstate the haven.

Another interesting anecdote refers to the lantern top of Colyton church tower, having been built as a beacon to seafarers using the haven. Unfortunately, as romantic as this may sound, the lantern tower was built long after any form of significant navigation ceased to reach the upper reaches of the estuary. On a practical note, Colyton church tower is only visible when viewed from the tidal limit of the estuary due to the intervening hill. Its navigational importance would seem somewhat irrelevant having navigated so far inland!

Coxhead writes:- *'Great efforts were made towards the end of the sixteenth century by Thomas Erle Esq., of Bindon to open up Axmouth Haven once more for shipping. He married Dorothy, daughter of William Pole of Shute, on 24th December 1581, and died on 16th March 1597. His work to re-establish a Harbour at the mouth of the Axe was carried on with great energy by his son, Sir Walter Erle, who died in 1665, but all their efforts were of no avail against the power of the sea. Thomas Erle's wife, Dorothy, was the sister of the celebrated antiquary Sir William Pole.'*

Writing in the early 1600s in his *History of Devon*, Sir William Pole similarly records the attempts of the Erle family in their endeavours to open up the haven:-*'It should appear that in ancient tymes, that there had been a haven and shelter for shippes in this place, for besides that it is a fayre bay, defended with high hilles on both sides, Seaton reacheth home unto this mouth of Ax, and anchors and other relicts of shippinge, hath bin found a good space higher up in the land, and tradition holdeth yeat the memorie thereof. At this place the river of Ax unladeth his waters into the sea. And it appeareth that here hath been a haven, by old works and piles, which have appeared by the endeavours of Thomas Erle, Esq., to have made a haven there [c.1583], and Sir Walter his sonne, which continued his father's labors and cost; but it fayled, and their labors and charges were lost.'* Sir William Pole died at Colcombe Castle, just to the north of Colyton, on the 9th February 1635.

It would appear that the Erles took the decline of the haven seriously and obviously expended a great amount of their wealth and effort in trying to maintain the estuary fit for commerce. The spiraling costs of the project may have prompted Sir Walter Erle to enter Parliament in 1614, having secured the parliamentary seat for Poole; a borough barely 5 miles from the family's main seat at Charborough. He brought in a bill 'for the repairing and maintaining of an ancient harbour and a new erected quay or pier near Axmouth', by which a supplementary levy on goods entering the port would be introduced to cover repairs to the pier. The bill received its first reading on 20th April 1614, but on 21st May its provisions were vigorously attacked by the Lyme Regis Member, George Browne, who feared the emergence of an economic rival to his own borough. The measure was committed, with Erle himself entitled as a Dorset burgess to help with its scrutiny, but the bill proceeded no further. It is unclear whether Erle spoke in support of his bill. His only other recorded business was a nomination to help survey old bills, mostly on religious topics which had previously passed the Commons, but not enacted.

Seventeenth century survey of the haven activity

In 1619 the Duke of Buckingham (George Villiers) carried out a survey of Mariners and Ships in South Devon. In this document it was recorded that both Axmouth and Colyton possessed nine sailors. Seaton and Beer recorded 80 and Sidmouth 103, the figures being a combination of sailors, mariners and fishermen. Sailors were specifically identified as those members of the ship's company below the rank of officers, professionally engaged in sailing commercial vessels. This would indicate that Seaton still had strong interests in the haven. Breaking down the total of 80, 16 were masters and mariners, 32 were sailors and 32 were fishermen. Interestingly some of the old local families show up in the records. The Dares were listed under the masters and mariners, a family name that crops up again in future maritime operations associated with the haven. Abbots, Webbers and Westlakes were all listed under the sailors and fishermen. In addition to recording the seafaring population Buckingham also documented local trading and fishing vessels. Those based at Seaton and Beer were as follows:-

Twelve fishing vessels were listed as being between 5 and 10 tons.
Trading vessels were recorded as :- The *Ascension*, 12 tons, the Mary, 14 tons, the *William*, 18 tons, the *Robert & John*, 18 tons and the *William & John*, 24 tons.

Vessels of this size whilst being comparatively small would have been typical of those involved with the coastal trade. Due to their displacement such vessels would have been incapable of working off the beach and were presumably based within the haven. At the time the estuary was variously referred to as either Seaton, Axmouth or Colyton, a result of changing ownership and promotion to gain favour with potential investors. It should be noted that the survey recorded no trading vessels at either Sidmouth or Ottermouth, implying that their trading operations had ceased by this time due to shingle encroachment and topographical changes due to coastal erosion.

A proportion of those mariners and sailors listed would have been involved with the developing Newfoundland trade. In 1623 the Council for New England authorised the formation of the Dorchester Company with the aim of funding an expedition to the colonies, specifically to form an agricultural and fishing colony in

New England at Cape Anne. The colony was initially populated by men from the Newfoundland fisheries who were employed in the shore-based activities of the trade. Sir Walter Erle applied and paid for an indenture to set up the venture. The number of investors grew quickly and not surprisingly involved many local gentry and merchants including Sir William Pole, Walter Yonge, William Fry and Richard Mallock (married to Walter Yonge's sister Joan). The company initially bought vessels associated with the fishing industry. The size is not recorded but presumably they were capable of trans-Atlantic voyages in order to transport the fish back to the West Country. As commented, the Mallock family had a tradition of involvement with various local enterprises. For a time, the family resided at Crabhayne Farm, located not far from Boshill Cross. They variously leased and owned the farm house, as described in two wills, the first referred to John Mallock who died in 1566, the second referred also to a John Mallock who died in 1610. Over three hundred years later the farmhouse was sold by the Hole brothers. At the time a box of old documents was discovered in the attic, some referring to the harbour and possibly the seventeenth-century reclamation of Seaton marshes. These were presumably of some importance, some having wax seals attached, unfortunately they were returned to the box and left in the attic – never to be heard of again.

As part of the Dorchester venture, it would seem that Sir Walter Erle was keen to set up trade utilising Axmouth Harbour and hence his efforts to re-establish its viability. Trade with the new world saw essential commodities transported westward in return for cod and furs. The aim of the Company was not entirely commercial; religious dissenters were at the forefront of the expedition, many originating from this corner of south east Devon which had a strong dissenting influence, centred in Colyton.

In 2005, following erosion of the mooring basin embankment, the Axe Yacht Club (AYC) carried out repair work to stabilise the perimeter bank. In the south west corner, directly down-stream from Axmouth Bridge, erosion had exposed what appear to be some old wooden piles. This particular area has probably not been disturbed since those early attempts by the Erles to improve the haven, some 350 years before. Having completed the repair works, the piles were once again buried beneath the regraded shingle bank and protected with gabion mattresses.

There is no certainty as to when the piles were placed there, but the location and depth to which they were buried would suggest they have been there for some considerable time. The compacted mud flat that once occupied this area was well established even in 1806, as shown by Searle's map.

If one considers the location of the piles, they are directly downstream of Axmouth Bridge with a north/south alignment. This is the most logical position in which to 'trench' a channel through the *'mighty ridge of pebble stones'*, as Leland suggested. Conveniently, the site uses the marl ledge extending from beneath the western extremity of Haven Cliff, providing a firm foundation. Whether the piles represent the Erles' work or the earlier attempt of Bishop

Low water, showing piles uncovered due to erosion.

The original mud flat before mooring basin excavation 1978. (John Chandler).

Lacey is uncertain, but it lends evidence to the reports of those early remedial works to maintain the haven's viability.

Tristram Risdon also comments on the work carried out by the Erle family, writing in 1630, *'The Erles of nearby Bindon, spent much time and most of their fortune in vain to improve the haven. It appeareth that in this place divers works have been attempted for the repairing of the old decayed haven, but of late years with better success than formerly by Thomas Erle, Esquire, lord of the land; who, when he had brought the same to some likelihood, was taken away by death, leaving his labours to the unruly ocean, which, together with unkind neighbours (by carrying away the stones of that work), made a great ruin of his attempt. But the now lord thereof, his son, hath not only repaired the first ruins, but proceedeth on with purpose to bring to pass that which before him his father intended, as well for the general good of the kingdom, as particularly for these parts.'*

Only ten years later we read in Sir William Pole's *Description of Devonshire* 'that it appears by old works and piles that there hath been a haven which Thomas Erle, Esquire, and Sir Walter his son, attempted to renew, but, after much expense, they were obliged to abandon the undertaking.' This indicates that Sir Walter Erle had some measure of success in rebuilding the harbour, following his father's attempt, if only for a short period.

Although the term abandoned was used it may not fully describe the state of the harbour entrance; for it would appear that limited navigation continued. An Axmouth collier, carrying a cargo of culm, was reportedly chased by Turkish pirates in 1638 and narrowly escaped capture. This would suggest that the harbour was still used by sizeable vessels, and for at least one ship it was the home port. Similarly, a House of Commons Journal states that in September 1643:- *'Two prize ships of Axmouth, that are now at Portesmouth, brought in thither with a Corn prize, shall be employed in the carrying of soldiers and other provisions, ready there and assigned for Plymouth.'* This directive was referred to the Committee of the Navy to take action, although it does not describe the circumstances under which the prizes were taken, it implies that Axmouth was still a viable port.

The great 'fish'

'On the 12th of July, 1622, there was a great fish came ashore at Seaton, which was 23 feet and 3 inches in length. The fork of his tail, from end to end, was 5 foot 1 inch. The compass about the middle of the fish was 9 foot and 9 inches. The said fish had no gills, but put out his water at his hole. His fins were like the leather which keeps the dirt from a coach wheel, without any gristles. His skin was smooth as an eel, but exceedingly black, except under the belly which was pale and white. His tail stood not as other fishes, at the ridge bone of his back, but from side to side he had not any scales. His teeth were big, round, and sharp. His flesh was very white, and felt like the fat of pork. There can be no mistake as to the species of fish, it was of the phocena or cetacean (porpoise or whale). Several hundreds of these fish run ashore or are driven ashore upon the Shetland isles at one time. Whether the blowing at the hole is that of air or water is still a disputed matter.'

The beaching of the great 'fish' caused much interest to the local inhabitants who would have rarely if ever seen such a mammal. Peter Orlando Hutchinson recorded a similar event in the mid 1800s on Beer Beach and produced a dramatic water colour of the stranded whale. More latterly a pilot whale was stranded on Seaton Beach in 1979, it was eventually washed into the estuary where it lay on the bank some 300 yards south of the Harbour Inn. Local coastguard Ron Russell reported it to the Natural History Museum. At 16 feet it was thought to be an immature pilot whale separated from its family pod by the prevailing storms. After some days due to the perceived health risks, it was removed and rendered down to become pet food.

Reclamation of Seaton Marsh

The potential for reclaiming Seaton Marsh came closer to reality when the manor of Seaton was purchased by John Willoughby in 1557. The area of marsh was considered to be waste land, but there were commercial advantages in turning it into grazing meadows. His great grandson of the same name eventually progressed the project after resolving legal ownership and tenancy issues. In 1660 Willoughby and his brother-in-law John Mallock of Stepps House, Axmouth, commenced construction of the embankment in order to drain a large portion of Seaton Marsh, some 170 acres.

The alignment of the embankment followed the historical parish boundary between Seaton and Axmouth, following the mid-stream course of the original estuary. The embankment ran north from the back slope of the shingle beach, parallel to the estuary, to a point just north and opposite Axmouth village. From this point it curved away to the west joining with the higher land in the region of White Cross, completing the enclosure. Reclamation further north was impractical since the salt marsh was at lower level and therefore not easily drained. This low-lying area was once a creek leading off the haven to the old settlement of Fleote and through which Stafford Brook flowed into the estuary. Today this area north of the original embankment forms the partially flooded Blackhole wetlands reserve. Stafford Brook now flows along the northern boundary of the reserve before joining the Axe.

The termination of the embankment lies close south of Fleote and *Fleet Hill*. A smaller subsidiary embankment led north, between the main embankment and Fleet Hill, this effectively spanned the entrance to the now silted inlet to Fleote. Historically a mill was located in this area. Seaton's 1840 tithe map names two plots close by as *Mill Hill* and *Mill Close*. The small embankment may have served to impound tidal water for the purpose of driving a tidal mill, equally it may have served to regulate water for the production of salt in the nearby pans. Alternatively, the mill may have been located to the north of *Mill Hill*, where it could have utilised Stafford Brook.

The historian Margaret Parkinson wrote a very detailed account of the reclamation titled, *The Axe Estuary & its Marshes*, published in the *Transactions of the Devonshire Association* in 1985. Initially it describes the formation of the marshes, land ownership issues and then the construction and drainage of the marsh. The account also provides a fascinating insight into the development of salt production along with the advantages of the newly drained pasture land. A brief précis of her account follows concentrating on the construction of the embankment.

The Willoughby embankment constructed 1660. (© The British Library Board Maps OSD 45 Part 4).

The bank was constructed using alder piles driven into the salt marsh close to the parish boundary; a secondary line was placed parallel to these, marking the base. The major part of the bank consisted of alluvial clay excavated from the western side of the bank. The excavations formed the main drainage ditch for the reclaimed marsh, running parallel to the new embankment. The clay was pitched to form a shallow angle on the outer edge to withstand the tidal pressure and surge from swell entering the estuary. The inner edge was pitched more steeply, with the two sides of the embankment separated by a level top, 4 feet in width. The surface was coated with a mixture of lime and chalk and reinforced using stone from *Beer Ebb*. The term *Ebb* crops up in numerous locations along the East Devon coast, describing the seaward extension of cliff rock falls (usually semi-circular) where the softer base material (mudstone) is washed away leaving a seaward crescent-shaped reef of harder boulders (lime/sandstone). Perhaps construction work at the time took advantage of a recent cliff fall. The stone was transported into the estuary using shallow drafted barges. Records show that it took some 300 barge loads to complete. Overall, the bank was finally covered with salt marsh turf in order to bind the protective covering as one homogenous structure. In addition, free stone quarried from Beer was used in the construction of sluices to drain the reclaimed land at low water. The sluice gates were elm boards, manually raised and lowered within grooved Beer stone surrounds, for the purpose of regulating drainage. The bank was obviously lacking in height since in 1669 it was raised to prevent over topping under flood conditions and was not fully completed until 1672.

Margaret Parkinson suggests that the embankment had increased the tidal range within the estuary, causing a funnelling effect. In reality this would not be the case since the flood tide has first to negotiate the narrow entrance, a natural constriction point. Even in the seventeenth century the entrance had become narrower (ref Leland's remarks in the previous century). The entrance regulates the impetus of an enhanced flood tide within the estuary. However, the embankment would have caused an increased flooding risk from spate conditions coming down the river, especially when combined with spring tides. By compressing the estuary, the embankment displaced an area of marsh that would have naturally accommodated a greater volume of water under flood conditions. The loss of this considerable area naturally causes flood water to back up within the estuary, artificially raising the water levels under extreme conditions.

She also suggests that the tidal range has reduced to a meagre rise and fall, which in a way contradicts the previous assessment. This is incorrect. The tidal range has not changed appreciably for millennia. It would seem the tidal range has been confused with the effects of local topography. The height of tides has remained unchanged, only that the low water height within the estuary has changed. Due to shingle encroachment, the course of the estuary has been forced beneath Haven Cliff where it drains over the marl rock bed, which in effect creates a shallow weir at low water. This retains the estuary at a higher level (1.5m) than that of chart datum, effectively causing an *apparent* reduction in range.

The embankment required continuous maintenance due to the effects of erosion caused by swell entering the estuary; the southern section was especially prone to this. Where the embankment terminated into the back slope of the shingle bank, roughly in the area of today's Trevelyan Road, was the worst affected. Even today, under storm conditions a considerable surge enters the harbour and penetrates up stream through the bridges towards the embankment.

Pulman recounts an occasion when severe flooding occurred in Seaton during the great storm of 1824:- *'The sea flowing up the street to such a depth that people had to be rescued from their bedroom windows, and the river and sea met over the Marshes and caused the loss of many cattle, though Seaton suffered little as compared with other places.'* The subsequent raising of the embankment by LSWR successfully prevented any further flooding from the estuary but the marshes continued to be flooded due to problems with the drainage culverts and occasionally by the sea over topping the shingle bank.

As commented earlier, construction of the embankment in 1660 prevented the tidal waters overflowing Seaton Marsh and filling the old creeks and inlets at high water. This quickly brought about a marked reduction in tidal flow within the haven. It is generally thought that a third of the original tidal volume ceased to enter the estuary during spring tides. This had a direct (and detrimental) impact on the scouring effect at the entrance. The reduced flow quickly resulted in a narrower and less navigable entrance channel.

The below LiDAR cross section provides an interesting comparison between the present-day estuary and the reclaimed marsh.

Estuary cross section 500m north of Axmouth Bridge (LiDAR). (Bryan Davis/Defra).

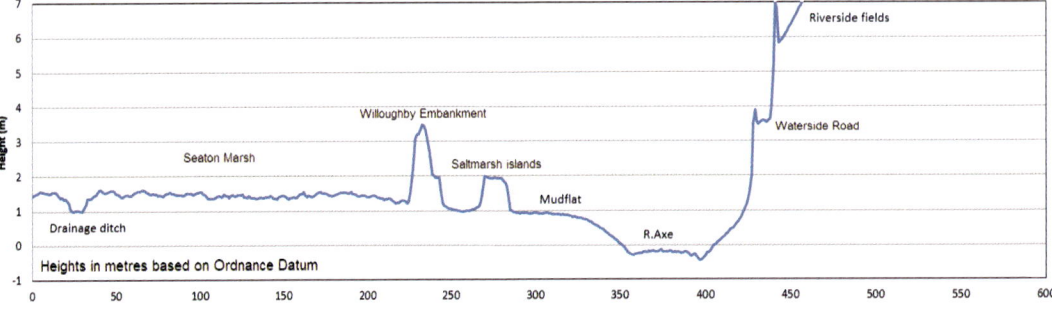

Generally, the level of the marsh to the west of the embankment is half a metre lower than the saltmarsh estuary islands to the east of the embankment. There may be an element of the marshes drying out, but since 1672 on completion of the embankment alluvial silt has been barred from the area; whereas the estuary islands continue to accumulate silt from the river.

What this does demonstrate, is that spring tides would have flowed over the marshes to a depth of half a metre. This represents an approximate volume of 375,000m^3, added to which the volume of the various creeks would increase the total to as much as 400,000m^3. This provides an illustration of just how much tidal volume was lost to the estuary, closer to half the quantity during spring tides.

Sir Walter Erle died in 1665, having survived the Civil War fighting for the Parliamentarian cause. The old medieval Stedcombe House had been destroyed by Royalists in 1644, leaving the estate without a manor house. Axmouth passed to his grandson, whose interests lay elsewhere in the family's larger Charborough estate and was sold in 1679 to Sir Walter Yonge, 3rd Baronet of Culliton. The ownership was short lived, as Sir Walter sold the estate in 1691 to Richard Hallett of Lyme Regis, who rebuilt the new Stedcombe House. Hallett died not long after, leaving his estate to his nephew Richard. In 1699 the young nephew, just twenty-one, returned home from the family's estates in Barbados with his newly wed bride Meliora Hothersall, from another influential plantation owning family on the island. Reflecting this, the Halletts adopted the name Hothersall throughout the following generations.

Stedcombe House.

Continued efforts to reclaim the haven

Despite the reclamation of the marshes efforts continued to reclaim the harbour, the commentator William Stukeley records in his *Itinerarium Curiosum*, published 1724:- *'In the early part of the present century (1700s) several of the farmers of Axmouth and the neighbouring parishes attempted to dig out the ruins of the ancient harbor, and each sent men for the purpose in numbers proportioned to the size of his farm. Considerable progress had been made, when a flood destroyed their labors and the attempt was given over in despair.'*

One can imagine the despair; the harsh forces of nature in such an exposed bay would be ever present. One can only marvel at the persistence over the centuries in the desire to improve the haven, presumably the rewards would have outweighed the expenditure, if only they had the ability to resist the forces of nature. Returning Axmouth to a working port would have benefited a large area of the surrounding hinterland. The only effective way to transport cargo in bulk was by sea. A port in the lower Axe valley would have greatly reduced the distances, rather than utilising the neighbouring ports of Lyme and the Exe; it would have represented a considerable saving in land transportation costs.

Stukeley continues by calling Seaton *'a little village at the mouth of the Axe, it has been a great haven and excellent port, of which they still keep up the memory. The shore is rocky, high, and steep, consisting of the ends of hills which here run north and south. The ground at the bottom, under the rocks, is many. The waves wash it down perpetually, undermining the strata of stone, which from time to time fall down in great parcels.*

At present this haven mouth, which is a good half mile over, is filled up with beach, as they call it — that is, coggles, gravel, sand, shells, and such

The Story of Axmouth Harbour

Example of an old pier constructed with wooden piles and rocks.

matter as is thrown up by the rowl of the ocean. So that the river water has but a very narrow passage on the east side under the cliff. The beach was covered over with papaver luteum corniculatum (Yellow Sea Poppy) now in blossom.' Consistent with previous accounts, the Axe remained diverted to the east below Haven Cliff. It would appear from the following, a substantial pier had been constructed to aid navigation:-

'Just by the present haven mouth is a great and long peer or wall jutting out into the sea, made of great rocks piled together to the breadth of six yards. They told me it was built many years ago by one Courd, once a poor sailor, who, being somewhere in the Mediterranean, was told by a certain Greek that much treasure was hid upon Hogsdon Hill, near here, and that this memorial was transmitted to him by his ancestors. Courd, upon his return, digging there, luckily found the golden mine, which enriched him prodigiously. So that at his own expense he built this wall, with an intent to restore the harbor. The people hereabouts firmly believe the story, and many have dug in the place with like hopes, and, as an argument of its truth, they say some of his family are still remaining that live upon their estate got by him.'

A romantic story, or an element of truth? Stukeley produced a sketch of the estuary at this time viewed from the top of White Cliff. It is reproduced in Pulman's *Book of the Axe*, showing certain details such as the salt pans within the enclosed marsh, the Barrow watch tower and distant Portland. Only if one looks closely, there is a small feature below Haven Cliff, but it does not provide sufficient detail to recognize it as the pier.

Stukeley's lithograph of the haven – 1723. (Book of the Axe).

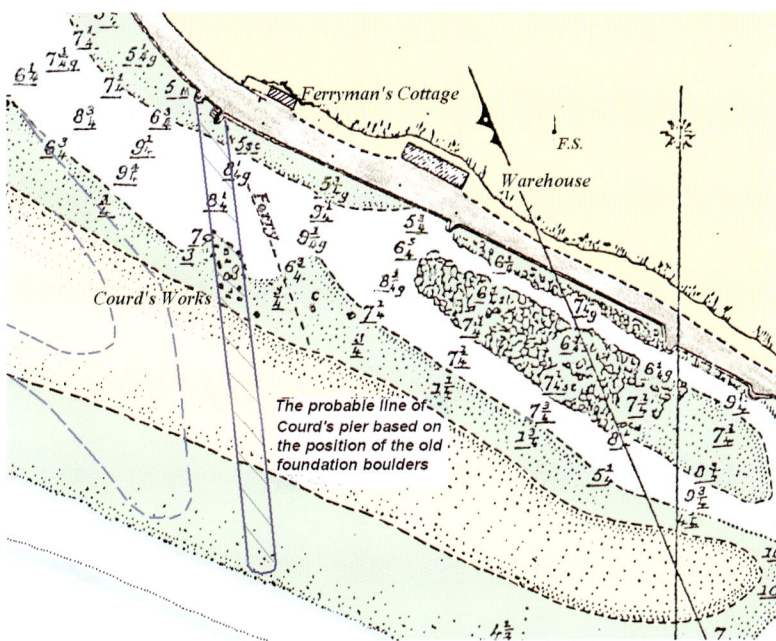

Location of Courd's pier. (UKHO Archive).

I believe there is an element of truth behind the existence of Courd's pier by the very fact that Stukely made such precise observations. The date of construction remains unknown except Stukely quotes it was built 'many years ago' (prior to 1724). This could easily place it during the Erles' ownership, indicating that perhaps it was the remnants of their works. Maybe Courd was the instigator in encouraging local farmers to *'dig out the ruins of the ancient harbor'* and through a mysterious legend his name became attached to the pier?

D.M. Stirling correctly assessed the situation in 1838, writing in his *Guide to the Watering Places on the South East Coast of Devon*:- *'Some remains of the old haven* (pier) *are still visible at the ferry. It appears to have been destroyed as much by the land flood, as the surges of the sea, the river having evidently forced its present channel through the centre of it.'* The comments fit well with more recent evidence of Courd's pier. Until a few years ago, fragments of what was probably this structure could still be seen embedded in the back slope of the shingle bank opposite Harbour (*Ferry*) Cottage. Stirling is probably correct in stating that the pier was breached more by *land flood*. The river channel has been continually deflected eastwards due to the shingle bank. The eventual force of the ebb tide combined with floods would have broken through the pier, leaving a section isolated to become embedded within the beach. During initial excavations of the mooring basin, carried out by the AYC in 1978, large rounded rocks (boulders) were removed from the mud bank. These partially buried boulders were inconsistent with the compacted mud bank of silt and shingle. The boulders were positioned such that if a line were projected north across the present river channel, it would connect with the harbour wall in the vicinity of Harbour Cottage. The pier would have been in line with the main body of the

Photo showing remains of Courd's works. (Michael Clement).

The Story of Axmouth Harbour

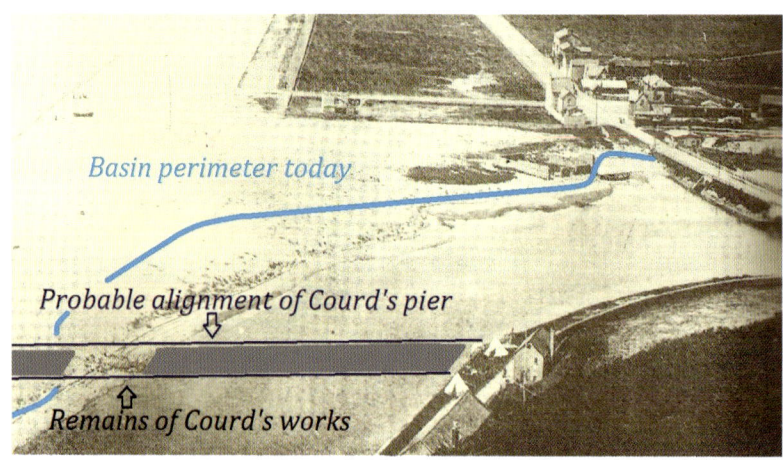

Courd's works from Haven Cliff. (Ted Gosling collection).

estuary to enhance the tidal flow and scour. Additional evidence is shown in both the Admiralty survey of 1852 and in photographs taken at the turn of the nineteenth century. The survey shows the rocks extending northwards from beneath the shingle bank into the river channel. Similarly, photos show remnants of the structure protruding from the back slope of the shingle bank. All these pieces of evidence indicate towards the last remaining remnants of an old training wall.

Strangely enough, if one looks closely at the 1890 OS map, the harbour area in question is titled *'Cords Works'*. Some have interpreted this as reflecting a rope works, perhaps connected with the nineteenth-century harbour development. However, its exposed location on the *'mighty ridge of pebbles'* is certainly no place for such activity. The distant memory of Courd's pier lived on sufficiently long enough to be recorded on the nineteenth-century OS maps – even if latterly misinterpreted!

The Pharos

Stukeley in 1724 goes on to say:- *'On the west side, near Seaton, upon a little eminence, is a modern [17c] ruined square pharos built of brick. They remember it sixteen foot high, and two guns lye there. They say there were formerly many great foundations of houses visible nearer the sea than the present town, but now swallowed up. And in all likelihood there stood the Roman city. More inwards, towards the land beyond the great bank of beach, is a marsh which the sea has made, landing its self up when its free flux was hindered. This is full of salt pans, into which they take the sea water at high tides. When they dig these places they find innumerable keels and pieces of vessels, with nails, pitch, anchors, six or eight foot deep, because it was formerly part of the haven. Anchors have been found as high as Axminster, and beyond it, tho' now there is no navigation at all.'*

In 1872 Sidmouth antiquarian Peter Orlando Hutchinson visited Seaton and commented on the Barrow:- *'We examined the great mound on which a fort was built to keep off pirates. I made it a hundred and fifty paces in diameter and Mr. Heineken made it about twenty five feet high, though they say it was once twenty feet higher. It is a heap of red earth and the esplanade is now carried over it.'*

Pulman similarly writes of the *watch tower* in 1875, referring to it as the Barrow – as though this was a recent name for it. He says, *'it has of late years been almost levelled. I can remember when it was of considerable height and size and had a billiard room upon it on the site of the ancient "pharos." The spot was for centuries used as a battery,*

The Pharos on the Barrow, viewed from White Cliff 1723. (Book of the Axe).

and had mounted guns. In the Calendar of State Papers for 1627 is a memorandum of a requisition to the Council from the Deputy Lieutenants of Devon, praying for "two sakers and two demiculverins out of the King's store," and remarking that "the country has already made bulwarks but wants great ordnance." They add that—" In former times, when there has been hostility between France and England, the bay before Seaton and Sidmouth, being very open, had been fortified with ordnance which is now unserviceable. This ordnance was probably given to the country by Henry VIII." In the year mentioned special attention was given to the defense of Seaton "against pirates and other enemies," and Sir Walter Yonge records in his Diary, under the date of June, 1627, that "there were, by consent of Sir Edmund Prideaux, Baronet, Sir William Pole, Mr. John Drake, Mr. Fry, and myself [Sir Walter], warrants granted out for assistance in the said fortification, namely—the first week Colyton hundred to send thirty men for every day; the next week Axminster hundred were to send thirty men for every day; the third week Hemyock hundred twenty men for every day; the fourth week Halberton hundred were to send twenty men for every day; and the fifth week Bampton hundred to send twenty men for every day; but for those who would not or could not come conveniently, being far distant, that they send after the rate of 8d, for every man per diem, and we of these parts would procure men in their places.'

Incidentally there would appear to be some confusion in the foregoing since Walter Yonge the diarist (1579-1649) was not titled, but his son Sir John Yonge was knighted in 1625 and became 1st Baronet of Culliton in 1661. The hereditary title lived on through his descendants which included the succession of a further two Sir Walters, the 2nd and 3rd baronets.

An interesting footnote within Walter Yonge's diary edited by George Roberts in 1848 casts doubt over the origins of the Barrow.

The long held belief that it was a natural feature is contradicted by the following – *'The great mound of earth thrown up on this occasion in order to the erection of a fort on the summit, stands on the broad shingle beach, a little to the eastward of the seafront, if it can be said to possess, of Seaton.'* George Roberts commented – *'By corruption it is now called The Burrow, instead of its correct appellation The Barrow. No one knew in 1845 how it came there, which proves how tradition often fails to perpetuate the recollection of really important transactions. The Barrow cost £241.'*

Walter Yonge wrote this note in 1627 indicating that the Barrow was indeed *'thrown up'* to accommodate a fort, the ancient pharos mentioned by Pulman. This contradicts many contemporary quotes which assume the Barrow was a natural feature. Perceived thought being that it formed an island just east of the western cliffs and was subsequently linked up by the eastward encroachment of the shingle bank. Again, this demonstrates how unsubstantiated accounts become engrained in local history!

Today the Barrow is a sad reflection of its former glory, the inland slope of the mound has been removed for the worst kind of 1960s development and public toilets have been built within it. The rise still provides a commanding view of the bay, but many years have passed since it presided over the entrance to the estuary. Undoubtedly the 'pharos' offered protection to the locality and guidance to shipping using the haven. Unfortunately, no records survive of any active service. It would appear that it led a very quiet life and that maintenance was not high on the list of priorities! Notably the Barrow in Victorian times changed its name to the *Moridunum*, in support of Seaton's claim to the Roman station. To assert its 'entitlement', *Moridunum* was spelt out in black pebbles inserted into the seaward-facing wall of the Barrow. Since that time, it has gone through a process of accommodating various shelters, from the initial elaborate Victorian pavilion to more modest structures, the last being a brick-built shelter of particularly ugly design, fortunately now removed – all a far cry from the Haven's guardian Pharos. An aerial photograph of the Barrow taken in 1925 shows a very regular semicircular shape inconsistent with a natural feature.

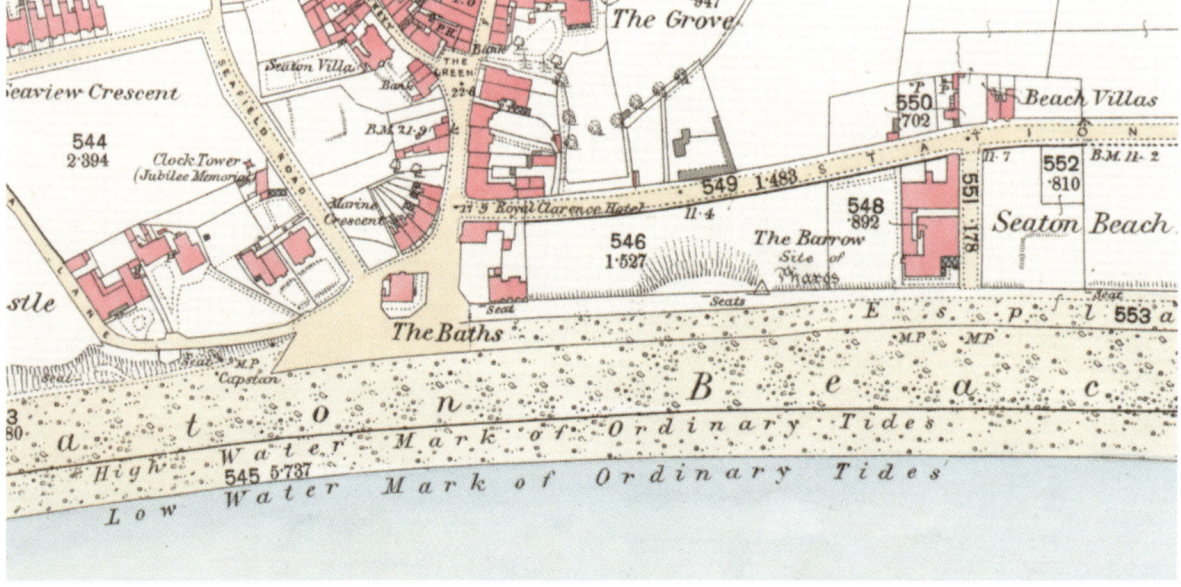

The original mound forming the Barrow – latterly the Moridunum. (National Library of Scotland).

Nineteenth Century Revival of the Harbour

By the end of the eighteenth century plans to develop the harbour had once again generated local interest, driven chiefly by the import of coal. The new proposal was ventured by the incumbent lord of the manor John Hothersall Hallett of Stedcombe, his ancestor, Richard Hallett having acquired the manor of Axmouth from the Yonges in 1691. The Halletts had made their wealth as merchants trading from Lyme, which was closely associated with their lucrative sugar plantations in the West Indies. The slave trade was at its height and huge fortunes were made as a result of it. A notable memorial survives in Axmouth church to the memory of the Halletts, dated 1749 quoting their association with the *Barbados Isles*. The Halletts' wealth was initially aimed at rebuilding Stedcombe. The old medieval manor house had been ransacked, burnt and raised to the ground during the Civil War. The new house is believed to have been built around 1697, although recent thoughts may place it slightly earlier. Whilst not a large country house, its symmetrical proportions sit well in the entrance to the combe, having a commanding view across the upper reaches of the estuary.

There are a number of anecdotes associated with Stedcombe. A local legend records that a certain Jew was murdered by the owners of the house during the 1700s. His faith would not permit interment in Axmouth churchyard so he was buried in the small woodland at the top of Stedcombe vale adjacent to the Lyme Road and which still retains the name of Jew's Plot. The result of this evil deed was a curse on the owners. The Jew would return and seek vengeance at the pace of one stride a year by which time they would be removed from the house. Presumably this has been fulfilled since the Halletts have long since gone!

Stedcombe's symmetrical shape has often been associated with Stephen's Ink, the profile likened to an ink pot. This association came about through a suggested family connection (a nineteenth-century owner was Sanders Stephens), implying the ink pot was modelled on the shape of the house. Another, that the building was a *calendar* house, having 52 windows and 360 panes of glass. Sadly neither are true.

More than a century passed before the Halletts took an interest in reviving the harbour. The effects of the Industrial Revolution were being felt even in this quiet corner of East Devon, resulting in an ever-increasing demand for coal. But the harbour had declined further; at times the tidal cycle was restricted to spring tides, due to the shingle spit encroachment. The Halletts recognised there was an opportunity to revive the harbour on a sound commercial basis. The following account from Pulman demonstrates the dire situation facing the haven.

'Prior to the erection of the pier, about 1803, [1809] the river did not regularly flow into the sea but remained kept back like a three-quarter tide and overflowed a portion of the Marsh, now lets at £7 to £8 an acre, and then for five shillings only. It was not only unproductive but rendered the

The Story of Axmouth Harbour

Searle's Map of 1806 – enlarged river mouth view (note, the Battery). (© The British Library Board Maps OSD 45 Part 4).

neighbourhood unhealthy and "agueish," as before mentioned. Even at high tides the stream had a flow at its mouth of not more than four or five feet, and at other times the water percolated through the shingle, as the Char does at Charmouth.' Under such circumstances, with the estuary maintained at a higher level, it would have been impossible for the reclaimed marsh to drain, especially the lower south east corner. The culverts beneath the embankment relied on the tidal cycle in order to drain at low water. Rain water and various streams emptying into the marsh would have been unable to drain, resulting in stagnant watercourses, producing Pulman's *'agueish'* conditions.

Pulman's account was written some seventy-five years later. How this information was passed on over that period is unknown. What it does illustrate is the perilous state the haven was in. If blocked on occasions to this degree it would have effectively allowed only spring tides to flow into the estuary, demonstrating how broadly the situation had deteriorated. No doubt during flood conditions the shingle would have been flushed out of the entrance, allowing the 'normal' tidal cycle to scour the channel. But without any form of training wall the entrance would have been susceptible to the vagaries of wind and swell, allowing the formation of an obstructing bar.

The production of salt would also have suffered as a direct result from the reduced flow – an industry totally dependent upon the daily influx of salt water entering the estuary. With the water level held back *'like a three-quarter tide'*, the estuary water would have become brackish until such time as the water broke through the shingle to resume the normal tidal cycle. Production of salt ceased in the late 1760s, indicating the minimal tidal ebb and flow.

With the river flowing into the sea close beneath Haven Cliff it would resemble the River Otter in its present-day state. The shallow Otter channel is much affected by the prevailing wind and sea state and has no permanent direction. Similarly, the Axe having no training wall would have relied on the unprotected base of Haven Cliff to provide limited seaward deflection of the ebb tide.

The encumbered entrance is clearly shown on Robert Searle's map of 1806 where the channel tended to flow more to the east than at present, with an extended shingle spit on the west side running parallel to Haven Cliff. Occasionally the entrance forms as such today, especially during neap tides when combined with heavy seas or a ground swell. The wave action and lack of scour allows the build-up of shingle to obstruct the channel. Fortunately, this lasts for only brief periods, the onset of spring tides and the training effect of the present-day pier, soon scours the channel. However, without a pier it is easy to imagine the situation described by Pulman. Left in this choked state, the estuary would suffer more readily the effects of silting. The residual seaward flow either passing over a much shallower entrance or 'percolating' through the shingle would promote silt to settle more readily in the reduced flow. This would accelerate the whole process, critically reducing the tidal volume, so essential to maintaining a clear entrance. Upstream Searle's map shows a significant channel running to the west of the large lower

View from Haven Cliff 2002 – extensive easterly bar.

saltmarsh island, possibly indicating the old channel prior to the 1660 reclamation. The map also shows within the northern section of Seaton's reclaimed marsh, the remnants of a distinct channel. Prior to reclamation this would have provided access to Fleet (Fleote) and Merchants Roads.

An interesting account describing the mouth of the Axe was written by the eminent Swiss scientist and geologist Jean Andre de Luc. He settled in England around 1772 and soon after was welcomed as a Fellow of the Royal Society. De Luc carried out a geological study of the south coast, (*Geological Travels – Vol 3*) which incorporated the section from Axmouth to Lyme Regis, prior to the famous landslip of 1839. On 6 July 1806 he took the opportunity to view the coastal geology from seaward in a small sailing craft accompanied by John Hothersall Hallett, whose father (Richard Hothersall Hallett) he stayed with at Stedcombe House. What follows is an interesting and accurate account of negotiating the harbour entrance just prior to the construction of Hallett's pier:- *'It will now be seen in what manner all the ridges of hills on this part of the coast are terminated towards the sea. Mr. Hallett had been so good as to have in readiness his own boat, with a sail and oars, to carry us to observe the coast on the eastern side, and his eldest son, Mr. John Hallett, accompanied us as our pilot. Though the tides have little influence within this filled up gulph (estuary), because of the narrowness of the channel which the Ax has preserved through the high beach. The river itself is so small, that, in common seasons, when the tide is out, the channel contains too little water for the passage even of a boat. It is necessary to wait for high water and if the wind sets in from the sea, the moment of the turn of the tide must be taken, in order that its current may assist in going down the channel.*

We took this moment accordingly for our embarkation, there was little wind, but a strong surge was coming in towards the coast, which would have rendered our passage dangerous, if we had waited any later. Sometimes a wave entering the channel lifted us up, and drove us backward; then, after it had passed, we dipped rapidly forward, and had there been less water, the boat would have been split or overset on the gravel. When we had gained the open sea, we had very pleasant sailing.'

The voyage continued along the coast to Lyme, viewing with geological interest the cliffs of Charton and Pinhay. De Luc then went ashore at the Cobb before returning to Axmouth – *'We reimbarked at about four o'clock to return to Axmouth; but when we arrived there, the tide was still low, and there was not sufficient water in the Ax to allow our boat to enter. We landed therefore on the strand, and followed this small stream across the beach, within which I saw it flowing on a bed of gravel covered with aquatic plants; a proof that, notwithstanding its inundations, it does not excavate this bed.'* Similarly, today, during settled summer weather if the channel remains stable, green seaweed (*Ulva Compressa Linnaeus*) takes hold on the loose shingle bed as it flows seaward. *'But where it crosses the beach, the case is different; for I was told by Mr. Hallett, that sometimes, after a long continuance of high winds from the south-east, a part of this bank was carried away and its gravel dispersed around over the bottom of the sea. With the first strong south-westerly wind, the waves brought it back, when, if the Ax happened to be low, it entirely closed the mouth of that river. It then discharged itself only by filtrating through the gravel, till it was again sufficiently swelled by rains to open a new channel.*

The place, however, since I observed it, has been guarded against this effect of the sea. I have lately heard that Mr. John Hallett, who was so good as to be our pilot in this little voyage, has secured a passage for boats in all seasons, by forming a permanent channel for the Ax across the beach, and defending it against the action of the sea by a cob like that at Lyme; a method which I saw afterwards employed in other places.'

A fascinating account of the river mouth prior to the construction of Hallett's pier, one of the very few that actually describes the outward passage in a small vessel. De Luc's account was translated from French and printed in England during 1811. Similarly, today navigation of the entrance requires strict observance of the tides! With a favourable wind direction and sufficient rise of tide I have often sailed (instead of rowing) my Axe One Design in and out of the harbour, but a healthy respect for prevailing conditions is essential if one is to avoid a situation so adequately described by de Luc! On his departure de Luc continued his travels westwards. His local guide Mr Tucker took him down to the beach where he boarded another vessel to take him along the coast to Otterton. Mr. Tucker pointed out the mound of red marl, the *Barrow* to his patron, who thought it part of the underlying strata. He may have held different views if aware of Walter Yonge's seventeenth-century account suggesting it was man made.

Recently discovered records show that a number of commercial vessels continued to be owned locally prior to Hallett's development of the entrance. This indicates that possibly during the late 1700s and into the early nineteenth century small coastal vessels were still able to access the harbour if on a limited basis, maybe during spring tides only. Many small sloops and cutters from as little as 20 tons to 50 tons were in local ownership. Such family names as Dare, Good, Gush, Head, Hammett and Miller occur frequently. What was noticeable with the coming improvements to the harbour, those same local ship owners slowly increased the size of their vessels, trading up from sloops and smacks to brigs and schooners, as will be seen later, all taking advantage of the improved facility.

During 1806 moves to revive the harbour were reported in the local press: *'A respectable meeting of gentlemen and inhabitants of the neighbourhood was convened by the lord of the manor of the adjoining parish of Seaton. At which a practical scheme was proposed for the recovery of the ancient haven. Although universally approved as a work of great public utility the design was not adequately supported. Subsequently however John Hallett Esq, lord of Axmouth in a most spirited manner commenced the work and has in a very ingenious way constructed and completed a commodious harbour in the mouth of the Axe capable of admitting vessels of 150 tons burden.'*

Although Richard Hothersall Hallett was still effectively lord of the manor (died 1814), the proposed revival of the port was initiated by his entrepreneurial son John Hothersall Hallett, who effectively took charge of the project. Revival hinged on improving access to the haven. Also taking into account the back drop of the continuing Napoleonic wars, Britain had just inflicted a decisive victory over the combined fleets of France and Spain at Trafalgar, and perhaps this provided greater optimism for safer trade within the Channel.

Revival of commerce was the overriding factor in restoring Axmouth to a working harbour but, primarily it was the import of coal, a proposal keenly supported by local merchants and gentlemen. This vital commodity had become invaluable with the coming of Industrial Revolution, but even the rural areas had come to appreciate the benefits of the new source of fuel, hitherto relatively unknown in the area. Coal was used in many local applications, one of the more important was the production of lime. There were many lime kilns in the locality and a number were set up close to the harbour. These have now disappeared with little trace, except for references to them on the old village maps. The remains of one such kiln can still be seen in the under cliff at the base of Haven Cliff's chalk outcrop, the blackened stone showing where the open kiln once operated. Another was constructed at the base of the cliff, close to the WW2 pill box at the harbour entrance.

Prior to the harbour's construction coal was imported by trading vessels beaching on the open foreshore, a hazardous operation, or by labourously transferring their cargo at anchor. Smaller barges would then be beached to discharge their coal onto the foreshore or brought into the river at high water. The advantages of a sheltered harbour from which to operate were clearly desirable to local ship owners.

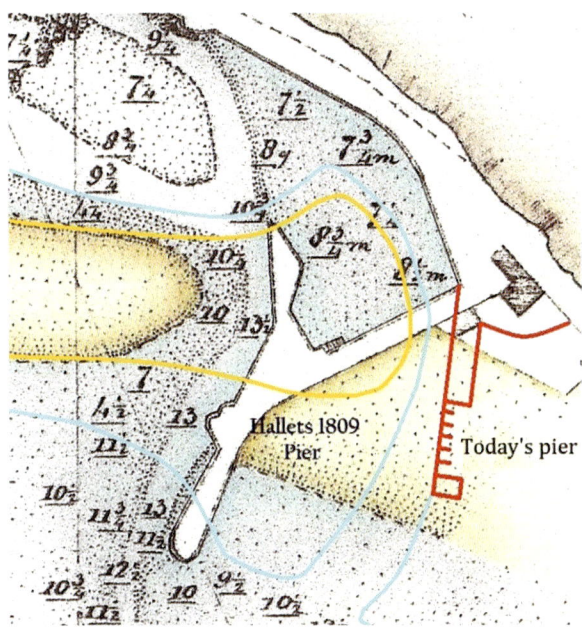

Hallett's pier design – the entrance channel today follows the line of the inner wall as seen on the right. (UKHO Archive).

For this to happen the entrance channel had to be stabilised both in direction and depth. The only practical way was to provide a training wall (pier) to direct the ebb flow, maintaining a scoured entrance.

There is no evidence of who designed the pier and holding basin, but costs were recorded, the sum of five thousand pounds is quoted by Pulman. Construction took place between the years of 1806 and 1809. A case note written in 1809 on behalf of J.H. Hallett described the harbour and its trade, with the clear intention of formalising harbour charges under a regulatory harbour authority, allowing provision for harbour maintenance. This culminated in the Axmouth Harbour Act, but not until 1830.

Within the notes the harbour entrance is described prior to 1809, before construction of the pier. The depths in the mouth were recorded as 12 ft 'pools', interspersed with shallows of only 4 feet even at spring tides. Additionally, up until 1806, an area of shallows some 200 yards within the entrance restricted navigation to all but very shallow craft (described as 'light boats'). This area of shallows would have been either the marl ledge extending south across the inner harbour channel (known today as 'The Rapids'). More probably it referred to the remains of Courd's pier, which similarly extended across the channel a little further upstream, effectively creating a shallow weir. Removal of both would greatly improve access to the estuary. In 1806 the only vessels using the harbour were Hallett's own fishing boat and occasionally other small 'skiffs' and 'sloops' entering for repairs by the Seaton shipwright John Ackerman. No doubt local ship owners if unable to trade regularly from Axmouth were at least able to keep one ship repairer in business.

Hallett broke with the tradition of trying to force a channel through the shingle beach within the middle of the Old Haven. Instead, he utilised the now deflected channel running beneath the unprotected base of Haven Cliff. An old untitled oil painting believed to date from the late 1700s shows the much older harbour wall terminating just downstream of Harbour Cottage (the old Ferryman's Cottage). The wall was the remnant of those earlier attempts by either the Erles, or more latterly Courd at which point an older pier projected south through the shingle bank.

Construction of Hallett's Harbour

Hallett's plan extended the old harbour wall beyond the Ferryman's Cottage, protecting the base of Haven Cliff. The wall terminated at the location of the present-day harbour mouth. From this point Hallett then built the pier seawards, but approximately 100 metres to the west. The pier was built such that it was detached from the harbour wall except for an interconnecting arm to the east, which formed the holding basin.

The design may have been partially dictated by local conditions. Constructing the pier to the west of the river channel and initially detached, would have allowed the tidal flow to pass temporarily undisturbed between it and the cliff base wall. We have no record of the construction, presumably a form of cofferdam would have been employed to excavate the shingle and access the underlying marl. Once exposed, wooden piles were driven into the marl bedrock providing a secure base for the foundation rocks and the eventual construction of the pier. Only when the pier was completed would the connecting arm have been constructed. This would have then cut off the tidal flow, forcing the river to exit through the shingle to the west of the new pier, establishing a new entrance channel.

It is hard to imagine the difficulties experienced in physically constructing the outer pier. It would have been a constant battle against the continual movement of shingle, especially excavating pebbles to construct the foundations, even when contained within a cofferdam. Time would have been limited to the low water period and only during periods of calm weather. Spring tides and floods would have presented further difficulties with the strength of the stream, all of which when combined together, reflect the tremendous achievement of establishing a pier in such an exposed location!

The design provided a small holding basin within the shelter of the connecting arm and new pier. It also had the effect of diverting the ebb through approximately 70°, causing it to flow seaward in a south, south-westerly direction. Ingeniously, at the point of diversion the ebb flow was deflected against a body of still water held within the holding basin. Whether or not by design, this body of still water had the added advantage of absorbing the frictional effects of the diverted ebb flow. Although, it is more likely that the holding basin was designed with the intention of providing berths during neap tides, the depths are greater near the entrance and downstream of the shallows, The Rapids (discussed later).

The original draught survey chart comments that the pier head was 18 feet above *ground*, whilst the final navigational survey comments that the pier head was 24ft 9ins above low water spring tides. This indicates that the base of the pier head had almost 7 feet of shingle surrounding it. The chart on page 53 shows a difference of three and half feet, demonstrating the changing heights in the shingle.

The restored harbour opens

The first large vessel (70 tons) to enter the newly constructed harbour, brought a cargo of culm in May 1809 – a comment in Hallett's case notes states it was the largest vessel to enter the harbour 'within the memory of man'. This suggests that vessels of this size had not used the harbour since at least the mid 1700s. Culm was described as a low-grade coal, broken down into small hard pieces of anthracite.

The newly formed entrance channel running parallel to the pier would have had a firm base of marl. The resilience of this hard base would have encouraged greater scour of the shingle spit to the west, maintaining greater channel width. At low water the channel alongside the pier would have effectively dried out with only the residual outflow of the river. This is demonstrated in the 1860 photograph showing a brigantine lying aground on the marl at low water just within the entrance. Over time the marl would have slowly eroded, deepening the channel, at the same time narrowing it. This would have also led to scouring of the pier's foundations. The present-day pier has suffered with this exact same problem. Over the years a deep scour hole has formed alongside the pier, requiring additional steel sheet piling to underpin the structure. Subsequently the channel width has narrowed and deepened, rather than being a wide shallower entrance.

Within the harbour the channel passed over the shallow marl ledge, extending from beneath Haven Cliff (The Rapids). The marl ledge still exists today, forming a natural sill within the harbour which impounds a certain amount of water at low tide. The remains of The Rapids can be seen just downstream of the old warehouse. At low water the ebbing stream flows markedly downhill over the ledge towards the entrance. This presented a problem for deeper draughted vessels, even at high water springs, restricting access to the warehouse quay and berths further upstream. So, in conjunction with the construction of the harbour walls a measure of dredging was carried out in order to cut two distinct parallel channels through the marl. Fortunately, the mudstone is fairly soft to break down, although it would have required considerable

Close up of pier 1870, shingle has partially infilled the holding basin. (Ted Gosling collection).

Axmouth Harbour chart 1852. (UKHO Archive).

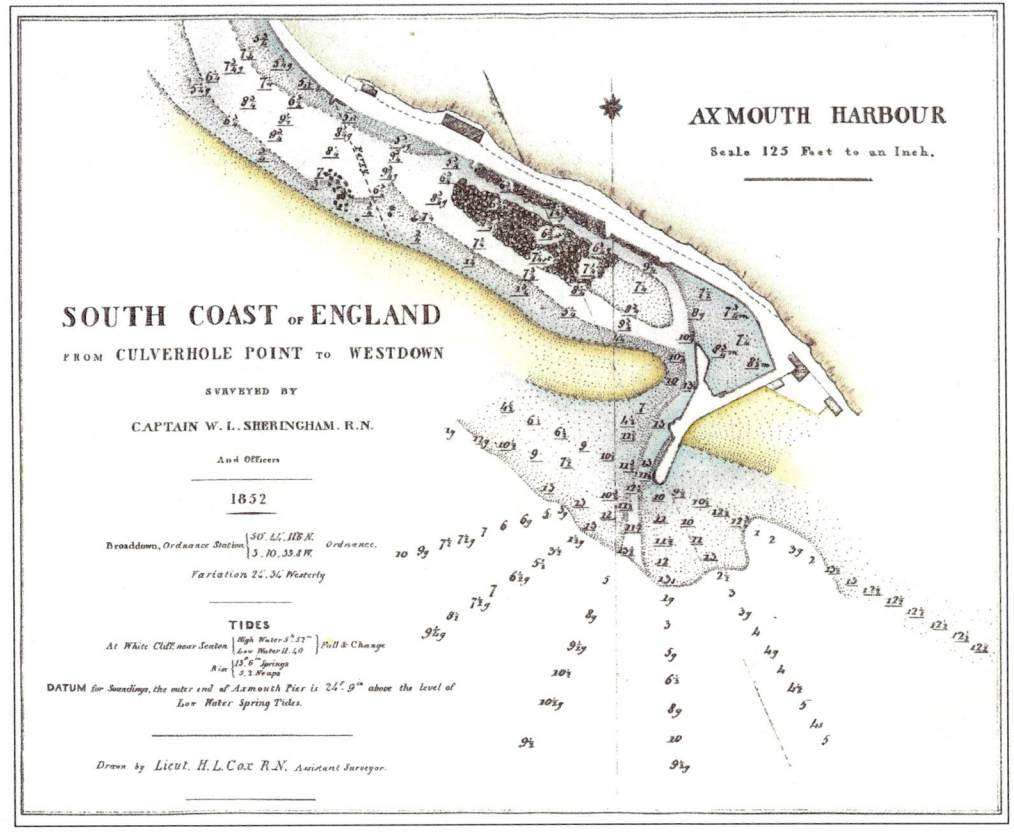

Top: Exposed remains of inner pier end 2008.

Right: Wooden piles exposed 1963. (Henry Pountney).

Old pier foundations temporarily exposed by scouring of the diverted channel due to storms 2021. (James Widger).

Below: Same wooden piles exposed Feb 2021. (Nigel David)

manual effort to achieve. The new channels are easily identified on the 1852 Admiralty chart; one runs close parallel to the harbour wall the other lies more to the south and close to the back slope of the shingle bank. A little further upstream the channel was cleared of any remnants resulting from Courd's old works, seen opposite the Ferryman's Cottage below.

The construction materials for the new harbour were all locally sourced. Much of the stone work came from the surrounding shore line, utilising boulders from cliff falls (cow stones) and no doubt any accessible stone from previous works. Unlike the majority of Lyme's Cobb, which was encased in neatly cut Portland stone! As stated, the new outer pier had its foundation on marl, wooden piles were first driven into the rock bed to provide an anchorage, then the stone work was built up around them. Again, Stirling comments, *'The stratum on which the new pier is erected declines gradually towards the site of the Old Haven, where it disappears, nor is it to be found in the sea outside. We may therefore infer that the principal cause of the failure of the old works* (Erle's & Courd's) *was its defective foundations.'*

Under certain conditions when the beach has been scoured on the west side of the entrance, those original wooden piles still appear, marking the location of the old outer pier. Again, they are thought to be alder since the timber is impervious to rot whilst submerged and loses none of its strength. In February 2021 a particular set of circumstances forced the entrance channel to the west and uncovered a significant amount of the old pier foundations, including fifteen piles, the most seen in a long time.

Similarly, the foundation stones of the inner end of the pier come to light on very rare occasions. This occurs when shingle has been scoured away from the back slope of the shingle bank within the entrance by exceptional flood water.

In 1833 D.M. Stirling wrote:- *'As an establishment of public utility, this is probably the greatest that has ever been effected in this part of the country. It proves extensively advantageous, not only to Seaton and Colyton, but to the circumjacent towns at a distance. Since the completion of this valuable work, extensive coal, culm, and timber yards have been erected on both sides of the river, and regular trading vessels to and from London, weekly, have been established.'*

The inner end of the old pier foundations exposed 2008.

Stirling also states in 1838:- *'ships of 150 tons were using the harbour. In the first half of the nineteenth century the harbour was used by small coasting vessels for unloading coal for the local lime-burning industry. They sailed away with cargoes of hides.'*

Similarly, William White, who published his book *Devonshire* in 1850, writes:- *'During the present century, piers have been constructed at the mouth of the Axe, where vessels of 100 tons burden can now discharge their cargoes in safety. The piers were those built by Mr. John H. Hallett of Stedcombe House in 1809.'*

Axmouth Harbour Act

On 8 April 1830, an Act of Parliament came into force entitled: *Axmouth Harbour. An Act for maintaining and governing the Harbour of Axmouth, and Works connected there with, in the Parish of Axmouth, in the County of Devon.* George IV. Sess. 1830.

This legal document by its very nature is quite drawn-out, but it is worth reading some extracts from the Act which provide an insight into the early life of the rejuvenated port.

The preamble to the Act recites:- *'Whereas John Hothersall Hallett of Stedcombe, in the County of Devon, Esquire, is or claims to be seised in Fee of the Manor or Lordship of Axmouth in the Parish of Axmouth in the County of Devon, and as Part thereof, of the Lands on both Sides of the River Ax, where the same flows into the Sea and for upwards of a Mile from the Mouth of the said River. And whereas the said John Hothersall Hallett about the year One thousand eight hundred and nine constructed a Harbour at his own expense on this Property, near the mouth of the said*

Axmouth Harbour Act 1830.

Import tonnage rates.

River Ax, with a Pier, Quays, and other Works connected therewith and hath since expended large Sums of Money in repairing, improving and maintaining the said Harbour and Works, and such Sums so expended exceed together the Sum of Five thousand Pounds.

And whereas the said John Hothersall Hallett and divers other Persons, by his Permission and upon Payment to him for the same, have hitherto used and employed the said Harbour for the Purposes of Trade and Commerce, and much Public Advantage has been derived there from.

And whereas the said John Hothersall Hallett is willing and desirous that the Public shall henceforth have the free and unrestricted Use and Benefit of the said Harbour and Works upon Payment to him, his Heirs and Assigns, of such Rates and Duties as Parliament shall think a reasonable Return for the Use of his Property and for the Money, he has expended and may expend.

And whereas it is expedient that proper Powers should be granted and that proper Regulations should be made and established, for the Repair, Maintenance, and Government of the said Harbour and Works, and of all Persons, and Ships or Vessels and Boats employed in or using the same; but such Purposes cannot be completely effected without the Aid and Authority of Parliament.'

The operative paragraphs of the Act recite:- 'May it therefore please Your MAJESTY, That it may be enacted; And be it enacted by The King's Most Excellent Majesty, by and with the Advice and Consent of the Lords Spiritual and Temporal, and Commons in this present Parliament assembled, and by the authority of the same, That the said John Hothersall Hallett, his Heirs and assigns being proprietors of the said Harbour, or the Guardians, Trustees, or Committees of such Heirs or Assigns as shall be Minors, or be under any legal Incapacity or their lessees for the time being, shall be and they and each of them are and is hereby authourised and empowered to put this Act into Execution; and it shall be lawful for such Proprietors, or their said Guardians, Trustees, or Committees, or their Lessees, from Time to Time, to alter and improve the said harbour of Axmouth in the Parish of Axmouth, in the county of Devon and the Piers, Quays, and other Works connected therewith, in such manner as they shall judge fit.

And be it further enacted, that the proprietors of the said Harbour for the Time being or their said Guardians, Trustees, or Committees or their Lessees, shall and they are hereby required, out of the Rates, Duties, and other Monies to be received and recovered by virtue of this Act, to maintain and keep in Repair the said Harbour at Axmouth, in the Parish of Axmouth in the county of Devon, with the Piers and Quays and other Works connected therewith.

And be it further enacted, That the Extent and Boundary of the said Harbour of Axmouth next the Sea shall be deemed and is hereby declared to be from the boundary Post on the beach which divides the Parishes of Axmouth and Seaton, extending down to Low-water Mark on the West to the Eastern extremity of the cliff commonly called or known by the name of Haven Cliff, extending down to low-water Mark on the East (the whole of the Property of the Shore between these Two Points being Part of the Manor of Axmouth and that the Extent and Boundary of the said Harbour within the said River Ax shall be deemed and is hereby declared to be to the South point of a Piece of Land commonly called or known by the name of the Slime, nearly opposite the Village of Axmouth, the whole of the Lands on both sides of the River Ax from the Mouth to the said Point of Land called the Slime, be in the Property of the said John Hothersall Hallett and the said Harbour so bounded shall be called Axmouth Harbour.'

Nineteenth Century Revival of the Harbour

William Newbery's watercolour of the harbour 1830. (David Mettam).

The last paragraph is interesting in that it defines the boundary of Axmouth Harbour, all within the land owned by the Halletts. The western boundary remains the same today, many do not realise that the beach east of Trevelyan Road is within the parish of Axmouth and not Seaton – its proper title is Axmouth Beach. This ancient boundary is a result of the old estuary forming the division between the two parishes. As the channel was forced further east by the encroachment of shingle, the original boundary remained in place, hence Axmouth now presides over land on the west bank of the Axe. The northern limit of the harbour is referred to as the south point of the *Slime*. There is no reference to this term on contemporary maps of the period. One can only assume that it refers to the point at which the salt marsh islands on the west side of the estuary terminate opposite Axmouth village.

The Act also authorizes *'John Hothersall Hallett and his successors in title to appoint officers to assist in the carrying out the provisions of the Act (appointment of Harbour Master & his deputy) to take tonnage duty, rates on goods, and to require Masters and Owners of British ships to produce registers of their vessels. The Proprietors of the harbour are also authorized to erect the necessary cranes, weighing machines ware houses and sheds for the proper maintenance of the haven.'* At the end of the act there is a schedule giving the harbour duties payable on a long and detailed list of commodities covering such a wide variety of items from coal, eggs and nails to furniture, gunpowder and cattle. John Hallett was involved in many entrepreneurial ventures, for besides developing the harbour, in 1835 he filed a patent for the improvement of manufactured cocks or taps for drawing off fluids. Coincidently at the same time a certain John Hallett of Axmouth was cautioned for smuggling, was there a connection? Hallett may also have been contemplating further development of the harbour, for in 1837 he contracted Hatchards of London to publish a pamphlet titled: *Correspondence relative to the exploring of forming a refuge harbour within the Portland and Start Bay.* Unfortunately, the pamphlet has disappeared into obscurity – it would have made interesting reading. Presumably the investment was not forthcoming, since further expansion of the port did not proceed, except for the construction of an additional quay at Squire's Lane.

In 1843 the following harbour dues were applicable:- Vessels of 10 tons burden and upwards were charged two pence per registered ton. Boats and vessels under 10 tons were charged one shilling. Vessels laid up in the harbour, two pence per registered ton per month, this after the expiration of the first month; ballast dues were a penny per ton. The layup dues demonstrate that the harbour had

The Story of Axmouth Harbour

1860 photograph of the harbour showing commercial sailing vessels, the only one in existence. (Barbara Bastin).

room to accommodate unemployed vessels, also that the harbour was safe for layup purposes. This was an advantage over Lyme which in certain storm conditions became untenable. The taking on of ballast was a common requirement where a return cargo was not available. Axmouth provided an almost unlimited supply of shingle for this purpose. Within the harbour certain areas were designated for dumping ballast to avoid fouling the working berths. There are two areas of fine 'pea' sized shingle not consistent with local pebbles forming low banks opposite the old higher quay – adjacent to Squires Lane. These two banks may be the remains of ballast deposited by the trading vessels, but may also be connected with material used during WW2 for the construction of dams, discussed later.

The new Customs House was constructed on the inner end of the pier alongside the holding basin. The building was naturally in an exposed position, one can imagine during winter gales the Customs House would often become isolated due to seas breaking over the harbour wall and pier. Eventually the building succumbed to storm damage and was washed away, only the rear wall of an adjoining store remains testament to its existence. However, two other harbour-side buildings remain from this period, the warehouse (today's *Harbour House & Moorings*) and the Ferryman's Cottage. The warehouse, essential to the harbour's commerce, had large openings on all three floors facing the quay, with small gantries extending from below the eaves to hoist up the cargo. The customs notice board was displayed on the wall facing upstream, detailing duties levied on imported commodities. Incidentally, today's inscription of *1776* on the southern gable end of *Harbour House* is a little misleading – the warehouse would have been constructed following the installation Hallett's new harbour wall and pier – c.1809. The Ferryman's Cottage is the oldest surviving property directly associated with the commercial port. It was originally called Passage House, subsequently Ferry Cottage and now Harbour Cottage. It may well pre-date Hallett's harbour, since the ferry had been in existence for a much longer period. The older part of Haven Cliff House which lies behind the early Regency façade may go further back as a 'passage house', being on the direct coastal route leading down to the harbour's eastern shore and the passage westwards across the river.

Navigation and pilotage

The 1860 photograph on page 60 is the most important representation of Axmouth Harbour's commercial operations. It is the only surviving photographic evidence showing trading vessels within Hallett's harbour, and it may well have been taken by Samuel Good, a pioneering Seaton photographer.

It was taken at low water from the western bank, looking downstream towards the entrance. There are two vessels pictured, the first being moored alongside the main quay adjacent to the warehouse. She is probably a topsail schooner, but if one looks carefully the main topmast has been sent down. Perhaps the crew were engaged in some maintenance, having lowered it to deck. Otherwise, if this was her rig then she may have come under the category of a 'Billy Boy' ketch, a seagoing development of the Thames barge originating from the east coast. These vessels usually had lee boards, and again the photo shows what may be a possible lee board in place but more likely, it is just a rope fender. Due to her size, general hull shape and greater freeboard, I would suspect she was a topsail schooner.

In the distance a second vessel lies downstream. She is appears to be a brigantine, square sails on the fore mast and fore & aft on the main mast. The shape of her bluff bow and curved stem typifies vessels from the early 1800s or even late 1700s. What is unusual is her position, lying aground just within the entrance; the inner end of the pier lies behind her stern. Maybe she had inadvertently taken the ground whilst entering on a falling tide, now having to wait for the next high water to come alongside? Both vessels are of similar size, and accord with references to the harbour accommodating vessels of 150 tons. These vessels typically had a loaded draught of approximately 9 feet (3 metres) and were sufficiently flat bottomed to comfortably take the ground at low water – and importantly, strong enough to do so when fully loaded.

Edward W. Cooke's 1861 magnificent oil painting of the harbour (overleaf) shows great similarities to the 1860 photo, with vessels moored alongside the main quay and in the holding basin at the entrance. Generally, the picture shows the harbour on a slightly grander scale than reality. However, its detail is excellent, depicting cargoes on the quay, even the mooring buoy and chain in the foreground used for warping vessels within the harbour. The ferry is underway with a horse and cart onboard. The large size of the ferryboat would have been difficult to handle considering the strength of the tidal streams. One suspects a certain amount of artist's licence has been used. A topsail schooner lies at anchor outside the harbour with just its masts showing above the beach. Typically, a south-west breeze is blowing, drying a line of laundry upon the *'mighty ridge of pebbles'*.

As an aside, there were only a few artists who painted Axmouth Harbour during this period. A well-respected Seatonian, William Newbery, painted some interesting water colours as did J.E. Fitzgerald, who later settled in New Zealand. A number of his local watercolours are now on display in the Canterbury Museum (NZ). B.J.M. Donne, a local Axmouth artist, produced a fine watercolour of the pier in 1875, with a considerable degree of accuracy, but sadly by then the outer section of the pier had been washed away.

Edward William Cooke's painting 1861. (© 2016 Christie's Images Limited).

The Two Sisters *of Seaton sailing in the bay 1836. A small sprit-rigged smack. J.E. Fitzgerald. (Canterbury Museum NZ).*

Today, local Seaton artist Barry Mason has produced many fine paintings of the harbour contemporary to this period. They show various vessels in the harbour, often referenced to actual shipping reports, providing a pictorial insight into the harbour's commercial operation in the days of sail.

Another common type of vessel using the harbour would have been the coastal smack. These single-masted, gaff-rigged vessels were the smaller work horses of the inshore coastal trade. With a maximum capacity of approximately 50 tons, they were derived from vessels formerly known as sloops and the earlier square sail carrying cutters. Being smaller, typically of around 50 feet in length, the vessels had the advantage of shallower draught allowing them greater access into the tidal estuaries and creeks of the West Country. Economically they were cheap to run, having just a two-man crew.

Coasting ketches were the last vessels to trade under sail in the West Country. They were derived from the coastal schooners, but having a handier rig for a small crew. This was achieved by reducing the fore mast sail area and stepping a smaller mizzen in place of the main mast aft. The rig could then be easily handled by a crew of three. Many ketches were originally schooner rigged, having been modified with a cut down sail area. The very last West Country ketches were actually built for purpose but these were not seen at Axmouth; they were constructed after the harbour had ceased to operate commercially. The smallest cargo vessels to use the harbour were the coastal barges of 10 to 15 tons. These small heavily-timbered vessels had used the harbour for hundreds of years. One of the earliest records of their use was during construction of the Willoughby embankment in 1660; transporting Beer stone for the reinforcement of the sluice gates to drain the marsh. These vessels would have used both sweeps and a sprit sail, but were very much restricted by sea conditions, generally keeping to sheltered waters. Their strength allowed them to be beached and take on a full cargo of stone, sometimes from the most exposed landings amongst the rocks and ledges beneath the cliffs.

The larger vessels using the harbour were restricted by their draught and hence limited to use during the period of spring tides, especially when fully loaded. Thus, with entry and departure restricted, cargoes would have been discharged and loaded over a few brief days to avoid the risk of being 'neaped'. This would have meant waiting possibly a week or so, for the next set of spring tides. The tidal cycle generally governed the frequency of sailings and therefore the larger vessels would have been limited to those few days around the fortnightly spring tides. Shallower-draughted vessels such as smacks, sloops and cutters had greater access to the harbour, especially to the entrance holding basin, operating even during neap tides. The harbour was quoted as having depths of 10 to 12 feet during spring tides and 7 to 9 feet during neaps. One suspects the neap depths were limited to the holding basin, although the spring depths alongside today's Fish Quay are comparable.

To gain maximum depth in the harbour, vessels entering and leaving would naturally use the period around high water with no tidal stream running. However, high water coincides with the maximum rate of the east going coastal tidal stream. This would have presented a problem for sailing vessels in making their final approach from seaward; a strong set to the east would have required careful judgement in making the narrow entrance. Additionally, onshore breezes tend to stall beneath Haven Cliff leaving a sailing vessel with little or no control. The solution to this was to warp vessels in and out of the harbour. A buoy was permanently moored (anchored) some 200 yards south west of the pier head. On arrival a vessel would initially secure to the buoy, a light messenger rope would be sent ashore with a small boat, usually performed by local boatmen known as *hobblers*. The messenger was then used to heave out a heavier rope (warp) to the vessel.

With the inshore end of the warp secured to the quay it was led to the vessel's forward capstan in preparation for entering port. Similarly, a warp would be secured to the buoy, in readiness for paying out aft. Through the combination of heaving forward and paying out aft, the vessel could be 'warped' into the harbour. Once into the harbour the vessel could be warped along the quayside to her berth. On departure a similar routine would have been used to warp the vessel back out to the buoy and safe water. An old photo shows a winch on the quay in line with the entrance, this may have been used in the process of bringing the warp ashore from the vessel. (Vincent Martyn, one-time Estate Manager for Stedcombe during the 1950s, commented that the mooring chain used for the buoy eventually ended up as a garden ornament – draped around part of the kitchen garden at Stedcombe.)

In general, the navigation of Axmouth Harbour would not have differed dramatically from the conditions experienced today. The length of the pier obviously extended sufficiently further seaward to enable the ebb tide to scour shingle into deeper water reducing the effects of the bar. The strong tidal stream experienced in the entrance would have been very similar and the entrance would have been just as exposed as it is today, especially with winds from the south east through to the south west. Of course, the greatest difference today is the use of motor power!

Seaton Bay is generally an exposed stretch of water, open to the prevailing south west winds. Mariners had to rely very much on their

The Story of Axmouth Harbour

Abraham Tidbury, the last Axmouth Pilot, seen in Queen St, Seaton. (Ted Gosling collection).

own experience and instincts when committing to enter a harbour set on a lee shore – especially one whose entrance demanded the added challenge of working closely with tides. In wider terms Lyme Bay is not the place to be caught in onshore gales. Many a sailing vessel found herself embayed in such conditions. With no port of refuge to run for (that was accessible at all states of the tide) options were severely limited.

In a similar vein, it would have taken great skill to enter Axmouth in anything but benign conditions. To assist a vessel entering the harbour, a pilot would have boarded in the approaches to offer local advice and guidance. Axmouth had its own licensed pilots, originating from local boatman who were well versed in the vagaries of the port. The licensed pilots were appointed by Trinity House, the national regulatory body, granted a Royal Charter by Henry VIII in 1514. George Miller was a long established Axmouth pilot serving the harbour for many year. He died in Seaton at the age of sixty-one in February 1858. The last known Axmouth Pilot was Abraham Tidbury, shown in the photo left, who was a resident of Queen Street, Seaton – he was born in 1813, just when the harbour was re-vitalised. No doubt he grew up close to the water learning from his father Isaac was also an Axmouth pilot. He died almost one hundred years later (1911) and was buried in Seaton churchyard

Similarly, local boatmen (hobblers) would have rendered services for running lines to enable a vessel to warp in and out. Trinity House records for the year ending 1857 show that there were 49 acts of pilotage from seaward into the harbour. All were classed as coastal vessels, with none arriving from overseas and all were British registered. As a rough guide this would indicate that two vessels used the harbour over each spring tide period throughout the year, although locally based small vessels would have been exempt from pilotage and would not have been included. The rates charged for pilotage were calculated according to the vessel's tonnage, the maximum rate being 150 tons. This is consistent with contemporary observations. One of the largest vessels to the use the harbour, was the *Alexis* of 150 tons. For example, a vessel of between 100 and 150 tons was charged 2s per foot inward and 1s per foot outward – the difference probably arose from the thought that it was easier to leave than arrive; today most ports charge the same for either inward or outward acts of pilotage.

During this period coasting vessels were regularly beached on open foreshores to discharge cargoes. This was a hazardous operation and could only be done in periods of settled weather. To be caught out in a strengthening onshore wind or rising swell could result in stranding or worse, being wrecked. Vessels would beach on a falling tide in order to allow themselves sufficient rise on the next tide to depart. On the approach it was usual to lay out a kedge anchor astern, laid some distance offshore providing the facility to heave the vessel off the beach at high water. Coal was delivered to Seaton regularly in such a manner.

Rates of pilotage for Axmouth Harbour.

64

The coalyard was situated just to the east of where Seaton's Marine Place now exists, shown in a very early photograph of Seaton, dated around 1850. The coalyard would have facilitated storage from either beach landings or coal transported from the harbour. Beach trading would have saved on harbour dues and pilotage, also the transport along the beach from the harbour, but with much greater risk to the vessel. Such activities were similarly carried out at Branscombe and Sidmouth as will be noted in the following extract.

In 1817 the famous local smuggler Jack Rattenbury described using Axmouth Harbour, and not under ideal conditions:- *'In January 1817, a vessel that had been to Sidmouth with coal, in a violent storm was driven into Loden Bay (Ladram?) where she was obliged to let go her anchor. She then cut away her anchor and ran ashore on Seaton Beach. Being a fine vessel and well adapted for coasting, a friend and myself purchased her off Mr Flinn, the owner. But she was so much damaged that it was with considerable difficulty that we succeeded in getting her into Axmouth harbour. There we had her properly repaired; and in June she was ready for sea, when my partner together with my son took the first voyage in her to Newkey after a cargo of slate.'* Again, this suggests there were ship repair facilities available in the harbour.

At the same time an article from the local press (January 1817) provides an insight to some of the problems faced with maintaining the harbour and its navigation.

'Axmouth Harbour has sustained much less damage than was at first reported. Two breaches were made about the centre of the piers, through which the sea poured with irresistible violence, and did great injury to the wharf, a house on the pier, and a road leading to the coal-yard; but we have the satisfaction of hearing that the piers are so little damaged that £20 or £30 will completely repair them. This harbour deserves to be better known. In 1806 the mouth of the river Axe presented, at low water a ridge of dangerous rocks which completely obstructed the navigation of the river. On these rocks the present proprietor of the manor, Mr Hallett, has erected a strong pier and by that means diverted the channel of the river into a deeper part of the bay. A western pier was also formed, but this was entirely swept away by the melting of the deep snow in 1814. Since that, it has been rebuilt and in such a manner that the floods which were always considered as unmanageable in this river, now find a passage behind the pier without doing any injury to the harbour. The first year after the erection of the eastern pier, the inhabitants of the neighbourhood were gratified by the sight of a loaded vessel of 60 tons entering the river, and discharging her cargo of culm on the pier. Since that time this harbour has been frequented by coasters of different sorts.'

Referring to the harbour in 1806, the comment concerning the ridge of dangerous rocks is probably describing the remains of Courd's pier. The rock foundations (as described previously) crossed the harbour channel from a point close down stream of the Ferryman's Cottage. Hallett removed the debris to allow vessels of a deeper draught to access the upper quay at Squires Lane and upper estuary. Similarly, during the same storm of 1817, Lyme suffered a breach in the main wall, this resulted in the use of Portland stone to rebuild a more resilient structure.

Another curious comment refers to both eastern and western piers. There has been no record of a west pier being constructed, nor does the Admiralty survey of 1852 shows any such construction. The confusion may have arisen due to the naming of Hallett's new outer

A topsail schooner entering the harbour in challenging conditions. (Nigel Daniel).

pier as *the western pier*, being constructed to the west of the original river exit, with the connecting arm to the main wall, *the eastern pier*.

The comment regarding the flood management probably refers to the culvert inserted beneath the inner end of the outer pier. This can be clearly seen in B.J.M. Donne's watercolour painted in 1875. The culvert would have helped relieve the pressure within the holding basin during the ebb tide and assist in scouring silt.

The article continues:- *'The largest that ever came into the river was the 'Alexis' of Sunderland, of 150 tons. Many thousand chaldrons of culm and coal have been landed here during the last nine years; and several vessels as well as boats, have found shelter there in gales of wind. Among these was a small sloop that had discharged her cargo at Sidmouth, and which was saved from destruction by running to the harbour in a gale of wind that sprung up suddenly from the south-west. A collier also, upwards of 100 tons, came there when the sea was so high that no pilot could venture out and though the master had only seen the place once at low water, yet he brought in his vessel himself, with all her cargo perfectly safe. These instances show that this work is not altogether so useless as its adversaries contend. At the same time, it must be confessed that it would be highly improved by an extension of the piers; which, if done with judgment, would unquestionably make it one of the most commodious and safe harbours on the coast.'* The *chaldron* (originating from the word cauldron) was a measure of dry goods, more essentially for coal. The defining weight has varied over the years and with locality: the London chaldron was defined as 36 bushels (a bushel equalling eight dry gallons), in present day measures equating to approximately 1.4 tonnes.

It's assumed the collier entering under challenging conditions was running before a strong onshore wind, the Master conning his vessel without the aid of warps or pilot's advice. Sailing into the Axe under similar conditions today would require a steady nerve and expert judgement; handling a much larger vessel deserved praise indeed.

The Dare family of Seaton had many shipping interests, during the early 1800s they traded far and wide, from Peru to the west coast of North America. Records show some of their ships were built at Bridport (West Bay). The *Mary Dare* was an armed merchantman thought to have been used as an escort for their vessels trading on the east coast of South America. The brig *Harry* is thought to have traded out of Axmouth under the command of Captain Harry Dare, whose telescope and rum glass can still be seen in Seaton Museum.

The 1824 storm

In 1824 a ferocious storm battered the south coast and caused much damage. Seaton was flooded by seas breaking over the beach and flowing into the village centre, and numerous properties were inundated. The marshes were completely flooded from the sea over topping the beach, temporarily returning the estuary to its former medieval breadth.

G.P.R. Pulman was an eye witness to the events. He later wrote an account of the storm in his *Rambles, Roamings and Recollections* published in 1863.

'A scene which I witnessed when a little child seems to rise up again and to re-enacted in terrible distinctness – the November Gale of 1824. Never within the memory of living man was there such a scene as that along the western coast. I had gone to bed, too young to be aware of the danger which threatened in the rising wind, the wild sky, the pouring rain, and the rumbling of the coming thunder. The house in which I was sleeping was some way up the street- a little below what is now the post office [in 1863 the post office occupied a site bordering the Square]. *I was awakened by an uproar going on, I knew not where. But the storm had reached its height. The thunder shook the house. The rain literally came down in streams. But what alarmed me most was the hearing of the sea outside my bedroom window.*

Yes, there it was – actually rushing up the street and bringing with it several of the boats which had been left upon the beach. Such a thing was never known before. I remember looking out of a window and, in the lightning, distinctly seeing the waves breaking through that handsome house upon the beach which was then in the course of erection. I saw it come out of the unglazed windows, and stream through the un-slated roof, and rush on – all green and foaming, covering the whole expanse of the sea beach and the Marsh as far as the eye could reach. [The building Pulman refers to may have been the Mansion House, now known as the Old Picture House on Harbour Road, adjacent to Beach Road].

The river, as it rushed to meet the roaring sea, seemed itself a sea. It rolled and leaped onward, with great strides of waves, bearing along the cattle which could not previously be removed from the Marsh. I saw the cows borne along one after another, their heads only visible, and appearing, to my childish fancy, like an enormous string of beads, widely separated from each other. I knew that everyone around me was quaking with fear, although they affected an indifference lest I should become more frightened than I was. Seaton itself was in intense alarm. Some of the houses nearer the beach were inundated, and the inmates escaped I know not how. Groups of people were assembled as near the river as possible, endeavouring to save the drowning cattle. Others were helping the inhabitants of the inundated houses in the town to remove their furniture, and all was commotion and alarm, while the Elements were at war, and the waters raging as if in madness. It was as if the deluge had come again. People said that it had. And mothers seized their children, and rushed with them cowering, through the streets. And strong men trembled.

I remember all this, and my childish fears, the dangers no doubt, were much exaggerated. But they were very great, and left sad effects behind them. No human lives were lost at Seaton. But the sea, in the Channel, the loss of life was terrible, and the destruction of shipping immense. By daylight the fury of the tempest was spent, and the waters had subsided from the streets. News of terrible effects of the gale arrived every hour, including the sweeping away of a portion of the Lyme Cobb, and Seaton people were thankful after the perils and dangers through which they had passed.'

Axmouth Harbour seems to have escaped relatively lightly, there are no reports of any damage to either the pier or the quays. Lyme's Cobb sustained considerable damage, the main wall was breached and a number of vessels washed out of the harbour and wrecked. Following this damage, major re-construction was required, using Portland stone to encase the old works, thus strengthening the Cobb, much as we see it today.

Development and operation of the harbour

Development of the harbour can be divided into various discrete areas. Initially there was the new pier and holding basin with the customs house quay tucked in behind. Moving upstream a new quay was developed with a large warehouse just below the Ferryman's Cottage – today's fish quay. Coal was discharged on the west bank, close to the present slipway adjacent to the old Axmouth Bridge, where a stone coalyard was built. Coal was also discharged

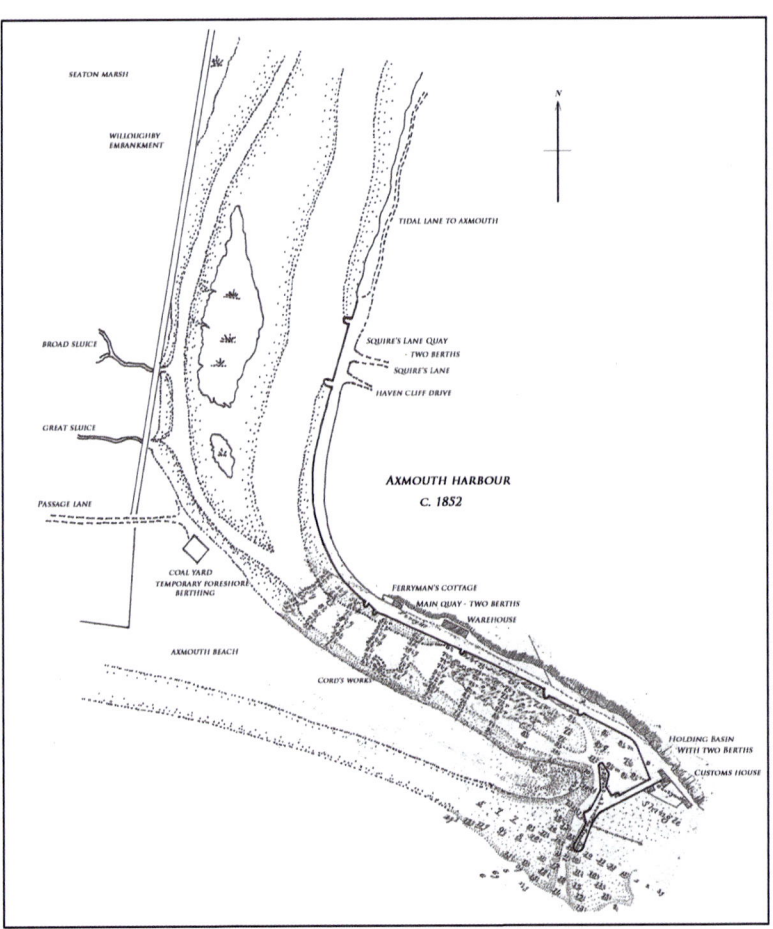

Extended harbour chart showing inner quay and berths. (UKHO Archive).

further upstream close to the Great Sluice, alongside the Willoughby embankment. On the east side of the estuary a new stone quay was constructed adjacent to Squires Lane. Smaller vessels could discharge nearly a mile inland using the village foreshore at Axmouth. Finally, an old stone quay just upstream of the village provided the last accessible point for vessels to come alongside. This was very much governed by the tide and limited to springs only.

Harbour layout – the holding basin

The holding basin at the entrance would have accommodated two, or perhaps three vessels in calm conditions. J.E. Fitzgerald painted some charming watercolours of the locality during the mid 1830s. The painting below shows three topsail schooners within the holding basin. The left-hand schooner has an awning rigged over the aft deck – since the painting was dated to August 1836, perhaps Axmouth was experiencing a heat wave! The Customs House is clearly seen in the background and two barges in the middle of the basin. These were used locally in the estuary and for short coastal passages – carrying heavy cargoes such as Beer stone and blue lias for cement production. With the lack of shore-side storage, it could be assumed that the holding basin was used more for trans-shipment, as the painting portrays. On later Ordnance Survey maps the track shown in the back ground led up to a lime kiln, not depicted in the painting. A coal-yard also existed between the cliff and the Customs House, although the main storage area for coal was further upstream.

A close up of the painting by Edward W. Cooke in 1861 is very similar and shows the same timber fendering around the inner end of the pier, but some thirty years later. This would have been essential in protecting vessels as they were swung into the basin and for warping in and out of the port.

Three schooners in the holding basin, J.E. Fitzgerald 1836. (Canterbury Museum NZ).

Detail of the painting of Axmouth Harbour by Edward William Cooke, 1861. (© 2016 Christie's Images Limited).

The main quay

Moving upstream from the holding basin a stone retaining wall linked up with the main quay. Sections of that original construction remain intact today, just upstream from the pier.

The main quay adjacent to the warehouse was constructed with projecting buttresses at each end. These would have provided a measure of shelter to the berths, protecting them from the swell under storm conditions and deflecting the strength of the ebb tide and floods. The main quay was built with a vertical face for vessels to lie alongside, whereas the remainder of the harbour wall was constructed with a slight incline for added strength. The main quay was sufficiently long to accommodate three moderately sized vessels. This allowed good access to the warehouse, dealing with a whole variety of commodities. The higher end of the main quay terminated in two smaller buttresses. Between them they sheltered the ferry steps and provided a berth for the ferry boat.

From the ferry steps upstream towards Squire's Lane, the harbour wall was of much older age and probably dates back to the seventeenth century works. A section of this wall remains although now underpinned with sheet piling. The photo below shows that original section of wall with the ferryman in the foreground. The area of low foreshore on the opposite bank gave access to the ford, but only at low water.

The main quay and ferry steps. (Barbara Bastin).

The old original wall upstream of the ferry steps. (Original F. Frith & Co photo print).

The coal wharf

Coal was the major import and secure storage facilities were set up on the west bank. Remains of the coalyard compound still exist; the stone-walled compound has been incorporated into the AYCs storage shed and a section of the stone-paved base lies next to the present-day slipway. Vessels would have dried out on the west bank at this location, where they would have discharged their coal into the compound. It is believed that a light railway existed from the coal compound westwards to the gas holders located in Station Road, where the coal was converted to town gas. An advert placed in the *Pulman's Weekly News* (June 1863) refers to the Coal Wharf, inviting the purchase of coals and other products; orders to be lodged with the Habour Master Alfred Bridgett. It stated that the coal was stored under cover at the wharf; presumably part of the compound was developed as a dry store facility. The wharf was located in the entrance to what was the old creek leading into Seaton Marsh then served by the Great Sluice. This was the main drainage outlet leading beneath the Willoughby embankment.

The west bank coalyard.

Incidentally, the photo below right has featured in recent publications suggesting that the view represents Hallett's 'training wall' supposedly taken in 1859. This is incorrect, the wall photographed is actually the boundary between Seaton and Axmouth. The stone wall still exists to the rear of the Trevelyan Road properties, built before the terrace was constructed. The top of the old coalyard buildings can be seen to left, behind the post.

Of course, during this period (1809-1877) Axmouth Bridge had yet to be built. The estuary would have provided a useful expanse of tidal water upstream of the harbour. There are references of vessels lying further upstream on the west bank alongside the Willoughby embankment. Some form of wharf may have existed to facilitate cargo operations, but there is no definitive evidence of this. For a brief period, this would have been a convenient berth tying in with newly developed railway and station (1867-1877). Plus, the channel already existed formed by the Great Sluice creek, leading to the west of the saltmarsh islands. This channel had its origins long before construction of the Willoughby embankment, acting as a major drainage creek from Seaton Marshes. During construction of Axmouth Bridge the small arch to the west of the main bridge was incorporated to span the old creek.

The cobbled coalyard today.

Boundary wall between Axmouth and Seaton. (Ted Gosling collection).

Squire's Lane quay

On the opposite side of the estuary, below Squire's Lane, a substantial stone quay was built with protecting buttresses at either end, similar in construction to the main quay. This provided sheltered berths, away from the effects of swell in the lower harbour, especially during storm conditions when the lower berths may have been untenable. These upper sheltered berths and the additional facility of mooring mid-stream, provided the harbour with an added advantage over Lyme. Due to the Cobb's exposed nature, vessels were known to break free of their moorings during heavy weather, only to be wrecked on the town beach.

The painting (overleaf, top) dated 1850, shows Squire's Lane quay with a schooner moored mid-stream. The two buttresses jut out into the river with a quay in between. A warehouse of some form is thought to have existed in the field opposite the quay on a piece of levelled ground adjacent to Squire's Lane.

The Story of Axmouth Harbour

Old watercolour looking upstream, showing Squire's Lane quay – 1850. (Ted Gosling collection).

Representative watercolour showing Squire's Lane quay, c.1855. (Nigel Daniel).

Present day remains of quay foundations.

Nineteenth Century Revival of the Harbour

Above: Alfred Leyman's painting of the riverside tidal lane – 1890. (Elford Fine Art).

Left: 1870 photograph of Squire's Lane quay. (Original F. Frith & Co photo print).

The above photograph shows Squire's Lane quay around 1870. It was taken from a position looking upstream, before the construction of Axmouth Bridge. Part of the quay had already collapsed – a sign of things to come; although the protecting buttresses at either end are still in place, a hole has appeared in the southernmost one. The photo opposite bottom shows all that is left today, a line of foundation stones on the foreshore below Squire's Lane.

Incidentally Haven Cliff House had been redeveloped by J.H. Hallett into his residence overlooking the harbour, whilst his father resided at Stedcombe House until his death in 1814. Following this, Hallett leased Stedcombe (as recorded in the 1840 Axmouth Tithe Apportionment) to Thomas Huddlestone, preferring to live close to and perhaps keep an eye on his new venture, whilst receiving revenue for Stedcombe. The family also built Southcott Villa, possibly as the dower residence. The property now renamed Millmead, is located on the riverside just south of the village, showing a few architectural features similar to Haven Cliff. During the 1950s whilst Vice Admiral Sir (Arthur) Francis Pridham was in residence the house became known as the Admiral's House.

Village foreshore berths

Smaller vessels such as smacks and barges were able to proceed upstream as far as Axmouth, the waterside road had yet to be constructed. The only means of access was via the tidal lane between the harbour and village. Sections of the old track still exist alongside today's concrete embankment.

The lane was impassable during spring tides, forcing travellers to use the footpath passing through the riverside fields. The upstream berths had one clear advantage in that the loading and discharge of cargoes avoided using the muddy lane to access the lower quays!

Alfred Leyman's painting of the village foreshore – 1890.

A sloop unloading on Axmouth foreshore. (Nigel Daniel).

Below and bottom left: 'Vicarage' quay at low water with Hawkesdown in the background.

Bottom right: The author's dinghy alongside 'Vicarage' quay – May 2021.

'Vicarage' quay

A little further upstream from the village, a drying creek (locally known as Vicarage Creek) extends along the foreshore adjacent to Little Broomhill meadow. The remains of an old quay lie at the edge of the saltmarsh, approximately 30 metres in length. A line of stones (cow stones – rounded and weathered, brought from the coastal foreshore) can be seen in a north/south orientation with a form of return wall which runs alongside the drainage ditch, just to the south.

The stones are placed on end, typical of quay construction, resembling the similar remains downstream of Squire's Lane quay. The foundations of the wall are set back to the east, possibly providing a measure of shelter from the main estuary. The drying creek is now a shallow inlet with only a couple of feet at high water springs. In the past, it would have been deeper, easily affording navigable access to smaller trading craft and barges during spring tides. Its location, similar to the village foreshore, shared the advantages of being able to bring goods further upstream, avoiding the tidal lane.

Axmouth vessels

Interestingly, during the harbour's renewed commercial importance there are accounts of ships trading considerable distances overseas. The first two such vessels, both with local names were the *Axmouth* and the *Stedcombe*. Whilst the *Axmouth* has no recorded connection with Axmouth Harbour, the *Stedcombe* was owned by local interests. The *Axmouth* is mentioned in accounts of early exploration of the Great Lakes. She was sailing in company with the brig *Wellington* and was reported to be a 30-ton craft. She was noted for being manually hauled across the 'portage' between Lake Erie and Lake Superior in 1817, the first such vessel to be delivered to the North West Fur Company.

The schooner *Stedcombe*, was originally owned by Bussells of Lyme in 1818. She was a schooner of 128 tons, measuring 67 feet overall, a beam of 22 feet and depth of 12 feet. Subsequently owned by George Clarke of Axmouth, the vessel sailed for Australia where she was involved in local trading. Sadly she came to an untimely end. She was sent to the Spice Islands in the Bandar Sea, east of Borneo to search for the missing Royal Navy brig *Lady Nelson*. The brig was thought to have been taken by pirates off Timor Laut in the Maluku Islands. Unfortunately, the *Stedcombe* followed a similar fate and was similarly taken in 1825, the crew murdered except for the two apprentices. Due to their young age and with the support of the local women they were spared, but held captive for fourteen years. Eventually the sole survivor named Joseph Forbes was rescued by the schooner *Essington*, his compatriot having died on the island. Forbes finally landed at the Dutch trading centre of Kupang to tell his tale. Kupang was famous for being the port where Bligh finally reached civilization following his epic voyage across the Pacific having lost the *Bounty* to mutineers. Strangely enough, in 2010 I laid a new fibre optic cable from the Sunda Islands across the Sawu Sea to Kupang.

A third vessel named the *Eagle*, a brig of 147 tons, had almost completed a trans-Atlantic voyage, having sailed from Quebec with a cargo of timber May 1843. Having nearly reached the safety of Axmouth she was stranded in the entrance and became a total loss. The vessel which measured 77 feet overall was comparatively small for such a voyage across the North Atlantic. But it demonstrates the degree of seamanship and navigation amongst the local community to perform trans-oceanic voyages; she was owned locally by the Head family of Seaton.

Arrivals and departures

Fortunately, during a period in the late 1850s *Pulman's Weekly News* (*PWN*) published regular notices of arrivals and departures in their weekly journal. Today this makes interesting reading and brings to life the comings and goings within the harbour. During the 1980s local Axmouth historian Graham Myers spent many long hours delving through old copies of *Pulman's* to gather information relating to the village. In doing so he also un-earthed information regarding the maritime trading activities of Axmouth Harbour. Through his diligence we now have a much clearer understanding of the level of commerce associated with the port. *Pulman's* published an article on 25 August 1857, which provides a good impression of the volume of trade:

'The harbour which is so highly favoured by nature presents at this time a very business-like appearance. On Wednesday 19th August no less than four schooners entered in splendid style and with two others already inside were soon safely moored in sheltered quarters. In addition to the trade of the resident merchant Mr. L .Halse, a vast quantity of timber is shipped off by Mr. T. Brice Esq, and the state of the quays shows what is doing in railway materials.'

This demonstrates the potential of the port's ability to handle more than just a couple of vessels as often quoted. Six vessels moored within the harbour would have been impressive sight for the small port of Axmouth and provides adequate proof of its renewed importance to the locality. Accommodating six vessels individually alongside tenable berths would have probably been close to the harbour's maximum capacity. Although it would have easily accommodated more vessels within the estuary, not requiring alongside berths.

The *Pulman's* article continues:- *'Axmouth may yet be destined to become a place of considerable importance, certainly as far as the harbour is concerned, that could be made one of the best on the English coast. It is spacious and its bottom is excellent. Persons of experience say that with the outlay of a small capital in deepening the river, and confining its head by a wall on the Seaton side, this wall meeting a small western pier, ingress and egress might be had at all times for vessels of heavy burden. No inconvenience would arise from the shifting beach, which now, at times, gives some little trouble.'*

The proposition of constructing a western wall to stabilize the entrance, indicates continuing difficulties with the movement of shingle. The suggestion of deepening the channel to allow access at all states of the tide would have entailed a vast amount of dredging. Whilst potentially a major improvement, its viability would have been very doubtful, let alone the immense work involved to expand on such a proposed scale. Axmouth was principally a port for coastal trade,

The pier from seaward – 1840.

governed by tidal access, which restricted the type of vessels able to use it. The reference to the excellent bottom confirms the suitability of the estuary for vessels to *dry out* at low water without fear of damage. The harbour was ideally suited to the smaller coasting vessels of the time, such as schooners and brigs, with smacks servicing the needs of smaller cargo consignments.

Pulman's quoted the number of vessels visiting the harbour for the two consecutive years 1856/57. Sixty-one vessels and 2819 tons of cargo were handled in 1856; in the following year this had increased to seventy-nine and 4050 tons. This shows a remarkable increase in trade and justifies Hallett's investment in rejuvenating the harbour. In less than fifty years the once small and very limited navigable creek had become a promising commercial hub for the East Devon district. Lyme being an ancient well-established harbour presented direct competition, but Axmouth possessed some advantages that Lyme could not offer. Axmouth had easier land access to the hinterland via the Axe valley and possessed greater storage facilities ashore for the numerous commodities handled by the port. Axmouth also offered greater protection to vessels once within the estuary. There were numerous occasions where vessels were literally washed out of the Cobb and wrecked on the nearby shore. Axmouth's Achilles' heel was its entrance. Although much improved it still suffered from the periodic build up of the shingle bar, having an entrance exposed to the predominant south westerlies.

Further quotes from *PWN* identify the vessels actually using the harbour. 10th November 1857:- *'Some alterations in the Axmouth channel course caused by recent storms has since reverted to normal. Ships in harbour reported as 'Elizabeth' of Brixham, 'Caroline' of Guernsey, 'Countess' of Durham and the 'Providence' of Grimsby. The latter will lay up for the winter. Nearly all the timber and hides washed from the quay in recent storms has now been recovered.'*

Amongst the sailing notices were some regular visitors to the harbour, for instance the schooner *Anne & Emily* (her master, Captain Searle) featured frequently. She was involved in the coastal trade and often only to adjacent ports such as Lyme and Topsham. For instance, *PWN* referred to coal being stockpiled at Axmouth and carried to Lyme due to lack of storage. Obviously, the estuary's surroundings provided much greater potential for storage opportunities on both the east and west banks, much greater than Lyme could offer. Unfortunately, the *Anne & Emily* came to an untimely end, wrecked at the Cobb in 1867. Other regular visitors were the *Jane* (master – Berry) and the *Providence* (master – Gush). Both these vessels were on regular voyages to and from Newcastle importing coal to Axmouth. There is also mention of foreign vessels arriving in the port, for instance in April 1858 the French chasse-marée, *Saint Nicolas* arrived from Rouen; these vessels were large three-masted luggers noted for their speed and smuggling potential. The Prussian schooner *Nodestern* arrived from the Baltic port of Rugenwalde in September 1858, whilst the Dutch vessel *Leo Simmige* similarly arrived from the Baltic in the same month, probably both were importing timber into Axmouth. The *Maria* arrived in October having sailed from Smyrna in Turkey – matching in distance some of the trans-Atlantic voyages from Canada.

The dangers of working cargo were all too apparent. Local resident Thomas Real was injured in September 1857 whilst ballasting a ship within the harbour. Falling into an open hold, or over an unprotected coaming was a common cause of death or injury. Another serious incident was reported in December 1857 when two men lost their lives. They were engaged in retrieving an anchor for the schooner *Johnson*, when their boat capsized drowning both of them; one was a Beer resident named Edward Abbott. On 14 February 1860 a 20-ton barge was wrecked within the harbour due to storms, although there was no record of any injuries. Another injury related to a fall which happened in June 1861. Axmouth resident Solomon Ayres fractured a leg whilst unloading coal from a ship. He was lucky to survive when a hatch board gave way, causing him to fall into the vessel's hold.

Tidal survey

In 1836 the British Association for the Advancement of Science wished to determine 'the level of the sea' in order to gain an understanding of mean sea level and any land movement. A Mr Bunt of Bristol was engaged to carry out the survey which required measuring the tidal range at three locations around the British Isles. The points chosen were Portishead, Bridgwater and Axmouth. Tidal observations were taken during January and July of 1838. Certain inequalities were observed and noted by Mr Bunt who had taken his levels within the bar at Axmouth. On the two different occasions it was observed that the bar had altered its position thus producing differing levels, some 1.29 feet apart. This was resolved by taking levels outside the bar to eliminate the error. So, it would seem that even with the benefits of the new pier, harbour users still had to contend with a degree of varying depths at the entrance.

The levels were recorded utilising fixed datum points designated by Mr Bunt. Two were set up at Axmouth, a granite block placed within the warehouse (kindly procured by J.H. Hallet), the other a copper bolt inserted into the church wall. The difference between the two levels was a little under 6 feet. An assumed zero datum point was arbitrarily taken at 100 feet below which the tidal heights were observed and compared. This resulted in mean tide level at Axmouth of 71.96 feet, whilst at Portishead it was calculated at 72.69 feet. From these mean levels, tidal ranges at each location could be evaluated. The discrepancy in mean levels was assumed to be due to two differing bodies of water, i.e. the English and Bristol Channels.

Interestingly the local antiquarian Peter Orlando Hutchinson visited the harbour in 1872 having heard of the granite blocks and wished to discover their whereabouts. From his diary he noted: '*We went to the river and crossed over on the ferry. At the ferry house we found an intelligent man called Stark or Start. For some years we have tried to learn something definite concerning the great stone laid down in between twenty and thirty years ago by some savants to mark the level of the spot, similar levels having been placed at intervals across the county northward to the neighbourhood of Bridgewater. It has been suspected that the land was slowly undergoing some changes of level, and by repeating the levels from time to time along the fixed points, any change will be ascertained. We found the stone inside the warehouse. We entered the western large door and found it at the right hand further corner. It was a block of granite measuring five and a half long, two feet four inches wide and apparently one and a half feet deep lying on the ground, or perhaps there is a bed of concrete under it. In the middle of the western or outer end there is inserted a brass or copper bolt, green with verdigris, about two inches in diameter, and from the centre of this I presume that the level was taken. We were both rather surprised at not finding a horizontal cut across the head of this bolt, as usual in the Ordnance bench marks to mark the exact level. On scratching the bolt with my nail, I fancied I could feel an indentation, but believe it was nothing more than an accidental scratch. Perhaps as afterwards suggested by Mr Heineken, there may have been a cap soldered on the head of the bolt to preserve such a cut from injury, if it should be there. To protect this stone from being meddled with, a massive arch of masonry has been turned over it. We could not learn where the next stone northward was placed. There is a copper bolt in the front of Axmouth Church (on the tower) put there I believe by Ordnance surveyors.'*

The datum stone within the warehouse – 1872.

Local cartography

Early coastal charts were lacking in detail and often quite inaccurate. Under the direction of the Hydrographer of the Navy, Captain Francis Beaufort, a programme of re-surveying the South West coast was conducted between the years 1851 to 1853. Captain W. Sheringham RN was tasked with surveying progressively westwards along the coasts of south Dorset and Devon. It was during these surveys that he charted Axmouth Harbour, leaving us with a very accurate survey of the harbour, conducted in 1852. The chart below was the initial draught survey of the harbour, this was then produced as a finished article for navigation. On close inspection it will be noted a line of what are presumably piles lie to the east of the pier head, this may have been some form of sea defence to protect the exposed Customs House.

The coastal survey techniques depended first on laying a marker buoy whose position was accurately fixed by celestial observations. From this point sounding lines radiated out at quarter point intervals, cross referencing their position from coastal features. Slowly a pattern of depth contours was built up from which the

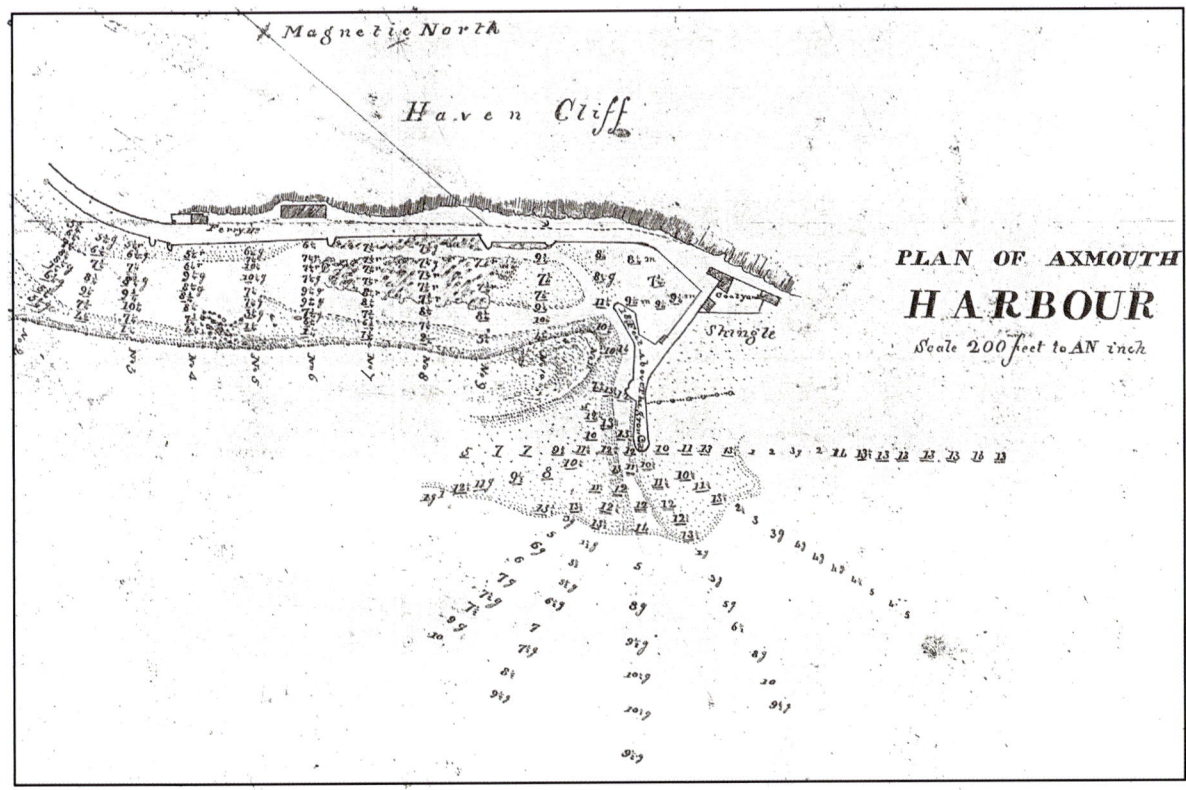

The original survey of Axmouth Harbour – from which the 1852 chart was produced. (UKHO Archive).

charts were drawn. Sheringham established a tidal monitoring station below White Cliff at Seaton Hole. On the foreshore a tidal pole was secured at the low water mark from which tidal height observations were made. Calculations were then made to record the tidal ranges and times of local high and low water. Similarly, the tidal stream was observed in a position approximately 3 miles south of Beer Head. This information is still used today, the tidal 'diamond' information on Admiralty chart 3315 originating from Sheringham's 1852 survey.

The Admiralty produced worldwide 'Sailing Directions', providing mariners with navigational guidance. The following is an extract from an early edition of the *Channel Pilot* (1878):- '*AXMOUTH.—Between Beer head and Haven cliff, is the broad and fertile valley of the Axe, apparently the ancient bed of a large river, though at present only an insignificant stream flows into the sea. At the entrance of the river Axe there is a small pier and landing quay; whilst under Haven cliff, which forms a prominent object from seaward, is a dock, which is said to accommodate vessels drawing 12 feet water. A short distance westward of the pier, stands the village of Seaton, which is favourably known as a pleasant watering place.*'

A similar account, but written from a landsman's perspective, *The Handbook for Travellers in Devon*, written by T.C. Paris in 1863, states '*It is a diminutive quay and pier at the embouchure of the river, which is a shifting opening, little broader than the vessels which enter it and sometimes completely barred by easterly winds. The view from this little pier is most charming; Culverhole Point is the furthest land eastward; Beer Head, called by fishermen Berry Wold to the westward.*' (Known earlier as Berreworth Point, as recorded in 1585). What a pity Paris didn't take some photographs!

Return of a seafaring village

With the foreshore drying berths and the old Vicarage Creek quay, the village would have once again taken on a maritime nature. In addition, William Rogers in his *Wanderings in Devon* (1869), commented on a jetty which had two or three boats moored to it, which is shown on the 1840 tithe map. An old photo also shows a small capstan and wooden landing stage just downstream from the village adjacent to Millmead. The jetty and landing stage would have provided a limited facility for gaining access to and from the river to avoid the muddy foreshore. These small jetties may have served ship's crews by providing a dry landing for those wishing to visit the village hostelries!

Photo of Waterside with jetty and capstan – 1890.

In regaining some of its seafaring tradition, Coxhead comments:-
'The Harbour Inn at Axmouth is of great age and parts of it date back to the days when the haven was in a flourishing condition. In the cosy warmth of the tavern parlour travelers would have heard many stirring tales of far voyages, desperate sea-fights and wild storms as the hardy mariners thronging the room exchanged their experiences.' Today's pub sign proudly displays the Harbour Inn's twelfth century origins.

'By its nautical name the Ship Inn proclaims its connection with the maritime past of Axmouth. It is comparatively modern and stands on the site of an ancient tavern of the same name which was in existence as early as 1483. The old building was unfortunately destroyed by fire on Christmas day 1879, and was replaced by the present attractive looking inn.'

Donald Payne wrote in his *Devon Harbours*, published in 1952:- *'Yet again a pier was built and for some years a small-scale trade was carried on. Two schooners, with mixed cargoes, plied regularly between Axmouth and London. Gradually other vessels appeared in the estuary bringing in coal for the lime kilns and taking away hides, flints and pebbles. Engravings of some hundred years ago often show four or five vessels lying at anchor in the estuary. It seemed as though, at long last, life was returning to the forgotten harbours of the Axe. Alas, to-day hardly a man or woman remains in Axmouth who ever saw the square tops'l schooners anchored by the Harbour Inn. I talked to Mr. Beer, one of Axmouth's oldest inhabitants, and an active, rosy-cheeked old man. We chatted together beside the water's edge. He could, he said, tell me all about the toll-bridge, "but they shipping days was afore my time."'*

Axmouth Coastguard

The Coastguard had an established base within the village, its origins stemming back to the Preventative Water Guard of the late 1700s (taken under the Board of Customs in 1822). Smuggling along this section of the coast was rife in the eighteenth and nineteenth centuries hence the presence of Coastguards within the village. There are many tales of smuggling routes through the village, to and from the beach at Culverhole Point (*Cuvr'l*), a mile east of the harbour entrance. The beach close the west of Culverhole Point provided a quiet landing spot at high water, with a path connecting onto the main Landslip path, ascending to the cliff top. This then gave access to the back lanes, such as Leggets, where an illicit cargo could be quickly spirited away into the hinterland of Combpyne and Musbury. Coombe Farm in the village centre was a recognised 'safe house' signified by a bottle end inserted into the wall. It's just visible, tucked beneath the dining room window sill, internally it was positioned in way of a window seat. A candle could be held close to the neck of the bottle, which shone a dim green light outside – sufficient to signify that coast was clear. Evidence of the more sinister side to smuggling is noted in Seaton's church records. In the list of vicars there is an entry for the Rev. Francis Drake, who was killed by smugglers on Bosshill, a mile north of Axmouth in 1769. Drake apparently waged a single-handed fight against the 'trade' but ultimately paid for it with his life.

The Coastguards were initially housed in a small terrace of cottages opposite the Forge in Higher Axmouth, although in 1851 the Chief Coastguard, John Archibald Hodgskins Lt. R.N. lived with his wife and daughter, rather conveniently in the Harbour Inn! There was also a pair of Coastguard cottages between the Harbour and Ship

View of Higher Axmouth with the old Coastguard cottages on the left – 1880.

The Story of Axmouth Harbour

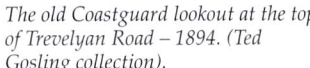
The old Coastguard lookout at the top of Trevelyan Road – 1894. (Ted Gosling collection).

Inns, now long demolished. The Coastguard's presence suggests there was a significant need to counter smuggling activities east of the River Axe. During the 1800s, a lookout was maintained on the top of Haven Cliff, equipped with a flag staff to communicate with the customs cutters offshore. The present-day footpath still leads across Frogmore field from where the terrace of coastguard cottages once stood opposite the Forge. The path then leads on to Stepps Lane before crossing the fields out to the flag staff on top of Haven Cliff. The two cliff top fields were known as Upper and Lower Beacon Field, presumably this refers back to an earlier time when beacons were an important communication link, such as heralding the arrival of the Armada. In May 1877 2 acres of the cliff top toppled into the sea. In anticipation of this happening the Coastguards had removed their flag staff.

Another Coastguard lookout used by the Preventive Service existed at the seaward end of Trevelyan Road, just on the boarder between Axmouth and Seaton. This was a substantial building owned by Sir John Trevelyan, decorated with crenellated tops; it eventually became a tea room. Ultimately the building was demolished to make way for the present Trevelyan Road terrace bordering the harbour.

Pulman's Weekly News reported on an inquest held at the Ship Inn on January 24 1860. A member of the Branscombe Coastguards, Raffell was drowned when his boat was 'upset' at Axmouth Harbour bar. It was described as a *melancholy accident*, and the deceased was buried in Axmouth churchyard. This demonstrates the dangers encountered at the entrance – even for the Coastguard.

On 24 March 1874 a lease was arranged between William Trewlaney Hallett and the Commissioners of the Admiralty in order to relocate and establish a Coastguard station at the top of Squire's Lane, above Haven Cliff House. The site above the harbour was leased for 99 years for the sum of £300, with an annual rent of £7. The substantial Victorian properties still have a commanding view of the Bay. An adjoining boiler house retains cast iron guttering with the 'fouled anchor' emblem on the down pipe, signifying the Coastguard's Royal Navy heritage, having originally been administered by

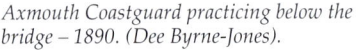
Axmouth Coastguard practicing below the bridge – 1890. (Dee Byrne-Jones).

the Commissioners of the Admiralty. The Squire's Lane Coastguard Station was linked by a direct footpath to the lookout and the flag staff on top of Haven Cliff. In January 1894 *PWN* reported a collision at sea off Seaton between a small steamer and a barque. Mr Stipling, Chief Officer of the Axmouth Coastguards reported that several crew members were missing and a number of bodies were later washed up on the beach.

The Axmouth Coastguard Station finally closed in 1948 following rationalization. A new station was built in Beer ending a long association with Axmouth Harbour and the village.

Axmouth Ferry

Axmouth Ferry was part of a series of ancient river crossings or passages along the south west coast. The *'passage'* is mentioned in ancient documents and was actively in use until the building of Axmouth Bridge in 1877. The passage formed an important connection within the ancient coastal ridgeway network, passing through much of south Dorset and into south Devon. The ferry provided a considerable saving in distance, Axe Bridge some 2 miles inland being the lowest permanent crossing point; and itself prone to flooding. In building the new harbour wall Hallett provided improved access for passengers using the ferry, with steps constructed close to the Ferry Cottage. These were incorporated between two small buttresses, providing a sheltered and more accessible landing. Although the landing on the west side of the river at low water would have been less attractive. The muddy foreshore led to Passage Lane, the track leading west along the beach to Seaton.

The 1860 photo of the harbour shows the ferryman's boat lying at the steps below his cottage. If one looks closely there would appear to be a span wire rigged across the river, this may well have been used by the ferry during the peak flow of the ebb and flood, especially on springs. By means of a snatch block free to travel along the wire, the bow of the ferryboat was attached to it, allowing the boat to manoeuvre back and forth across the stream with little effort. It also had the added safety factor of preventing the ferry from being swept out of the harbour during the maximum ebb! Clearly, this couldn't have been permanently rigged, since it would have restricted navigation to the upstream berths. Alternatively, the line may have been a messenger rope rigged in preparation for warping a vessel in or out of the harbour.

Edward Cooke's 1861 painting of the harbour shows a larger flat-bottomed ferry in operation with a horse and cart aboard. The vessel is being manoeuvred by a long pole to punt it across the river. In reality handling a craft of this nature could only be achieved during periods of slack water. The ferry more commonly used was of a conventional type, having space for foot passengers only, horse and carts were left to wade across the ford at low water.

The photo overleaf dated 1870 clearly shows the Ferryman's Cottage, warehouse and Customs House near to the entrance. The inner end of the pier is also clearly visible, although there appears to be a build-up of shingle within the holding basin. The ferry boat lies on the foreshore awaiting customers. On 16 October 1866 Thomas Hart who held the lease for the Axmouth ferry was summoned to appear at Axminster petty sessions for nonpayment of the poor rate.

The new Squires Lane Coastguard Station. (Dee Byrne-Jones).

Fouled anchor emblem on CG downpipe.

Axmouth Harbour Ferry – 1861. (© 2016 Christie's Images Limited).

The ferryboat on the foreshore. (Ted Gosling collection).

Accounts for Axmouth ferry in 1870 reveal that £31 was received in tolls, wages cost £15 and repairs £5, presumably the remaining £11 was his lordship's profit.

Axmouth village ford

Commentators have suggested that a ford once existed across the estuary at Axmouth, in effect a continuation of the village street. Today there appears to be a line of stones and gravel crossing the river adjacent to the village. This is misleading, since it is the protective scalpings placed over the sewerage pipe that crosses beneath the Axe leading to the main Seaton plant. The pipeline was installed beneath the river bed during the 1970s. It followed the alignment of an old wall (jetty) extending from the east bank as shown on the Axmouth tithe map of 1840.

Viewing it today one could easily be misled, assuming it was once a ford; it even creates a slight weir effect at low water. If such a ford had existed then it runs contrary to the theory that the estuary was historically wider and deeper. Even today the depth of water (at low tide) is some eighteen inches and with soft mudflats to negotiate on either side, it would have made for a hazardous crossing. Further, reviewing LiDAR surveys of the adjacent Seaton Marshes shows no sign of any trackway or path leading across the reclaimed marshes. Leland wrote of his passage across the salt marshes from Seaton to Axmouth, *'I passed from Seaton at the ebb over the salt marshes and the River Axe to Axmouth.'*

This was interpreted by Margaret Parkinson in her paper *Axe Estuary and its Marshes* (1985), that Leland had used a ford opposite the village. Parkinson's claim is based upon a seventeenth-century entitlement to Mrs Elizabeth Starr who continued to have leave to cross the marsh on what was considered an old right of way. This was to access Sir Walter Earle's land following construction of the Willoughby embankment. Due to the boundary location between to the two parishes, Earle's portion of saltmarsh would have only been accessible from Seaton Marsh. Understandably there would have been a right of way to access this land since the River Axe effectively cut it off from the rest of Axmouth parish.

In fact, Leland did not describe where or how he crossed over the river; I would suggest that perhaps he used the ancient ferry crossing rather than a ford. One also has to bear in mind that this was prior to the construction of the embankment, therefore the estuary would have been of greater proportions, making a ford at this location even less likely. Additionally, had Margaret Parkinson been able to access today's LiDAR mapping she may well have drawn a different conclusion. There is nothing to suggest a direct route across the marshes, no raised path is shown as one might expect, and in fact a large silted up creek lies across the suggested route.

Axmouth Harbour ford

More latterly, a ford certainly existed further downstream. This provided transport across the estuary at a point close to where the old Axmouth Bridge now exists. The ford was very much dependent on the state of the tide, only permissible at low water. This site provided firmer compacted shingle banks on either side of the river, allowing easier access at low water. The firm river bed at this point permitted 'fording' by horse and cart. A photo taken prior to construction of the old bridge (c.1870) shows the gravel 'slipways' leading down to the crossing, linking Passage Lane to Waterside, the tidal lane leading to Axmouth. The 1840 tithe map shows both the line of the ferry and ford. The ford's location was also confirmed by D.M. Stirling in 1838, when commenting on a wreck within the estuary, now referred to as the Axe Boat (see page 128) lying a little further upstream. *PWN* reported in February 1877 that the new bridge was almost complete, and interestingly commented on the ford, *'it is said to be dangerous to use following recent flooding which affected the depth and currents'*. The construction of the bridge had constricted the flow, resulting in greater scouring and increased depth of the river channel, ending the use of the ford.

Photograph taken before the bridge – 1870. (Original F. Frith & Co photo print).

The Story of Axmouth Harbour

Reports of storm damage

On 3 September 1864 John Hothersall Hallett died, and with him the last days of Axmouth Harbour's maritime trading. It was no coincidence following his death that the harbour started to decline. J.H. Hallett had done so much to revive the Old Haven and through his efforts Axmouth Harbour had once more become a thriving port. Without his ambition and continuing drive to maintain the harbour, his descendants soon lost interest in its viability. The estate passed on to his nephew William Trelawney Hallett, who showed little business acumen. Signs of poor management followed, eventually leading to the sale of the estate including Axmouth Harbour, thus closing a long chapter of Axmouth's connection with *'they shipping days'*.

Pulman's Weekly News reported the following, on 12 December 1865, that Axmouth pier was said to be in a state of partial ruin. A further report on January 30 1866 reported that storms had washed away the roadway below Passage House including part of the harbour wall and that the pier head had entirely gone. This heralded the final decline of the harbour's commercial operation. With the pier head demolished the scouring effect of ebb tide would have diminished and the entrance once again was subject to the effects of the shifting shingle bar. In January 1867 *PWN* reported further storm damage, Axmouth Harbour House (the customs house situated near to the pier) which was unoccupied, had its windows damaged and the interior inundated by sand and water due to severe storms. The severe storm saw the river rise up to Axmouth's churchyard gate (no doubt having flooded the cottages on the corner) and sheep were washed out of the river, miraculously some were rescued.

In *A Log-book of a Fisherman & Zoologist* by Francis Trevelyan Buckland the following statement was taken from W.T. Hallett's foreman Mr Beard:- *'On the 12th April 1868 a huge bore came unexpectedly in from the sea at Axmouth in Devonshire. When surveying the estuary of the River Axe in company with the Chairman of the Axe Salmon Fishery District Mr W.T. Hallett of Stedcombe House, I observed that the entrance to the river was blocked up to a great extent by an enormous accumulation of shingle. I was told that in April a most remarkable wave came in suddenly from the open sea. The sea had been previously perfectly calm and there was no wind whatever, the water must have risen suddenly as far as I could make out at least twenty or thirty feet. Mr Beard foreman to Mr Hallett gave me the following particulars. The first ground sea was seen on 12th April 1868 about three or four miles out at sea, it reached the shore about half past*

Axmouth, the high tide almost covers the lane.

four o'clock pm and continued till nine o'clock. About eight o'clock just at the turn of tide it was tremendous. None of the newspapers appear to have noticed this phenomenon at all.'

The comments of Mr Beard are detailed and could be attributed to one of two effects. The initial description lends itself to that of a tsunami. It mentions an initial singular wave seen at some distance approaching the shore, typical of such phenomena, but there is no mention of the sea receding ahead of the wave breaking onshore, a typical characteristic of a tsunami.

A second and perhaps more probable cause is the effect of a storm generated many miles away. On these rare occasions the swell travels over vast distances and as it proceeds into shallow water it is slowed and increases in height. If conditions are right the increasingly steep long period waves reach the shoreline as a heavy groundswell causing untold flooding and damage. This would seem to be the cause of the event in 1868 since it had persisted over a period of at least four hours when it reached its peak, presumably taking a further period to subside. There is now some thought that these events maybe caused by what is termed a meteo-tsunami. They are triggered by rapidly moving weather events that cause a sudden change in atmospheric pressure, moving at the same velocity as the waves. They can generate small waves in deep water, but like conventional tsunamis the waves grow much larger as they move into shallow water, not as a single wave but as an extended period of large waves.

The Times reported the event, but it was dated 23 April rather than the 12th. It reported a *terrifying and extraordinary event* which struck the coast of Devon and Dorset. All was calm on April 23, 1868 when 20ft to 30ft waves reared up out of the Channel and with a deafening roar crashed into Lyme Regis, overwhelming the Cobb. Farther along the coast Burton Bradstock was inundated as waves swamped the beach. The road to Bridport became impassable and the waters surged up the River Brit and flooded the inland town of Bridport. Budleigh Salterton in east Devon was also struck by flooding waves. Similarly, extraordinary events were reported in Plymouth. *'The swell caused the sea, at high tide, to cover the breakwater with one white foam, which occasionally enveloped the lighthouse. The waves at times ran 20 or 30 feet up the steep rocks at Bovisand, and the spray rose a hundred feet or more. Such an unusual swell induced many masters and seamen ashore to go to the citadel and the Hoe to witness the extraordinary scene.'*

A remarkably similar event occurred just over one hundred years later in 1979. The occurrence of this extreme wave action was due to an Atlantic storm many hundreds of miles away, generating a huge groundswell. In 1868 there was no mention of Axmouth Harbour sustaining any damage except for the shingle accumulation. Although only a year later further storm damage started to affect the viability of the port. For on 9 February 1869, PWN reported *'very high seas on Sunday week, old Axmouth inhabitants said not occurring since the memorable high water of Nov 1824. The well-built outer pier constructed by Mr Hallett had held, had that given way the sea would have overwhelmed the beach, railway station and gas house. The inner pier gave way and the marsh was a sea itself up to Axmouth church.'* This is slightly at odds with the previous report of January 1866 where it reports that the pier head had gone.

Commercial Decline

The harbour slips back into obscurity

The harbour had continued in full operation for approximately sixty years, until as Pulman writes in the *Book of the Axe* (1874):- 'Across Leland's "mighty rigge of pible stones" which choked the estuary and now composes Seaton Beach,—across the ferry over the Axe near its mouth, at the easternmost end of the beach,—and the visitor finds himself in the parish of Axmouth and at the foot of the bold and lofty eminence called Haven Cliff. The view from the top of this cliff, and from all the other points of the range of which it forms the southern extremity,—and especially from Hocksdon Hill, which towers above the village,— is not more extensive than beautiful, and produces a striking effect upon the stranger of taste who beholds it for the first time, while it never palls upon those most familiar with it. What is left of the harbour at the mouth of the river, as stated in my account of Seaton, is the unaided work of the late J. H. Hallett Esq., lord of the manor, and uncle of W. T. Hallett, Esq., his heir. Strictly speaking, the visitor would be within the parish of Axmouth before crossing the ferry, where the boundary posts on the beach no doubt mark the western bank of the river at the time of their erection.

It is much to be regretted, for humanity's sake as well as for the sake of local commerce, that the once famous harbour should be left a useless ruin. But the deaf ear of the Government continues, as heretofore, to be turned against appeals for help, and it has long been found useless to make

B.J.M. Donne's watercolour of the pier – 1875. (Seaton Museum).

The old pierhead looking west. (Ted Gosling collection).

them by private individuals. A few years ago, two trading vessels sailed regularly to and from London, and other vessels used the harbour. But the introduction of the railway transferred the considerable carrying trade of the neighborhood from the water to the land.

The operation of the tides and shingle pressing the mouth to the eastward, along with the diminution of the volume of the river, as already referred to, and the discontinuance of harbour repairs—all this is sufficient to account for the present dilapidated condition of the place. A considerable portion of the inner pier, forming a portion of the old work, was washed away in a gale on Sunday, January 31, 1869.'

An interesting watercolour accurately shows the harbour entrance in 1875, which is slightly at odds with Pulman's account, since it shows the outer section of the pier missing, but it does endorse his report of 1866. The painting by local Axmouth artist B.J.M. Donne (1831-1928), shows the remains of the outer pier foundations and a few wooden piles. I feel this picture provides a more realistic portrayal of the harbour, even taking into account the obvious decline. The harbour wall is far less grand and smaller in scale than that painted by Edward Cooke, but the detail is accurate. Careful examination shows a culvert under the inner section of the pier. This may well have been inserted to create a circulation of water within the basin to reduce silting – previously discussed. By this time it was of little importance since the basin looks to be partially filled with shingle, no longer able to accommodate larger vessels. Incidentally Donne is buried in Axmouth churchyard, the grave marked by an elaborate headstone decorated with a large clam shell.

The painting above looks westwards from the east side of the entrance. It is a poor-quality reproduction, showing the reduced pierhead on the right with the rock remains extending seawards; centrally, in the far distance, one can just make out White Cliff. The painting may well be one of William Newbery's works.

Pulman continues:- *'I shall merely observe here that since the washing away of the pier at Axmouth, three or four years ago (1869), a "bar, or shoal," has evidently begun to form off the mouth of the river, which itself is also undergoing change.'* The 1878 Channel Pilot made the following comment:- *'Axmouth harbour is the private property of Mr. W. Trelawny Hallett who gave notice, 12th April 1877, that the piers, quays, and other works had been greatly damaged during a gale, and that in consequence the harbour was unsafe for the use of ships or boats.'*

The harbour crane. (Ted Gosling collection).

Similar crane type – Mangrove Bay, Bermuda – 2016.

Sadly, once again the harbour had fallen into decline. There were a number of contributory factors this time. The age of the steam railway had arrived in East Devon – a direct competitor to seaborne trade. The building of Axmouth Bridge barred access to the estuary and a lack of funding all contributed to the harbour's demise. Pulman's reference to a bar forming off the mouth of the river shows that Hallett's design had been effective in keeping the entrance channel scoured. The loss of the outer pier soon allowed the shingle bar to re-form, a situation that prevails today.

Donald Payne wrote:- *'But just as a revival of sea-borne trade was clearly under way it was scotched. Early one morning in the autumn of 1867 gangs of workmen appeared among the salt pans and mud flats of the estuary. Piles were driven into the marsh; tracks were laid; the railway came to Seaton.*

The same railway line that takes away trade also brings in visitors. But I for one feel that when the last vessel has cast off from a deserted jetty it leaves that anchorage the poorer for its passing. Thus, it was with Axmouth. Less than a decade after the single-line railway had reached out to the neighbouring town of Seaton, the River Axe was closed to commercial shipping. Across the mouth of the river, where once a ferry had plied for hire and where for generations a horse and cart had crossed at low tide, a concrete toll bridge was built which no trading vessel could ever hope to pass.'

The coming of the railway must have had an enormous effect on local trade. Quite suddenly there was no reliance on wind and tide. One can imagine the reluctance of Hallett to keep the harbour going in the face of such competition. Harbour repairs were always a challenge to perform in such an exposed position, and with decreasing revenue it would have been difficult to justify the expense. Faced with a backdrop of general decline, the estate lost interest in the harbour allowing it to slowly decay.

Payne's account of the railway construction omits to say that it actually utilised the embankment constructed by Willoughby in the seventeenth century. This provided a convenient raised and level route to the terminus located on the back slope of Seaton Beach. Without the embankment one wonders if the railway would have been built at all? Construction of the railway required raising the embankment a further 3 feet to ensure it remained above the flood waters of the Axe; it was also widened by 10 feet. Material for this was taken from the adjoining strip of estuary salt marsh, bordering the embankment.

The old crane shaft – April 2020.

Its removal formed a channel some 40 feet (12m) wide running parallel to the embankment, from the Broad Sluice, upstream to a point opposite the village of Axmouth, almost a mile in length. This channel does not appear on Searle's map of 1806, lending evidence to its formation during the railway line construction. This feature remains today as a shallow channel separating the embankment from what are now salt marsh islands and is still navigable at high water in a small boat. The lower section of embankment adjacent to the Seaton Station platforms was eventually encased in concrete to give it better protection. Prior to the construction of the bridge the lower embankment was more exposed to the effects of swell entering the harbour in heavy weather.

The railway eventually opened in 1868, bringing a new trade to the area, besides the commodities that were once brought by sea. Visitors had arrived, generating a new form of income that Seaton quickly adapted to. Sadly, the harbour took no place in this new form of development and quietly slipped from importance.

Today there is little physical evidence of the harbour's commercial operation. The now converted warehouse provides two harbour side residences, Moorings and Harbour House. On the west side of the harbour the old coalyard has been absorbed into the yacht club's compound, a small section of the old cobbled yard is still visible alongside the slipway. Upstream, a line of foreshore stones are the only remnants of Squire's Lane quay. Close to the harbour mouth, a cast iron stump of a crane remains in place. It served to load and discharge vessels berthed in the holding basin, tucked in behind the old pier.

The crane can be seen in the lefthand photograph opposite, along with a recent photo of a similar design I took on the quay near our cable base at Mangrove Bay, Bermuda – a survivor from a different era.

The English & Bristol Channels Canal

In 1825 an act was obtained for the construction of the English & Bristol Channels Canal. The proposed canal route was due to run from Seaton Bay and terminate in the River Parrett near to Bridgwater. It was claimed that sailing vessels could save 220 miles by using the canal, avoiding the generally windward passage down Channel, which could take many days during the winter. Although not directly associated with Axmouth Harbour, the canal's construction may have had a detrimental impact. The construction of a harbour at Beer would have been in direct competition to Axmouth, being in the more sheltered part of the bay and available at all states of the tide it would have quickly established itself as a preferable harbour.

A substantial port was to be constructed encompassing Beer Roads, with a locked inner floating basin. From Beer the canal led inland beneath White Cliff and via a series of locks skirted close west and north of Seaton before following a path along the Axe Valley to a point east of Chard. The canal's dimensions were to be 90 feet in breadth, 15 feet deep, capable of allowing vessels of 200 tons to transit the 44 miles. The canal would have reached 345 feet above sea level at its summit, requiring 29 locks. Having reached the plateau area east of the Blackdown Hills it then required a further 29 locks to reach the Bristol Channel. Extensive surveys were carried out to confirm levels, although not be confused with Bunt's tidal survey some ten years later.

Two reservoirs serving the canal were to be constructed, each at the head of the Rivers Axe and Yarty; of course, both rivers feed into the Axe estuary. Reducing their natural flow would have impacted on the all-important volume of water required to maintain the harbour entrance and could have been catastrophic for both the harbour and estuary.

Due to lack of funding Telford's scheme never came to fruition. The advent of steam and growing size of vessels effectively sealed its fate to the drawing board.

Axmouth Bridge

An Act of Parliament was passed in 1863 in order to build the Seaton branch line and to construct a bridge over the River Axe. The finance was raised through the Seaton & Beer Railway Company. The directors eventually sanctioned £3000 of stock to be raised for the bridge construction in 1875. *PWN* reported that preparations were under way to commence construction of Axmouth Bridge in November of that year – it was reported that an architect had arrived with several horses and a quantity of cement! The bridge was be constructed of mass concrete, a pioneering method at the time. By September 1876 work was nearing completion and in November it was opened to pedestrians; the first carriage to negotiate the bridge was that of Colonel Hallett of Haven Cliff. In the following January one of the piers suffered some damage as a result of floods. The bridge was rendered temporarily impassable due to some *'imperfections'*, which ultimately resulted in subsidence.

Following remedial work, the bridge was declared open to all vehicles on Thursday 29 March 1877. At the same time the passenger ferry across the Axe ceased, ending the ancient passage. Fees were transferred to the new Bridge Keeper who resided in the newly built toll cottage. *PWN* reported: *'The advantages to the public are doubtless great, and if anybody can be induced to erect villa residences along the charming site along the Axmouth side of the river, they would very soon find tenants, and the prosperity to both Axmouth and Seaton would be that extent enhanced.'*

Thankfully, waterside development never did proceed due to the lack of access. The muddy tidal lane to Axmouth remained the perfect obstacle for another forty years. With the coming of Waterside Road attitudes had fortunately changed; with covenants applied, the riverside fields were preserved for posterity.

The bridge construction was another blow to the harbour's viability. It immediately prevented vessels from accessing the Squire's Lane quay, Seaton embankment and Axmouth village. Although by this date commercial traffic was much reduced it effectively sealed any thought of future expansion utilising the estuary. The bridge also had a side effect of creating a form of weir. The flow of the river was constricted by the construction of the western approach embankment, through which a small arch was inserted to allow the old Great Sluice channel to drain. The raised approach effectively created a barrier across more than half the width of the lower estuary. The river channel was then confined to the eastern side of the estuary, spanned by the three arched bridge, another factor in slowing the ebb tide and contributing to the effects of silting.

Axmouth Bridge - 1890.

The bridge was designed by Philip Brannan, a self-styled architect. The building contract was signed with William Jackson of Westminster. Records show the initial intention had been to construct a single span across the river. However, the authorities were not confident of mass concrete construction, requiring two buttresses to support three arches. Soon after completion of the bridge (May 1877), the *imperfections* previously reported, resulted in subsidence of the western pier, and the insufficient foundations suffered from the effects of tidal scouring.

Fortunately, the structure has been able to withstand subsidence. The west pier sank whilst the east pier remained in place, resulting in sagging of the centre arch. In fact, comparing photographs over the intervening years, shows how it has continued to slowly sink. In 1956 the road surface was removed and iron girders were placed over the central span to relieve the loading on the central arch. The girders were covered with a heavy timber decking and then re-sealed with tarmac. The raised highway required additional wooden railings to protect pedestrians. In 1988 further remedial work was carried out whereby the road surface was removed and high tensile steel girders put in place of the old steel and wooden structure. This resulted in lowering the road surface to its original height. The concrete structure of the central span has now been relieved of any load bearing except for supporting its own weight. Nevertheless, a large crack remains visible in the underside of the central arch where it has sagged out of 'true'. Micro piling through the western pier and western abutment has stabilized the structure.

A deep scour hole lies immediately downstream of the western pier. Recent floods have deepened this, and ultimately this may result in the demise of the bridge. Amazingly, whilst the old bridge continued to take road traffic, the structure noticeably shook with the passing of larger vehicles; one felt it was not the place to loiter!

The Toll Cottage was similarly constructed of concrete along with the bridge. It was constructed on the western approach, extending over the adjoining tidal mudflat, supported on two substantial

The Story of Axmouth Harbour

Lithograph of the Toll House – 1880.

concrete arches. This allowed the tide to wash beneath the cottage, it also had a flight of steps leading down to the river – good for an early morning dip! Over the years, infill of the adjoining mudflat and saltmarsh has left no visible indication of the very solid foundations, and unlike the bridge it has shown no sign of subsidence.

Trading ceases

To all intents and purposes the harbour had become obsolete, its *'dilapidated'* condition all too apparent; contemporary opinion had effectively written it off. However, the harbour was still accommodating smaller craft. *PWN* reported in September 1884 that Zeno Good and William Power, boatmen, were fined by the Harbour Master Robert Start (in post from 1857) for evading harbour dues!

Coxhead writes in his paper of 1970:- *'Up to the year 1868, when the branch railway line to Seaton was opened, two vessels were still trading regularly between Axmouth Haven and London. The coming of the railway sounded the death knell of this coastal trade, and, to make matters worse, on Sunday, 31st January, 1869 an exceptionally severe gale swept away the greater part of the pier at the mouth of the river. A ferry service used to connect the Axmouth side of the river with Seaton until the present bridge was opened on 24th April 1877.*

Prior to this event, coasters were able to moor alongside a wharf situated by the railway station at Seaton. For a few more years small coasting schooners continued to use the haven, but before the end of the nineteenth century this traffic had also ceased.'

Donald Payne writing in his 1952 *Devon Harbours* provides a further insight. This description of Axmouth and Seaton, with quotes from local 'worthies', is a delightful snapshot of life around the harbour during the mid twentieth century. It also draws on those memories reaching back into the previous century, providing a fascinating insight into those last days of sail. *'Perhaps, Mr Beer suggested, the son of the former Harbourmaster, who now lives in Seaton, could tell me more about the old times. So, I left Axmouth, asleep in beauty and contentment beside its forgotten river. The distance to Seaton is close on a mile; first along a straight narrow road parallel to the river Axe, then across the toll bridge at its mouth. This was the bridge I have already mentioned, that was opened in April 1877 and made free to the public some thirty years later. At its western end is a little concrete cottage which once belonged to the toll-keeper—Mr. Ware, the Harbourmaster lives there now.*

Mr. Ware's title, I must explain, is more or less a courtesy one; there's little for him to do nowadays except collect the odd half crowns for harbour dues. His main business is his garage, and there I found him, a dark-haired, youngish man, covered in oil and grease, tuning up the engine of an ancient Morris. I asked him first about his house—was it really all concrete? "Yes," he replied, "every bit of it, roof doors and even the window frames." "And I suppose it was built at the same time as the bridge?" "That's it," he agreed, "1877. It's the oldest concrete house in England, and the coldest, I'll be bound!" He added that the bridge was also entirely concrete, and it too was the oldest of its kind in the country. Together we walked to the parapet opposite his cottage and looked across at the now deserted harbour. Just to seaward of the bridge on which we stood the Axe turns sharply eastward, almost at right angles to its former course, and then, some forty feet broad, flows dead straight and parallel to the sea. For nearly two hundred yards a substantial quay, deserted and in some need of repair, borders its landward bank; while to seaward lies the "mighty rigge of pibble stones," growing mightier year by year. At last, hard by the cliff, where the ruins of the old Custom House stood before they were washed away by the gales of January 1915, the river makes its last turn south and, as in Leland's time, "at a very small gut goith into the sea." Near its mouth is a constant turmoil of sound as wave upon wave drags its quota of smooth rounded pebbles across the entrance, pebbles which the river must eternally sweep aside before it gains the sea.

"No wonder we don't get more than a few dinghies in" said Mr. Ware looking in disgust at the seething mass of shingle. "And we're still only allowed to charge half-a-crown for harbour dues, so there's never any money to try and improve things." Lucky for him, I thought, as I made my way into the town, that he's got his garage. Seaton town may be only a mile from Axmouth, but in all the things that matter the two are poles apart. Axmouth looks with dignity at its past; Seaton looks with courage to its future. And its main hope for the future, as the town obviously realizes, is to make itself attractive to the crowds of tourists who flock here, by road and rail, each summer.

Personally, I heartily dislike the holiday camps, amusement arcades and chromium-plated snack-bars that inevitably spring up in the wake of trippers, but there's no denying the fact that I'm in a minority, and these amenities – all of which Seaton can offer – are appreciated each year by countless thousands. If you want to know more about this side of Seaton, I suggest you buy a guide-book. I for one was far more interested in the dozen small fishing boats drawn up on the wide arc of shingle beach, in the dignified old shops of Fore Street and in meeting some of the local worthies – men who had spent their whole lives in Seaton, and can remember the days when it was a simple, unknown fishing village.

First, I called on Mr. Real, who is a son of the former Harbourmaster. A tall gaunt man in his late fifties, I followed him into his office and soon we were talking of the days when his father was in charge of the River Axe toll-bridge.

"Father had to collect fourpence from each horse and cart that crossed the bridge," he told me, "a penny a leg for animals in harness and a ha'penny a leg for those not in harness. One old farmer, I remember, was a proper miser. When his cart reached the end o' the bridge he'd stop, unharness his horse, and make his son pull it across!"

He went on to tell me of Mr. Sanders Stephens, owner of the Manor, who in 1907 put up more than £2,000 to have the toll-bridge made free to the public. "He was a proper old martinet," said Mr. Real, "but a very straight man. He admired anyone who'd stand up to him. Trouble was, there were only two men in Seaton who weren't afear'd o' him: my father was one, and t'other was the undertaker!"

Mr. Stephens, it seems, used to own practically the whole lower reaches of the Axe Valley, including the river and harbour. When he sold the railway company a right of way through his land, he made them agree never to allow trains on a Sunday — nor during his lifetime did one ever run.

Mr. Real went on to tell me how in the old days the river used to flood at high tide right across the valley. "It was Sir Walter Trevelyan," he said, "who first built an embankment where the railway now runs, and so drained the marsh [in fact it was an earlier owner, John Willoughby who built the embankment]. *Before that ships could anchor right 'longside the parish church." I was able to confirm this when I later found traces of rusty and ancient mooring rings in the Church-yard wall; also when I saw a fragment of plate, probably from some locally-made dinner service, which Mr. Turner had dug out of his garden — the design on the plate clearly shows three ships anchored hard by Seaton church. I also learnt that the coast-line here changes almost from day to day according to wind and tide; and that some forty years ago the mouth of the Axe was blocked by shingle for more than a week, so that the pent-up river flooded the whole valley.*

With stories such as these we passed a very pleasant afternoon. "But," Mr. Real ended, "I can't tell you much about the shipping that used to put in here. You're a dozen years too late for that. There's not a man left in Seaton who ever saw the cargo-boats a-sailing in. But you'd best go and see Mr. Akerman at Jasmine Cottage, he knows more than any of us about the old days here." And so, thanking him for all his help I went in search of Mr. Akerman, whose sudden death just as this book went to print was such an unhappy loss for the town he loved. I found him not at Jasmine Cottage but checking over stores in his ironmonger's shop in Fore Street a friendly and fascinating place, full of strange implements and every possible variety of tackle. Along one side of the shop a full twenty feet stretched a massive mahogany counter, a fine piece of timber. "That," said Mr. Akerman with pride, "came from a Finnish timber ship, the barque 'Berar'. She was wrecked in 1896, some three miles along the coast, just west of Charton Bay."

Soon, it seems, her cargo was being plastered up against every cliff between Seaton and Lyme. It quickly became known that any timber salvaged would bring in money, though fetchers could not be keepers. So, Mr. Akerman's father, with three others, went off to the wreck. They took with them a hammer and a bag of 6-inch nails. Soon they had knocked together a raft, which they dragged back to Seaton, with much difficulty, against a stiff breeze. A couple of days later they went out again, taking this time three long seine-net warps and 50 fathom of rope; then, by kedging along, they brought back another two hauls. Their share of the salvage money came to £7 between the four of them. "And," his eyes twinkled, "a few odd bits o' timber like this bench of mine!"'

Churchyard Mooring Rings

I believe the comments regarding vessels lying alongside Seaton's St. Gregory's churchyard, should not be taken too seriously. We know that the marshes were enclosed by Willoughby's embankment in 1660, long before the Trevelyans came on the scene. Even in the late 1600s the salt marsh was well established with only small shallow creeks reaching the inner edge of the marsh. There is no evidence to suggest deep-water channels afforded navigation close to the churchyard. One can only assume that the comments refer to much earlier times, perhaps in connection with the origins of *Merchants Roads*, indicating a period in the 1300s. As to the mooring rings located in the churchyard wall, if they were indeed for that purpose, they must have been installed prior to the marsh reclamation in 1660. The construction of the embankment would have barred any form of navigation from the tidal estuary into the marsh. Realistically, small mooring rings placed in a vertical wall would provide insubstantial security for anything larger than small punts; larger vessels would require more substantial mooring posts (bollards). It should also be noted that the churchyard wall is on a raised bank well above the marsh level.

Generally, Seaton Marsh floodplain is at a level of 1.5m above OD, this is equivalent to a tidal height of 3.9m (an average spring tide). The marsh level will have not changed significantly from 1660 since there has been no silting effect from the estuary. Therefore, access

Commercial Decline

Seaton church, above the marsh.

across the marsh to the churchyard wall would have required the existence of a deeper creek to allow any form of navigation. LiDAR mapping shows no creek pattern in this particular area which tends to indicate the rings may have been for some other purpose. Sadly, the rings have now disappeared with no photographic record as to their exact location.

The wreck of the *Berar*

The *Berar* had, as described by Payne, become embayed, unable to sail off a lee shore under storm conditions; her fate was sealed. None of the local harbours would have been able to accommodate a vessel of her comparatively large size (902 tons), nor would they have been accessible under heavy weather conditions. Obviously Mr Akerman had a keen eye for salvage and found the timber recovery worthwhile. The mahogany counter in Akerman's hardware shop (Fore Street, Seaton) was salvaged from the *Berar* and survives to this day (2023). It's been the scene of countless transactions and no doubt has overheard more than its fair share of gossip – if only it could tell its own story! The *Berar's* figurehead (the head of a female) was also recovered. For many years it graced the entrance hallway of local fisherman Ken Tolman's thatched cottage in Queen Street, Seaton. On his death the figurehead was presented to the Seaton Museum, along with other artifacts recovered from the wreck. A lignum vitae dead-eye from the *Berar's* standing rigging was recovered in 1988, and it is now displayed in the Pilot Bar of the Harbour Inn.

The *Berar* was built by William Pile of Sunderland in 1863 for the shipping company Tyser & Haviside. The vessel was constructed of iron and built as a full rigged ship. Presumably she was cut down to a barque at some later date. She had two near identical sister ships, the *Himilaya* and the *Trevelyan* (coincidently a name very much associated with local Seaton landowners who also had interests in the North East of England). The vessels were built for trading with India, carrying a combination of cargo and passengers.

The Story of Axmouth Harbour

Wreck of the Berar *– 1896. (Ted Gosling collection).*

Berar *split in two, revealing her timber cargo. (Ted Gosling collection).*

With the opening of the Suez Canal, sail could no longer compete with steam on the run to India. *Berar* was transferred to the New Zealand and Australian immigrant trade under charter to Shaw-Savill. Following this she was used for transporting indentured labour from India to Fiji and to Guyana (she was the first vessel to use Fiji's new quarantine facilities on the island of Nukulau, east of Suva, an island I have visited many times for weekend barbeques whilst stationed in Fiji aboard *Pacific Guardian*). Eventually *Berar* ended up under the Italian flag and it was whilst on passage from Borga, Finland to Seville, that she encountered heavy weather in the Channel. She was driven into Lyme Bay and unable to claw her way off the lee shore became embayed. She stranded on the rocks midway between Charton Bay and the Slabs, during the night of 7 October 1896. All 16 crew managed to get ashore safely, but the ship became a total loss, breaking in two a few days later, spilling her cargo of timber onto the surrounding beaches.

Remains of the Berar *at low water – 1988.*

At low water springs the remains of the wreck can still be seen, lying just within the eastern boundary of Axmouth. Iron frames, floors and plating are still visible. The section appears to be the after part with the prominent stern post. Other pieces of the wreck lay close by amongst the rocks and kelp, including a capstan, lifeboat davit and a section of an iron tubular spar. Just to the north east of the wreck lies Peek's Harbour, a narrow inlet cleared of the foreshore boulders on the western side of Charton Bay. The landing was cleared by the Peeks of Rousdon.

A few years earlier in 1866, the Austrian brig *Clement Auguste*, a wooden sailing vessel was wrecked on the western edge of Charton Bay. This was fortuitous for Sir Henry Peek who shortly after commenced construction of his cliff-top mansion at Rousdon. The vessel was carrying a cargo of Sicilian marble, of which the majority was salvaged, auctioned off and used in the construction of the main staircase and dairy of the house. One can still find small broken fragments of cut white marble amongst the foreshore rock pools originating from the wreck.

Beach trading continues

Francis Kilvert, clergyman and Victorian diarist, travelled to Seaton on Monday 7 August 1871. The day was fine and hot. He described the beach scene, a mixture of early tourism and the legacy of coastal trading by sea.

Staying at the Pole Arms, he was greeted with a typical bright summer's day. Eager to look at the foreshore, he proceeded down Fore Street to the beach. It was busy with the new phenomenon of day trippers. These early tourists had just arrived on the train. They were keen to enjoy the seaside and in a somewhat liberated way to Kilvert's thinking; people were observed paddling in the sea with no shoes or stockings!

The beach thronged with people whilst somewhat incongruously, a fully loaded collier was moored close to the beach. Her cargo of coal was being discharged into local barges which in turn transferred it ashore to waiting carts at the water's edge. As each one was loaded, it required six horses to haul the coal up the beach, leaving deep furrows in the shingle. Having reached the top of the beach, they were emptied into the coalyard, described as the *wharf*. To save time, the horses were freed from their reins, except for the lead, which careered off back down the beach, showering pebbles in all directions, with the other five following in hot pursuit. This caused much annoyance to the visitors – children were pulled aside to avoid being run over! With raised tempers, the situation became a little out of hand, but the arrival of the local policeman soon restored an element of calm. Amongst all this activity, local boys took advantage of the mayhem. They could be seen darting in and out, even in the sea, recovering large pieces of coal which they swiftly carried away on their shoulders.

From aside, Kilvert reflected on the eventful scene, noting the contrasts between the dark-hulled collier and galloping horses, with the wonderful backdrop of White Cliff's brilliance, the azure sea and blue sky; commenting that the light seemed even more intense than Cornwall!

The collier would have 'moored off' having first laid out a kedge anchor aft and run a mooring rope to the top of the beach, secured using a capstan and mooring post. Conditions appeared to be settled, but the master had decided not to beach his vessel. Beaching would have negated the use of barges. Perhaps the tides were not convenient for re-floating, or he was keeping an eye on the weather, any sign of a swell building could result in the vessel being stranded. The comment referring to the *wharf* describes the old Seaton coal yard, a stone-walled compound situated just east of the present seafront roundabout, now occupied by a pub and restaurant. The harbour at this time was still accessible but with the outer pier gone, it would have been more difficult to navigate.

In May 1877, a large section of Haven Cliff 'fell into the sea', as reported by *PWN*. The Coastguards had anticipated the fall and removed their flagstaff. Presumably fissures had opened up prior to the slip, which was assessed to be nearly 2 acres of the cliff top.

Around this time the deaths of two notable local characters were reported. On 27 April 1880 Captain W.H. Moore (RN), ninety, of Cliff Castle, Seaton; it was thought he had served at Trafalgar as a very young midshipman. The other, was local artist William Newbery, who at the age of seventy-nine died on 8 March 1887. He left some interesting water colours of local scenes, especially those of the harbour and beach.

Newbery's painting of Seaton Beach – mid 1800s. (Elford Fine Art).

The upper quay in ruins – 1900.

A period of quiet inactivity

By the end of the nineteenth century the harbour had ceased to function commercially, the outer pier had completely disintegrated, leaving only a line of foundation boulders that partially obstructed the river's exit. The harbour's demise was twofold. Besides the arrival of the railway, the Halletts had fallen on hard times, rumours of the estate's mismanagement were circulating, so it was little wonder that harbour maintenance had ceased. William Trelawny Hallett of Stedcombe died on 2 December 1889, he was the last Hallett to hold the title of lord of the manor. Following his death, the estate, including the harbour was offered for sale at public auction, pursuant to an order of the High Court of Justice (Chancery Division) made in an action: *Acland v. Hallett 1890*.

Peter Orlando Hutchison noted in his diary – October 1st 1890:- *'Another old Devonshire family come to grief! Hallett of Stedcombe "sowed up". Report says extravagance and mismanagement. Stedcombe House and 1500 acres of land advertised to be sold; together with the Advowson and Vicarage of Axmouth, and also the Manor & lordship.'*

He continues, 30 October 1890:- *'Today the Stedcombe Estate was put up to auction at the Half-Moon in Exeter, comprising some 1500 acres, Manor, Lordship, endowment and Vicarage of Axmouth. The estimated value £2,100 per annum. The first bid was £31,000. It was finally knocked down at £35,600 to Mr. S. Stephens, of Brook St. Grosvenor Sq., London. A comment appeared following the sale to the effect that the auction failed to repay the second mortgage outstanding and that the third mortgage would not get a farthing, due to the ruinous depreciation of the property market.'*

The harbour and estate after exactly two hundred years in the ownership of the Halletts was sold to Samuel Sanders Stephens, deeds dated 2 February 1891. Sanders Stephens had little interest in the harbour and thus ended a period dating back to the 1400s. The lord of the manor no longer had ambitions of resurrecting the harbour and finally accepted that any further commercial development of the haven was impractical.

With the disappearance of the outer pier the entrance channel slowly shifted more to the east following the line of the inner harbour wall, as it does today. The crumbling remains are shown on the OSGB map dated 1888 (above), with just the connecting

The Story of Axmouth Harbour

Remains of pier – 1890. (Ted Gosling collection).

Right: OS Map 1888. (National Library of Scotland).

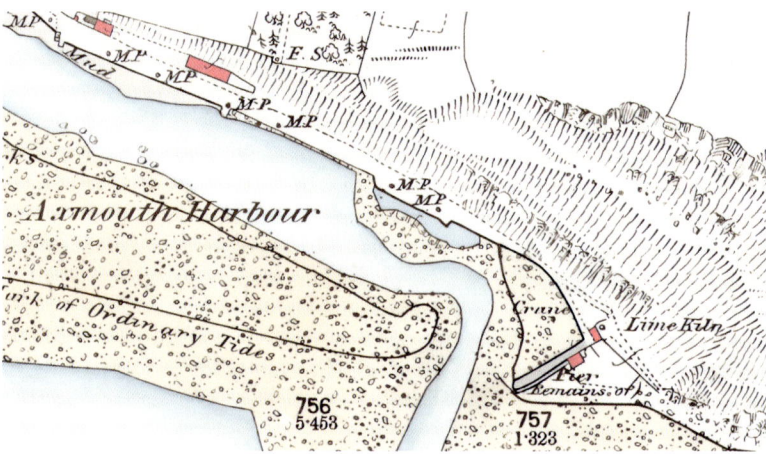

Haven Cliff - showing the remnant of the pier and Customs House.

Sketch of the pier remains -1905.

arm projecting into the channel, with the old Customs House still in place.

Photographs of this period depict very little activity in the harbour, except for the odd rowing boat. In the photograph (left) the crumbling remains of the Hallett's pier can be seen forming a kind of slipway at the entrance. Remnants of the pier caused shingle to build up on the east side of the entrance, partially concealing the inner harbour wall, but also providing protection for it. The old Customs House became the estate's temporary 'summer house' until that too succumbed to storm damage and was washed away in 1915. The only reminder of the building's existence is the rear stone wall that now has a viewing area and seats above it, which in turn was once a lime kiln during the harbour's commercial operation.

The photograph top taken at a similar time shows the Customs House intact but only the foundations of the old pier. The channel still flows to the west of the seaweed-covered rocks. A large build up of shingle and stones fill the foreground, what was originally the holding basin.

The sketch (left) shows the seaward extension of the foundations, the river still flows to the west of pier remains.

Commercial Decline

The old tidal lane leading to the bridge. (Fife Cultural Trust).

The Halletts last connection with the harbour

The last connection with the Hallett family occurred in February 1908 with the death of Colonel Clements Thomas Hallett (Bengal Lancers). As the younger brother of W.T. Hallett he had continued to reside at Haven Cliff House, overlooking the harbour; the Colonel's wife continued to live at Haven Cliff until her death 1918.

Waterside Road – the tidal lane to Axmouth

Although Axmouth Bridge had been constructed in 1877 the riverside road to Axmouth remained a tidal track. In 1891 it was reported that shingle had been thrown up onto the track, requiring an official inspection of the retaining wall near to the bridge. It had previously been maintained by the Halletts as part of the harbour works, but the new estate owner, Sanders Stephens was reluctant to continue with the expenditure, arguing that it should be a matter for the Axminster Highways Board. The poor condition of both the tidal track and footpath was raised by Axmouth Parish Council in 1895, but no improvements were forthcoming. There was a proposal in 1913 to construct a raised road linking the village with the bridge, but the villagers rejected it on the grounds that the plan did not incorporate the riverside footpath. Even after heavy rains and gales had caused the river to flood the lower village in November 1916, nothing was done to improve matters. And that's how it remained until after W.W.1 when in 1924 construction started. The road was raised to a level thought to be above the highest tides, the carriageway widened and a foot path was incorporated on the landward side. Sections of the new road encroached onto the estuary, the gently sloping foreshore in front of Millmead and the approach to the village disappeared under a concrete embankment. Mid-way along Waterside sections of the old tidal track still remain as a reminder of quieter days when the pace of life was still governed by the ebb and flow of the tide.

Further cliff falls

The *Devon & Exeter Gazette* covered a story in their 2 April edition of 1931:- '*Not since the great landslip of 1839 has such a huge quantity of cliff fallen as at Axmouth. Early Sunday morning, thousands of tons fell from Haven Cliff, on which lie the Axe Cliff golf links. The fall occurred not fifty yards from the mouth of the River, and a new mass of rock protrudes into the sea forming a promontory nearly three hundred yards in length. The occupants of Harbour Cottages, situated about three hundred yards*

The extended slip below Haven Cliff.

away, did not feel or hear any crash, as the boulders and earth slid away rather than fell. The slide has greatly altered the appearance of the cliff, and a further fall is expected.'

The cliff fall caused the upper stratum of both chalk and greensand to topple seaward over the underlying Mercier mudstone (marl) cliff, possibly initiated by the copious spring that flows over the impervious marl of Haven Cliff. The debris completely engulfed the lower cliff face and beach below, extending some distance seaward from the base of the original cliff. The slip had changed the whole profile of Haven Cliff, and with the upper promontory gone it appeared less in height with a long sloping incline towards the sea. Once the fall had stabilised vegetation took hold and due to the reduced gradient, a path was established leading from the beach into the under cliff. This area was curiously named 'Elephant's Graveyard' – a name it retains today with various improbable explanations! Over the intervening years wave action has eaten into the fallen debris, leaving only the larger boulders seaward of River Ledge which now form rock pools at low water. The majority of the loose, finer material that formed the slip has gradually eroded away; the old footpath no longer exists and the once concealed marl cliff is slowly re-appearing.

Prior to this in 1909, a cliff fall, just east of the old warehouse completely blocked the harbourside lane to the river mouth (the warehouse had already been converted in the late 1800s, at the time 'Moorings' was the residence of an ex RN paymaster). In January 1910 the Old Ferry Cottage was gutted by fire, the seventy-year-old occupants, Mr and Mrs Jacob Type were rescued by their neighbours from the Moorings. The fire brigade was summoned by ringing Seaton's' Jubilee clock bell!

The harbour remained neglected for the next fifty years. The remnants of the old projecting arm eventually disappeared, allowing

The converted warehouse – 1922. (Original F. Frith & Co photo print).

the shingle to be washed out of the entrance, revealing the inner harbour wall once more and leaving it exposed to the elements. The photograph (right) shows the last remnants of the old Customs House and the exposed termination of the wall.

The crumbling state of the seaward end of the wall was temporarily halted with the infill of bulk cement. Makeshift shuttering was put in place and cement was poured into the void, but with no foundation it was soon undermined. The rest of the harbour wall was occasionally patched up, but with no programme of regular maintenance.

The last remnants of the Customs House. (Ted Gosling collection).

Seaton beach remained undeveloped until the coming of the railwa. Up until this time the only buildings were the Trevelyan's mansion house close to today's Beach Road and the Coastguard lookout at the top of Trevelyan Road. As the railway link became established, station buildings were constructed alongside the Axe, the Station-Masters house was built at the bottom of Trevelyan Road. This building was typical of the Victorian terrace house design, except it was never developed into a terrace! The Trevelyans had designs for seafront terraces of a much grander construction, resembling Brighton or Eastbourne, none of which materialised. The ambitious plans can be seen in two lithographs at Seaton Museum, showing their rather ostentatious aims. In 1910 the Trevelyan Road terrace was built, not to the grand designs originally proposed, but none the less a handsome row, more fitting with the surroundings. These properties remained isolated at the end of the beach (just within the Seaton boundary) for many years, until piecemeal development slowly colonised the *mighty ridge*.

The only sign of activity within the harbour was the conversion of the old warehouse. This was completed in 1902, when the building was converted into to two separate properties and has been occupied ever since.

Several fishery in tidal waters

An interesting case was brought against local fisherman Harry Snell in 1939 by Miss Maud Sanders Stephens owner of Stedcombe Estate (Stephens v. Snell, Chancery Division 06/07/1939). It was alleged that illegal fishing of salmon had been conducted by netting the tidal waters of the river mouth without license. The case was settled in favour of the manor, due to proof of ownership of the tidal river bed and thus the fishery. This anomaly reverted back to a time before the Magna Carta (1215). Ownership was substantiated by reference to the grant of the manor of Axmouth and its fishery by Richard de Redvers (Norman nobleman), to the Abbey of St. Mary of Montebourg. Importantly the grant was reconfirmed by either Henry I or Henry II, predating Magna Carta.

By common law of England, the public has a right to fish in tidal waters, the claim to a several fishery is a claim to exclude the public from that right; but the prerogative right of the Crown to grant that right was taken away by the provisions of Magna Carta. In this particular case the grant was made prior to Magna Carta and therefore remained unchanged. In an inspeixmus charter by 'Lord Henry of good memory, formerly King of England, *I grant the manor which is named Auxemud in Devon, with the church of the same manor and a fishery, and two draughts which are there, to drag with nets.*' The term *draught*, refers to a designated area or 'patch' used for netting, this

Salmon netting at the harbour mouth – 1950s. (Michael Clement).

may refer back to two separate channels within the haven. During the Dissolution the manor reverted to the Crown and the status quo remained. The tidal River Axe remains one of the few rivers in the UK where ownership of the tidal river bed lies in private hands (now Bindon Manor Estate and EDDC), exclusive of Crown Estate jurisdiction.

Stedcombe Estate was very protective of its fishing rights. This was not the first time that the fishery had been contested. In the late 1700s the Rev. Richard Hallett brought an action at the Exeter assizes against Sir William Templer de la Pole of Shute. He sued Sir William for trespass on his several fishery, the trial before jury found in favour of the plaintiff, Richard Hallett.

Similarly, Miss Stephens' father, Samuel Sanders Stephens (who happened to be High Sheriff of Devon at the time) brought a case against his neighbour Sir Edmund de la Pole of Shute for trespass of fishing rights and once again the verdict was found in favour of Stedcombe. Sadly, salmon stocks have declined to such an extent that netting is no longer viable (or permissible) and ceased in the late 1970s. Similarly, the salmon trap set up just below Axe Bridge by the Ministry of Agriculture & Fisheries to tag salmon and sea trout was removed in the late 1960s due to the scarcity of the fish.

Salmon were caught by shooting a net from a rowing boat as it crossed the outer river mouth entrance. This was done on an early rising tide as the salmon prepared to enter the estuary. A post set in the River Ledge rocks beneath Haven Cliff acted as an indicator, once this was covered by the incoming tide netting ceased. It is unclear as to where this ruling originated; it may well have been set by the estate as a means of conservation.

Change in Emphasis

The first signs of change in harbour usage

The only sign of any activity within the harbour was the use of the odd small craft for recreation. This was an early indication of change in the harbour's use from trade to leisure. The arrival of the internal combustion engine was also significant in this change. Negotiating the harbour entrance was never easy, especially under oars or sail. The introduction of motive power in small boats provided a means to partly overcome the difficulties of navigating in strong tidal streams. Sometime between 1929 and 1931 a group of young boating enthusiasts began to use the estuary and harbour on a regular basis. This led to the formation of a club in the summer of 1936. The title chosen was the *Seaton Sailing and Motor Boat Club* (SS&MBC). Meetings were held at the Geisha Café (at the junction of Trevelyan and Harbour Roads) and the club ran occasional dinghy sailing races on the tidal estuary.

World War Two

All too soon World War Two intervened, the beach was closed off and a barricade of steel scaffolding with barbed wire was erected to discourage invasion landings. At the same time the Landslip and under cliffs were mined. The estuary was temporarily dammed using sand and gravel bags to form two barrages, creating an impounded stretch of water. The dual purpose was supposedly for landing seaplanes, whilst deterring invasion via the estuary.

The first yacht to appear in the harbour, lying in the old Great Sluice creek.

The upper barrage was positioned opposite Squire's Lane and the lower opposite Harbour Cottage. Both failed fairly quickly due to their inadequate strength, unable to hold back the volume of water. Interestingly a German aerial reconnaissance photograph taken on 29 September 1940 shows the two dams, both having been breached. Other war-time activity saw the construction of the Taunton Stop Line, a defensive line across the South West peninsula. A series of pill-boxes starting from Axmouth Harbour led inland along the length of the Axe Valley and onward to the north coast of Somerset. The first pill-box was built below Haven Cliff close to the site of the old Customs House at the harbour entrance. These structures made of either brick or concrete were located along the eastern side of the valley disguised in hedgerows and woodland. Some were more prominently placed, one lying close to the river bank downstream from Axe Bridge, its position becoming precarious as the bank erodes away from beneath it. Linked with the Stop Line, a concrete plinth gun emplacement was positioned at the base of the cliff. It was located close by the footpath leading up to Elephant's Graveyard, just to the east of river mouth. This provided a sweep of Axmouth and Seaton Beach in the event of enemy troops landing. It is thought that a 6-pounder Hotchkiss gun was installed on the plinth. Coastal erosion has now washed away both the path and the plinth.

During the war, local fisherman Tom Newton living in Harbour Cottage (the old Ferryman's Cottage) was presented with the OBE for bravery. Early one December morning in 1940 he noticed a live German mine enter the harbour on the flood tide, dragging with it

Tom and Irene Newton – 1941. (Michael Clement).

part of its mooring cable. By his actions he prevented the mine from drifting up stream towards the bridge and importantly the railway station where munitions were being transferred to Beer quarries for safe storage. Tom kept the mine away from any obstacles using an oar and then guided it back down river when the tide turned. He eventually beached it at the river mouth, having waded into the water to ensure it landed safely. The mine was then neutralised by the Coastguard. The *Western Morning News* reported his heroic act and interviewed him at his cottage:- *'There's something to be done here, I said to myself, or some things going to happen. I got hold of an oar, the mine being sufficiently close to the wall to reach it. As it bobbed up I carefully "nursed" it with the oar pushing it away until I had manoeuvred it to a sandy bit of beach. It took about two hours to do that. When I had landed the beggar, I told the Coastguards who removed the live horns.'* Tom's wife remarked to the reporter how he had stuck to his job, whereupon Tom said *'Yes, you women would hang over the wall, until I told you to get the **** out of it!'* Tom went to Buckingham Palace the following April for the investiture, and the King remarked *'It was an extremely plucky thing to do, and I congratulate you on your escape.'* Tom operated one of the Seaton Beach fishing boats *Tib* (E201 – Tom, Irene, Barbara) for many years; he continued to sell fish from his blue Austin van until his death in 1971. The rusting shell of the old mine lies buried under the shingle, having been unearthed and reburied during subsequent dredging operations.

One Axmouth vessel, the yacht *Iolanthe* took part in the evacuation of Dunkirk and survived to return to the harbour. The last occasion Axmouth sent vessels to relieve a situation in northern France was during the siege of Calais, and that was in 1346! During the war a local branch of the Admiralty Ferry Crew Association (AFCA) was formed between Axmouth and Seaton, its purpose was to move small craft inshore along the coast in support of Royal Navy wartime operations. The association drew on local mariners of which the following were all members of the Seaton Sailing and Motor Boat Club. The team was led by Robert Redvers-Lewis (skipper), Vincent Martyn – Mate, Tom Hills – Engineer and Roy Perry – Deck Hand. The branch had responsibility for the coast between Weymouth and Exmouth, and remained in existence for a few years after the war. Axe Yacht Club minutes of 1951 record Lewis as still leading the branch and at the time the association was still open to membership. Eventually the AFCA was amalgamated with the Royal Naval Mine Watching Service to form the Royal Navy Auxiliary Association in 1963. On its disbandment, Vincent Martyn became the Honorary Little Ship Club Port Officer for Axmouth. One wonders just how many Little Ship Club members visited the harbour?

The converted lifeboat – Fiducia – 1950. (Jim Bennett).

Post Second World War

From 1945 it took some time for life to resume to some sort of normality. Robert Redvers-Lewis a member of the original SS&MBC, resided at Harbour House (the old warehouse which had been badly damaged by fire prior to the war). He had purchased two ex-RNLI boats with the intention of commercial fishing. It was aboard the *Fiducia* that a meeting was

Vice Admiral Sir Francis Pridham. (HMS Hood Association).

held in 1947 from which resulted the formation of the Axe Yacht Club (AYC). Redvers-Lewis was elected as its first Commodore and Vice Admiral Sir (Arthur) Francis Pridham elected as its President.

Sir Francis had grown up locally attending Allhallows School in Honiton prior to its relocation to the Rousdon estate. He joined the Navy in 1901, in 1919 as First Lieutenant aboard HMS *Marlborough*, he took part in the rescue of members of the Russian Royal family from Yalta (Crimea), including the Dowager Empress Maria, mother of Tsar Nicholas II.

Later in 1936, he took command of the battleship HMS *Hood* and at the time assisted Emperor Haile Selassie during the invasion of Ethiopia by Italy. At the end of WW2, he retired and moved to *Millmead* (then referred to locally as the *Admiral's House*), the riverside residence just below the village. He took a great interest in the yacht club and regularly attended the regatta prize-giving ably assisted by Lady Pridham.

At the time Lloyds Register of Shipping (Yachts) confirms the establishment of the AYC in 1948, although for a very brief period the Seaton Sailing and Motor Boat Club continued in parallel. Some of the members of the SS&MBC were reluctant to reform the club as the AYC, but within a short period of time, probably by late summer of 1948 the SS&MBC discontinued. Some of the SS&MBC founder members (Ray Wilkins, Ron Harwood and eventually Ken Tolman) moved to become founder members of the AYC, thus maintaining the thread of continuity back to 1936.

During this period the AYC had very little in the way of facilities apart from an open beach and shallow tidal estuary. The Club's HQ was a white painted shed located on what is now the garage forecourt opposite the AYC entrance. The club house was known as the 'Hut' and used on an informal basis, being leased from Stedcombe Estate. In 1951 the estate gave permission for the building of a more permanent structure on the top of Axmouth Beach. With the valued help and support of local builder and AYC Commodore Ben Turner, the forerunner to the present-day clubhouse was established. At the 1952 AGM a disagreement arose, due to membership irregularities, resulting in a spilt of the AYC. A contingent left to form the breakaway Seaton Sailing Club, taking with them the recently formed fleet of Wildcats – a locally designed (Illingworth) plywood performance dinghy. The SSC established its base initially in a small beach hut at the top of Trevelyan Road, but eventually moved their HQ along the seafront, close to the *Moridunum*. The SSC continued for a number of years, sailing the Wildcat fleet from the open beach, but eventually it was wound up with the remaining members being welcomed back into the Axe Yacht Club.

Meanwhile the AYC was left with 52 members, little funds, a part-built clubhouse and no established racing fleet. Fortunately, the club's Vice Commodore, Jack Drew of Axmouth had been working on the introduction of a more traditional type dinghy for the AYC. He designed the 12-foot clinker-built dinghy which became known as the Axe One Design, and this was subsequently adopted by the AYC as its official class. The AODs were ideal for both launching off of Axmouth's open beach and for sailing on the

HMS Marlborough *– signatures of the Russian Royal family*

AYC Prize giving 1955 – Commodore Jim Archard, R. Donnithorne, Ron Harwood, Lady Pridham, Audrey Davis & Sir Francis Pridham.

estuary at high water. The AYC soon established a series of summer races both in the bay and on the estuary. As an amateur boat builder, Jack constructed the first eight hulls in his workshop above the family butchers in Taunton.

The part-finished boats were then brought to Axmouth to be completed by their respective owners. The boats' construction used a combination of timbers, mahogany, ash and elm. Incidentally the elm came from the woods behind Stedcombe House, courtesy of Vincent Martyn (Stedcombe bailiff and estate manager). The first boats took to the water in 1953, with the fleet eventually numbering 19 in the early 1960s. Following the initial nine boats some were also built by local boat builder H.J. Mears, but this was at a time when more economic and more modern lighter GRP dinghies were starting to appear and by the mid 1970s the class had ceased to race.

In 1953 Vincent Martyn (also Club Treasurer), was able to secure a lease from Stedcombe Estate for that part of the beach on which the club house was built, formalising the club's tenure. Later, he purchased the sailing lifeboat *Fidelius* from Robert Redvers-Lewis. Launched as the *Baltic*, she was built by Saunders in Cowes in 1916 and stationed from 1916 to 1936 at Wells, Norfolk. Under her new ownership she was renamed *Marvin*, remaining in the harbour for many years.

Post war a large motor torpedo boat (MTB) was laid up on the western foreshore just downstream from the bridge, which eventually required the aid of mechanical diggers to remove the mud that built up around it in order to leave the harbour.

In the meantime, due to a long period of neglect, there was a great danger of losing the entire length

The original Agrad. *(Ray Wilkins).*

The Story of Axmouth Harbour

Seaton Sailing Club HQ at the top of Trevelyan Road – Wildcat *in foreground - 1953.*

AOD No.1 Whimbrel *in the bay – 1954. (Margret Northcott).*

Smew *with* Fidelis *in the background - 1950s.*

The harbour mouth – 1960. (Henry Pountney).

of the inner harbour wall. Where the wall terminated at its seaward end (river mouth) the limited repairs of the early twentieth century had become undermined with the wall slowly collapsing. This was again temporarily halted under the guidance of the estate manager, Vincent Martyn; mass concrete was poured into the shuttered stub of the wall. In addition, a capping parapet was added along the full length of the wall from the bridge to the river mouth – providing a little more security when walking along the quayside. The old commercial quay next to the warehouse had by this time silted and was only suitable for mooring shallow draughted craft.

To provide a limited number of berths, moorings were laid by the AYC in the middle of the old river channel downstream from the bridge. One notable vessel that occupied a river mooring for many years was Ray Wilkins' *Agrad*. She was a 37' ex-Naval pinnace from Devonport. In the 1950s she regularly plied the coast on summer outings to Lyme, Weymouth and Torbay and often crossed the Channel to Guernsey and St Malo. Many years later under new ownership *Agrad* voyaged much further afield to Gibraltar and the Mediterranean.

A couple of Axmouth yachts made some quite remarkable voyages. *Johanna* reached the west coast of Scotland for a summer cruise, whilst Brigadier E.E.Nott-Bower with his wife as crew, sailed down the Atlantic coast to the Mediterranean, returning via the French canals. He wrote a fascinating book of his voyage aboard *Smew*, titled *Ten Ton Travel*. The voyage was conducted in the early post-war years and had many challenges, from prevailing austerity, to lack of supplies and a very troublesome engine! On her return the yacht was based in Axmouth for a number of years. Nott-Bower continued to sail from Axmouth, often contributing further accounts of voyages to the yacht club newsletters.

Under the auspices of Stedcombe Estate, Vincent Martyn in association with Wally Barnes built a concrete jetty projecting from the west bank, 100 yards downstream from the bridge. The jetty built in 1955 reached out into the main stream of the river, spanning the original creek running from the Great Sluice and once servicing the old coalyard. The jetty provided a valuable facility for a number of years, affording access to additional alongside berths and moorings.

A new AOD exits the Taunton workshop – 1953. (Irene Drew).

The harbour mouth – 1963. (Original F. Frith & Co photo print).

The Story of Axmouth Harbour

The old jetty – 1963.

Fiducia and brand-new jetty – 1955 (Copyright Francis Frith Collection).

1966 Mark Davis, Bryan Davis and Nigel Daniel in conversation with Vincent Martyn aboard Marvin, *Ray Wilkins in the foreground. (Bryan Davis).*

Agrad.

It was at this jetty that Vincent Martyn moored his converted lifeboat *Marvin*. The photo (opposite bottom) shows her laid-up at Axmouth with Vincent Martyn aboard taking to a very young author with Mark and Bryan Davis. Ray Wilkins, in the foreground owned the Admiralty pinnace *Agrad*.

Unfortunately, the jetty's foundations, or lack of them were its downfall. Tidal scouring of outer end caused it to crack and subside, whilst wave action undermined the inner end. It was eventually demolished in the early 1980s to make way for an enlarged mooring basin.

A tragic accident happened on the river in 1955. Two lads were sailing an international 14 type dinghy up the river when their mast struck the overhead power cables that spanned the estuary from Coronation Corner across to Seaton Marshes. Unfortunately, both were killed in the incident. The electricity board reacted quickly and re-routed the cables under the river bed to remove the danger entirely.

During this period a couple of fishing boats used the harbour wall and a few moorings were laid above the bridge by the boat builder H.J. Mears. Harold Mears was apprenticed in Exmouth building mine sweepers during WW2. In 1945 he moved to Beer and set up his own boat building firm. In 1958 he moved to the present location just upstream from Axmouth Bridge. Paul, Harold's son, took over the business in the late 1980s and now Paul's son Alex is working with him, still building traditional clinker-built boats as well as fitting out GRP fishing vessels.

The jetty shows signs of subsidence.

The Story of Axmouth Harbour

The harbour in 1964.

On the death of Maud Sanders Stephens in 1959, Stedcombe Estate was sold, effectively ending private ownership of the harbour which dated back to the time of Henry VIII. The position of Harbour Master remained, in name only. Harold Mears took on the role following the retirement of Mr Ware. Harbour charges adjacent to and including Axmouth Beach were devolved to the AYC in 1962, for the grand sum of £70. This was the forerunner of the eventual formalised leasing arrangement that continues today. In February 1964 the AYC approached Jack Daniel, resident of Trevelyan Road with the aim of fulfilling a newly appointed position as yacht club beach master. This started a long association with the AYC, lasting until Jack's retirement in 1988. The position was many-fold and what started out as a voluntary post collecting visitor fees developed into a full-time occupation of maintaining facilities, from clubhouse to moorings. Fortunately, the club could also rely on an active group of volunteers who could turn their hands to most tasks! Naturally, Jack's wife, June became drawn into the administration of the club, taking on the post of assistant treasurer, including membership; which conveniently focused much of the back ground management close to the club's HQ.

In 1965 the final vestiges of WW2 protection measures were removed from the harbour. A matrix of scaffold piping had been laid on the beach as an invasion deterrent. Much of this had corroded and become embedded in the shingle. Some sections had been washed over the shingle bank and lay as an eyesore on the harbour side. These were finally dragged out, cut up and disposed of, but even today small sections still reappear gradually corroding away.

During this period the first small amount of dredging was conducted by the AYC. The area between the jetty and the bridge provided a reasonable sheltered basin but with a drying mud bank crossing it. The bank was lowered and the old Great Sluice channel partially filled to provide a level base. Once complete it allowed craft to dry out at low water without resting awkwardly on the step bank, thus avoiding the risk of flooding as the tide rose up. It was the first step in a long line of future dredging activities to improve mooring facilities.

Another local enterprise to set up at Axmouth harbour was the company Pebble & Flints. It started just after the Second World War, employing locals to pick pebbles from Axmouth Beach and eastwards to Culverhole Point (also from Branscombe Beach). The

Change in Emphasis

Pebble storage hoppers.

Pebble & Flints – a young author being escorted home – 1964.

pebbles were generally of a particular size (grape) and individuals were paid by the bucketful. The company used the old coalyard within the AYC compound to house its tractors, store sacked pebbles and process them for many uses, such as grinding the constituent parts in the manufacture of paint and toothpaste. Larger stones were gathered for ornamental pavings and garden ornaments. The pebbles gathered east of the river mouth were graded and stored in hoppers constructed on the site of the old Customs House. Metal chutes allowed the pebbles to be transferred into lorries for transportation.

It is difficult to estimate the quantity of pebbles removed. The concession for extraction which included both Axmouth and Branscombe Beaches was 1000 tons per year. Concerns regarding degradation of beach material resulted in the licence being revoked. Without it the company could not survive, and so it was wound up in 1973.

Local fishing fleet

During the late 1970s Seaton's fishing fleet continued to work off the open beach in the summer months, with a fleet of eight traditional clinker-built boats ranging from 22 to 26 feet. During the winter the fleet laid up on the foreshore within Axmouth Harbour. Due to the vagaries of the harbour mouth this was the only time that Seaton fishermen would venture into, and out of the harbour! Interestingly one of those old Seaton fishing boats was still in service until 2010. *Swallow* belonged to father and son, Dit and Ron Wilkins, a heavily constructed clinker-built beach boat, 22ft in length and carrying the registration of E29. She was built in Exmouth by Lavis and spent a long hard life working off the open beach. In her early days she often set her lug sails to assist her home, one of the last fishing boats to do so. Eventually the Wilkins retired and *Swallow* moved to Lyme as a tripping boat under the new name *Maid of Lyme*. Ultimately, she ended up back in Exmouth.

As time progressed Seaton's fishing fleet slowly reduced in numbers. With improvements at the harbour entrance those remaining gradually relocated to the harbour. The building of Seaton's sea-wall did not help matters, as during storms it restricted the space for hauling up the boats. Today, the long tradition of

Swallow E29, Exmouth – 2010.

Seaton fishing boats – early 1970s.

working boats using Seaton's open beach landing has ceased. The fleet provided the town with a vibrant focal point, for both visitors and locals, it was the last vestige of Seaton's historic connection with fishing – sadly, now gone.

Some notable vessels

A couple of notable craft entered the harbour around this time, the first more especially for its large size, the other for its deep draught. The first was *Mervic*, an ex-World War One American submarine chaser. These vessels were built in their hundreds by the Electric Launch Company in Bayonne, New Jersey. Some 550 were sold to the Royal Navy during WW1 and shipped across the Atlantic aboard transport vessels. With a length overall of 80 feet (24.4m), she was the largest vessel (and still is) to enter the harbour in over a hundred years. She arrived at high water on a calm summer's evening during 1967 and gently nosed into the bridge to swing (unintentionally opening up the hood ends of her planking as the stem made contact!), berthing alongside the harbour wall just downstream of the bridge.

There she remained in semi lay-up for a year or so before departing under the new ownership of local resident Frank Manning and Brian Stien. With a change of ownership, she took on a more colourful life. Initially she spent some time in the Thames, then

Mervic in the south of France.
(Frank Manning).

headed down through the French canals to the Mediterranean. The voyage was not without incident; a misunderstanding whilst passing the locks resulted in a lock keeper firing a shotgun at the vessel! Fortunately, no one was injured and *Mervic* continued on her way – although the story reached the national press in the UK: *France fires on British vessel!*

The second notable vessel entered the harbour in a similar fashion to Jack Rattenbury's account of 1817. *Nevenda*, a graceful 37-foot deep keeled yacht, was caught out in a summer gale during 1967. Seeking shelter, she had anchored in Beer Roads, but dragged and ended up being driven ashore on Beer Beach.

Nevenda *alongside the jetty 1969. (Bryan Davis).*

The stranded yacht suffered hull damage with some planking stove in. She eventually became a write off, her valuable lead keel was removed by the local boat builder Harold Mears and her keel-stepped mast was sawn off at deck level. Fortunately, she avoided being broken up and was salvaged by local Axmouth lifeboatman Bernie Webber. With the hull damage temporarily patched up, she was placed on greased timbers and slid down the beach to be re-floated. The short passage across the bay and into the harbour almost ended in disaster. The yacht leaked so badly that she only just made it to the jetty before completely sinking. This was much to the relief of George Dart who was towing the yacht in a small open boat which itself was in danger of being dragged under. Over the next year Bernie repaired the yacht, using some unconventional methods. The original lead ballast keel was replaced with ex-Seaton railway lines welded together and covered in cement to form a 'bulb' keel; the mast was re-stepped on deck in a tabernacle. Re-launched under the new name of *Phoenix*, she continued to have a colourful life, surviving many more exploits in various Channel Island cruises. One notable incident occurred when Bernie and his new wife Sylvia got caught out in a gale off of Portland Bill. A Navy mine-sweeper stood by offering to take the honeymoon crew off, but ever resourceful Bernie declined. With Sylvia manning the bilge pump, *Phoenix* made it into Weymouth – just! The yacht was originally designed and built by Charles Sibbick of Cowes in 1901, having been converted from a yawl to sloop in 1933.

The harbour is sold to the local authority

On 7 March 1966, one of the contributory factors in the demise of Axmouth Harbour as a nineteenth-century trading port, was itself axed by Dr Beeching. The branch line from Seaton Junction to Seaton Station finally closed after just ninety-eight years in operation. Once the provider of cheap transport for both goods and passengers, the railway was itself superseded by improved road transport.

In 1967 the harbour was sold to Axminster Rural District Council and within the transfer of ownership, the AYC continued to maintain its lease of the beach and moorings.

On 10 July 1968 the Axe Valley suffered torrential rain causing extensive floods, resulting in damage to riverside properties and cars being swept down the river. The flood water also swept recently cut hay from the fields into the river. This caused spate conditions and

Collapse of the harbour wall – 1971 (pebble hoppers in the background).

with the added effect of the hay, boats were wrenched from their moorings and washed out to sea. One 18ft clinker launch named *Iffy* was eventually found off Portland and taken into Weymouth, no worse for its unaccompanied voyage!

In 1971, the estate's earlier repairs to the seaward end of the harbour wall collapsed into the entrance. The concrete infill had been undermined by tidal scour and wave action. This made entry to the harbour even more hazardous with large blocks of concrete causing obstructions close to the wall, right in the narrowest part of the entrance channel!

Maintenance of the harbour continued in an ad hoc way, Axminster RDC was presented with the same issues as the previous owners, with very limited funding for repairs. Ultimately, the council surveyor decided the only course of action was to pour more concrete into the void of the collapsed wall! This had the effect of producing an even greater quantity of unstable and unsupported concrete mass – having absolutely no regard for navigation.

Within the harbour, vessels were discouraged from mooring alongside the quay wall due to its fragile condition, although the residents of Harbour Cottage and the Moorings maintained berths adjacent to their properties. Notably, Doug Brown of the Moorings ran an old clinker fishing boat named *Gwendolin* from the quay, but then subsequently a 30ft launch named *Bounty*. Having originally been built as a passenger ship tender, she had operated as a tripping boat from Padstow and then St Ives. *Buccaneer* as she was originally named, was delivered by a local crew from St Ives to Axmouth, arriving in the harbour one foggy Sunday morning in April 1969; it was quite a novelty to see a vessel enter the harbour with navigational lights! Re-named *Bounty*, she had a long career based at Axmouth. Initially, trippers were taken on excursions along the coast to Lyme and Sidmouth, but the venture was always hampered by the tidal constraints of the harbour; her size and narrow beam made her impractical for operating off the open beach. Eventually she was sold to local Axmouth farmer/fisherman Roger Webber who converted her for trawling. She continued in this role for a number of years, with many local youngsters experiencing their first taste of 'deep sea fishing' aboard her. *Bounty* had one distinct advantage over the other local boats, being slightly larger and more powerful, she notched up some notable successes in the Beer Regatta trawler races!

Small signs of improvement

By the early 1970s the harbour entrance had truly become the *'very small gut'*. Harbour users not only had to contend with a constantly shifting shingle bar, but strong tidal streams and an obstructed entrance. Within the harbour, The Rapids, originally excavated by the Halletts had become filled with stones, rocks and small boulders. The debris had accumulated in the channel from ad hoc repairs to the harbour wall – it truly lived up to its name on the ebb tide! The area effectively formed a weir, retaining water in the harbour at low tide and restricting the depth at high water. Use of the harbour was restricted to a couple of hours around the high-water period, especially during neaps. During spring tides, it had the effect of accelerating the tidal flow, a further limitation. However, one solitary boat owner, Chris Duke, aided by his spaniel, used to spend hours at low water with a large rake and garden fork painstakingly removing small rocks and boulders from the Rapids and piling them up against the harbour wall. He reckoned his 'dredging' work eventually allowed an extra half hour of access either side of high water for his small fishing boat!

More noticeable improvements within the harbour which had begun in the late 1960s continued. The AYC, due to increased demand for moorings decided to embark on a concerted dredging project. It had already created a line of trot moorings from just below the bridge downstream to the old warehouse. It must be remembered that the work was planned, organised and carried out by volunteer labour from within the Yacht Club. A nucleus of AYC

AYC members clearing rocks – 1973.

individuals led the way. Jack Bradshaw, Jack Daniel, Fred Wilmot and latterly Ian Rogerson, were determined to see improvements made to the harbour. A basin was initially excavated between the bridge and the old jetty in 1969. This provided an additional thirty moorings for yachts and motor boats up to 8 metres in length. As a by-product the spoil from the dredging was used to provide greater hard standing within the yacht club's compound and was also used to reinforce and consolidate the 'mighty pebble ridge'. The fluidised silt and mud permeated the shingle to form a solid base, and once established (dried) could not be distinguished from the rest of the beach. A slipway was also created leading into the basin, adjacent to the bridge.

Unfortunately, the harbour entrance remained in its precarious condition for a further ten years. In fact, during the summer of 1973 a small 14ft boat managed to become wedged under a section of the overhanging collapsed wall. The vessel sank but the owner managed to get free unharmed. Subsequently the AYC decided to improve things and hired pneumatic drills and over a summer weekend managed to break down the offending section and reduce the obstructing concrete blocks.

Construction of the new pier – 1978.

Following much lobbying by the AYC and prompted by dangerous incidents, Civil Engineers Lewis & Duvivier were contracted in 1973 by Axminster RDC to draw up plans for stabilising the harbour entrance wall, with further additional phased improvements. Unfortunately, this coincided with local council re-organisation and the proposal was shelved. In 1974 ownership of the harbour was transferred to the newly established East Devon District Council. The situation continued unchanged for a few more years. But with increased lobbying from the AYC, EDDC was encouraged to dust off the proposal, since it had become obvious that further deterioration was inevitable unless something was done. Also, under the Axmouth Harbour Act of 1830, the council had an obligation to maintain the scheduled harbour.

Due to the rapidly deteriorating condition of the wall, the initial phase of Lewis & Duvivier's improvement plan received approval in 1977. This consisted of a new short pier extension, 20 metres in length encasing the crumbling entrance wall. Constructed of sheet steel piling driven into the underlying marl, it was then back filled

The mudflat before dredging the mooring basin 1971. (John Chandler).

with concrete. The piling was also extended inwards some 20 metres to underpin and strengthen the original inner wall. Finally, the new concrete pier was stone faced to improve its appearance and to allow it to blend in with the existing wall. The improvement work also involved clearing the entrance of the old concrete obstructions. The new pier was completed in 1978, the first major works since J.H. Hallett's pier of 1806.

On completion, the new short section of pier provided a slight improvement in the scouring effect of the ebb tide, helping to somewhat stabilise the bar. An unexpected side effect of the design created a set towards the new wall when navigating the entrance, especially during the maximum strength of the tidal stream. This was due to the sharp angular direction of the pier. Had it been designed with a more sweeping curve, the problem may well have been averted. Ultimately the extension provided the long-needed security to the crumbing harbour wall, finally stabilising the deteriorating condition.

The newly formed mooring basin and protective spit – 1978.

Following the work in 1978, a section of inner harbour wall collapsed near to the bridge affecting access to the harbour side properties. Follow-on work continued with piling and underpinning between the bridge and Harbour Cottage.

Demand for moorings steadily grew, and the improved entrance gave impetus to improvements within the harbour. In 1978 the AYC embarked on a major excavation and dredging project. This time a larger basin was excavated from the western bank downstream of the concrete jetty. It was during these operations that wooden piles first came to light, indicating earlier projects to 'trench' through the shingle. The basin was excavated downstream to a point opposite Harbour Cottage, where under the direction of the South West Water Board (rivers) it was deemed that some sort of protection was necessary. This involved constructing a small buttress formed from stone-filled wire gabion baskets.

The enlarged basin could now accommodate a total of 120 moorings, which was increased further when the old concrete jetty became unstable and was demolished, thus joining the upper and lower basins to form one large expanse of water.

Fishing rights sold

In March 1978 the fishing rights of the tidal Axe were sold at auction in two lots, the 'sole and several fishery' between Axe Bridge and Axmouth Bridge and rod fishing between Axmouth Bridge and the sea. They were acquired by Sir John Loveridge of Bindon Manor for the sum of £19,600. This included the right to net migratory salmon at the river mouth and in the upper reaches but subject to licence from the then S.W. Water Authority. The rights were sold by Ms Judith Fiske the sole remaining descendent of Saunders Stephens family who originally owned the estate, estuary and harbour. She retained the right of one rod for herself and her successors in perpetuity.

The Story of Axmouth Harbour

Above: Wave tops the beach - AYC Clubhouse.

Top right: Seawater running into the boatyard behind Trevelyan Road.

Below: Seawater pouring into the boatyard.

Bottom right: The harbour channel almost blocked.

Swell without storm

The following winter produced one of the greatest coastal floods seen in living memory, but under very unusual conditions. 13 February 1979 started quietly with an overcast sky, a light northerly (offshore) wind and with neap tides prevailing.

The author, living in Trevelyan Road was awoken at six o'clock in the morning when through the dark, waves could be observed breaking over the seafront, with water pouring down the road. As daylight came the situation worsened with large waves topping the seafront and flooding into Seaton's esplanade properties. To the rear of Trevelyan Road, waves were breaking over the top of Axmouth Beach and surging into the yacht club compound, smashing boats and huts in their path. Fortunately, in the half-light I managed to take a series of photographs which demonstrated the waves' destructive action. To the east of the AYC clubhouse the *'mighty ridge of pebbles'* was being breached by waves over-topping the shingle spit. The newly excavated basin was partially filled with shingle and the harbour channel below the basin was almost blocked, narrowed to within a few feet of the harbour wall. The long-established protecting beach was much reduced in height, allowing waves to surge over it in storm conditions.

Seaton's Harbour Road became totally flooded with numerous properties and businesses affected. Seawater also flowed into

the holiday camps inundating what used to be the old salt marsh. By late afternoon the swell had subsided and the full extent of the damage could be assessed. The AYC clubhouse had been partially demolished; many boats were damaged and beach huts destroyed. A considerable volume of shingle was washed into the harbour, both into the basin and the channel downstream of the old warehouses. The constriction presented a potential flooding problem for the lower Axe in general. The local authority responded by deploying excavating machinery to partially clear the channel of shingle. Once partially cleared the backed-up

AYC damage photographed the following day 14.02.79.

river water within the estuary started to take effect and scoured much of the shingle seaward. As a result of the storm, the *'mighty ridge of pebbles'* was not so mighty! Consequently, when walking along the eastern harbour wall to the river mouth one had an unbroken view of the sea due to the much-reduced height of the beach. It took a number of years of 'normal' wave action to restore its former height.

As a consequence of this unusual and destructive ground swell the AYC's insurers contended that since no storm conditions prevailed at the location of where the damage occurred, they declined to pay for the reconstruction of the clubhouse!

The cause of this havoc was a severe storm far out in the Atlantic generating a large swell of a particularly long wave length. Such waves can have a period of up to 20 seconds, compared with the 5-10 second period of local storm waves. The swell was of sufficient

Shingle swept away from the base of Haven Cliff – 1989.

height to retain its destructive force into the shallower coastal waters of the western English Channel and Lyme Bay. It resulted in many cases of flood damage along the south coast. This rare occurrence had great similarities to those recorded in 1904 and 1868.

A similar event in the winter of 1989, but less dramatic, swept the shingle beach away from the base of Haven Cliff, extending towards Culverhole Point. For a period of time the cliff was left unprotected with waves washing against it at high water. Slowly during the following summer, the beach re-established itself. Today the accumulation of shingle is far greater than for many years.

Recognition of the harbour's renewed importance

The inner harbour wall continued to be patched as and when sections crumbled, despite this a few local fishermen started to use the quay and a limited amount of dredging was conducted to allow berthing alongside. After a few more notable collapses, one especially close to the residential properties, a programme of piling and rebuilding was put in place by EDDC during 1985. The quay adjacent to the properties (the one-time trading berths and warehouse) was replaced in its entirety and the berths dredged for greater accessibility to form the new 'Fish Quay'.

The original Lewis & Duvivier plan was in three phases. The first to stabilise and restore the harbour entrance, resulting in the short 20 metre pier head was completed in 1978. The second phase involved stabilising the whole length of the harbour wall from bridge to mouth with steel piling to underpin. The third phase planned to extend the pier a further 65 metres seaward, almost to the mean low water spring mark. Its purpose was to stabilise the entrance channel and prevent the shingle bar from forming. In a way this replicated Hallett's design, forming a training wall to concentrate the flow of the ebb. Although phase three was shelved, phase two effectively materialized in a piecemeal process as sections of the harbour collapsed.

Wrecking?

The Guernsey-registered trawler *Fairway* based in Brixham had got into difficulties some 6 miles south of Beer Head in November 1978. The 175-ton vessel had just come out of refit but suffered a clutch failure. The weather was not good, with a severe south-westerly gale building, the skipper and crew decided to abandoned ship. Before departing, the vessel was anchored and the crew were then taken off by the Torbay Lifeboat. Eventually she broke free, I distinctly remember seeing the trawler drift across the bay in heavy seas heading towards Culverhole Point. The lifeboat stood by, but in the deteriorating conditions was prevented from getting a tow aboard and returned to Brixham, leaving the *Fairway* to its fate. She eventually stranded on the rocks just west of the Slabs below the old Landslip Cottage. News travelled fast, some individuals boarded her on the falling tide, laying their claim to salvage. Beer Coastguards arrived soon after but were prevented from boarding so stood by to prevent any looting from the vessel, having already found some of the vessel's gear concealed in the Landslip. The Receiver of Wrecks was informed and the vessel was declared 'lost property'. Following this the fishermen departed but still held out for their claim of salvage. The coastguard and police then assisted the vessel's owner in removing the more valuable equipment. Later that night looters struck and removed numerous items including its Decca Navigator – registered and only operable with the owner's license! Some two weeks later after being declared a total loss a syndicate of Seaton fishermen purchased the vessel for £100 (her original value being placed at £65,000). No doubt the paltry amount reflected the inaccessible position of the wreck with regards to salvage.

Fairway ashore east of Culverhole Point.

The vessel had been driven ashore on a particularly high tide and any thoughts of towing it off were dashed by the offshore rocks which had ripped a large hole in the wooden hull. Additionally, the Nature Conservancy Board was concerned at suggestions of forming a track through the Landslip or along the beach from Axmouth in order to recover the more valuable brass, copper and bronze items including the propeller. A tracked vehicle managed to traverse the beach from Axmouth but was eventually abandoned along with the wreck. In the end little was retrieved, although the syndicate maintained they had recovered their initial investment, but with little profit! Eventually the trawler was deemed to be a hazard and the army was brought in to demolish it by the use of explosives. The remains of the vessel still lie on the foreshore amongst the rocks, with fractured machinery and twisted metal work which once formed the engine floors.

Another fishing vessel was wrecked and looted on Seaton Beach in February 1982. The 40-foot converted lifeboat had 'broken adrift' from its berth alongside the quay at Harbour Cottage and was swept out of the harbour. Another version reported that the vessel had 'accidently' slipped its moorings when being moved. In either event the boat ended up being stranded on Seaton Beach adjacent to Burrow Road. The vessel's owner, a Lyme fisherman arrived to secure the boat, only to find looters had removed the brass navigation lights and steering wheel. Unable to salvage the vessel it was eventually stripped of any recoverable items and burnt.

Fishing boat ashore on Seaton Beach – 1982. (Seaton News).

The Story of Axmouth Harbour

Buccaneer wrecked at the river mouth – 1985. (Seaton News).

In August 1985 a local fishing boat *Buccaneer* also broke free from alongside the quay. The 24-foot trawler was locally built by Mears. A severe summer storm produced sufficiently rough conditions to chaff the moorings and wrench a mooring ring from the quay. The vessel was swept out of the harbour and wrecked on the beach just east of the river mouth. The heavy swell took little time in breaking up the boat, leaving little to be salvaged.

New Axmouth Bridge

During the late 1980s discussions took place for the replacement Axmouth Bridge due to its deteriorating condition caused partially by the ever-increasing road traffic, coupled with its unstable foundations. After much local consultation regarding the siting of the new bridge it was decided to construct immediately upstream of the old bridge. The new bridge was completed in 1990, whilst the old bridge was restored and pedestrianised, retaining its claim to being the oldest surviving concrete bridge in the UK – with the status of being one of the youngest Ancient Monuments. There has been recent speculation regarding the line of steel piles and protective rocks laid across the river immediately upstream of the new bridge, suggesting they are the remains of works carried out during WW2. In fact, they were installed as part of the new bridge construction, forming a protective weir against erosion of the new bridge piers. The weir was constructed such that it is almost level with the river bed, making it visible only at low water.

Bronze Age Sword in Axe

During construction work on the bridge piers in November 1989, a 15-inch (39cm) bronze sword was recovered from the river bed. Archaeologists believe the flat rapier originates from the Bronze Age and may have been thrown into the river as a religious gesture. The rapier's original surface has been lost by erosion or corrosion, leaving a pitted patina. The hilt, which has its top end missing, preserves part of two rivet holes. The rapier now resides at the Royal Albert Museum in Exeter, awaiting display, having been treated for the effects of prolonged salt water immersion.

Medieval wreck – the Axe Boat

Construction of the new bridge has resulted in deflecting the tidal stream. The angle of the piers and walled infill on the eastern bank deflects the in-coming tide to the west, upstream of the bridge. The deflection of both the flood and ebb tide has gradually caused the main river channel to move westwards, causing greater scouring of the west bank, especially on the flood.

This is visibly apparent by the erosion of the salt marsh island just upstream. Scouring has also revealed the remains of what is thought to be a small sixteenth-century trading vessel, now termed the Axe Boat. The surviving wooden structure is in remarkably good condition having been preserved within the fine silt and gravel of the estuary. As the gravel on the west bank has been scoured, the upper parts of the vessel have become visible. It is lying on a north-westerly heading, more or less upright with its wooden frames protruding from the shallow incline of the bank.

Interestingly D.M. Stirling's *Guide to the Coast of South East Devon* written in 1838 quotes the following:- *'In the month of November, 1837, was discovered, at low water, in a deep part of the river a little above the fording place, the remains of a vessel of about seventy tons burthen, which in all probability has remained in that situation for upwards of three centuries.'* This description matches remarkably well with the position of the Axe Boat. The 'fording place' being immediately upstream of the old Axmouth Bridge. Pulman used this very same quote in the *Book of the Axe* but modified it such that it implied the wreck was some way inland from the entrance, Stirling's firsthand account positions it accurately.

Since its re-discovery in 2002 Southampton University has carried out investigative work to establish the vessel's age and type, radio carbon dating places it between 1400 and 1640. The construction is carvel with heavy closely spaced frames. The vessel's dimensions are approximately 50ft in length (15m) with a beam of 15ft (5m). The interior hull is also planked – known as ceiling, this provided additional strength and formed a smooth inner hull surface preventing cargo from falling between the frames into the bilges. This helped to protect the cargo from contamination and allowed bilge water to be pumped out from the intervening space; it also provided a smooth surface for ease of handling cargo. The vessel was built with a heavy longitudinal keelson, remarkably well preserved along with the limber boards – the removable boards giving access to the bilge. The construction is thought to be of oak throughout, with treenail fastenings, although the keelson is secured with iron clenched bolts. Round ballast stones were found in place along with traces of coal, possibly indicating a former cargo. The wreck has yet to be fully investigated and may well reveal more detail, however scouring continues and protection has been added to prevent further erosion. In May 2009 further investigations were carried out, clearing a complete cross section of the hull and some artefacts were recovered – a very well-preserved elm bowl and a wooden spade. The information regarding the Axe Boat has been compiled by Jon Adams and Kitty Brandon of Southampton University.

Medieval wreck – just north of Axmouth Bridge – 2015.

If indeed the wreck is of seventeenth-century construction, then it provides an interesting clue as to the course and depth of the estuary at the time. Whilst positioned on the present west bank its location when abandoned may have been more central to the old estuary. Although the majority of the wreck remains buried, its keel lies only a matter of a metre or so below the present river bed, a further indication to the old estuary's original depth? D.M. Stirling's account would certainly suggest it being more central in the channel. Positive dating will provide more definitive answers.

The Present Day Harbour

Retaining the harbour's natural character

Since the late 1960s there have been various schemes and proposals to create a yacht marina at Axmouth. The majority of these schemes were based on uneducated and un-researched assumptions. The first such scheme was proposed in November 1971 – The Axmouth Feasibility Study. The study instigated by both Axminster RDC and Seaton UDC offered very little for the improvement of the harbour. It concentrated on flooding Seaton Marshes, creating an enormous stagnant boating lake with waterside properties. There was no means of access to Axmouth Harbour or the sea, the only provision being a ramp and slipway to cross the tram line (suitable for dinghies only). A restaurant was proposed for the exposed site of the old Customs House at the harbour entrance and from there a form of cable car to reach the summit of Haven Cliff! The study was full of inaccuracies but it had one beneficial aspect in generating such local opposition that the Axe Vale & District Conservation Society was formed in order to oppose the project and protect the estuary and the marshes.

During the 1980s the Fishermen's Association tried through various bodies to gain support for more sustainable improvements to the harbour entrance. The construction of Seaton's new sea wall (completed in 1980) restricted access for the use of fishing vessels on Seaton Beach, this saw a slow migration to using the harbour in preference. A consultative committee was set up by local councillors and representatives of the Fishermen's Association. EDDC as harbour owners were reluctant to offer any financial assistance. So, the cause was taken up by local MP Sir Peter Emery, who lobbied various ministries for financial support. It was taken further with representations by Euro MP Lord O'Hagan for EC funding to support a feasibility study for the improvement of the harbour entrance. Ultimately, no financial support was forthcoming. Subsequently the Fishermen's Association under the guidance of Dick Bastin, managed to secure a small amount of funding for dredging work. Following restoration work of the inner harbour wall, the quayside berths were dredged and made usable once again. But importantly, Dick also cleared the downstream section of channel in the area of The Rapids. The latter involved removal of accumulated debris, mainly rocks and boulders which had accumulated from various repairs going back over many years. It included removing an amount of the underlying marl, which achieved significantly greater access in terms of depth of water either side of high water – a great benefit to harbour users in general.

In 1988 to provide a formal body for the governance of the harbour EDDC incorporated the Axmouth Harbour Management Company. The company which manages the harbour to this day is formed by members of the two main lease holders using the harbour – the Axe Yacht Club and Fishermen's Association. The non-profit making company holds the head lease for the harbour, with sub-

The Present Day Harbour

leases held by the AYC and FA. The AYC administer the west bank and mooring basin, whilst the FA manage the eastern side quay. The role of Axmouth Harbour Master is held by a member of East Devon District Council staff, with responsibility for policy matters affecting the harbour. The day to day responsibilities are devolved to two volunteer Assistant Harbour Masters appointed by the Axe Yacht Club and Fishermen's Association. Whilst not full-time posts, they are responsible for ensuring compliance with the EDDC byelaws in respect of the harbour. The harbour is actively managed within a policy of phased improvement whilst retaining its natural and traditional character. In 1998 a section of the 1830 Axmouth Harbour Act was repealed under a revision order to allow enactment of new byelaws and redefine the harbour limits to include the harbour approaches from seaward. Encasement of the harbour wall from the entrance to the Fish Quay was carried out in 1996 – re-enforcing the foundations and completing the earlier remedial repairs of 1985, securing the harbour wall in its entirety from the entrance to the bridge. This effectively completed phase two of the original 1974 proposal.

Further marina schemes were proposed by private speculators without any understanding of the physical constraints restricting its development. A marina generally implies a harbour with access at all states of the tide, available in most weather conditions and with deep water berths. None of these important factors were addressed. Two marina schemes were proposed, one by Denness & Ridett Development (1989), the other under a different guise, The Axmouth Harbour Development (Ridett – 1991). The schemes generated support from various local bodies, unfortunately demonstrating a naive understanding of the fundamental difficulties that such projects presented. Both plans ignored the physical constraints presented by the harbour entrance and glossed over any improvements in

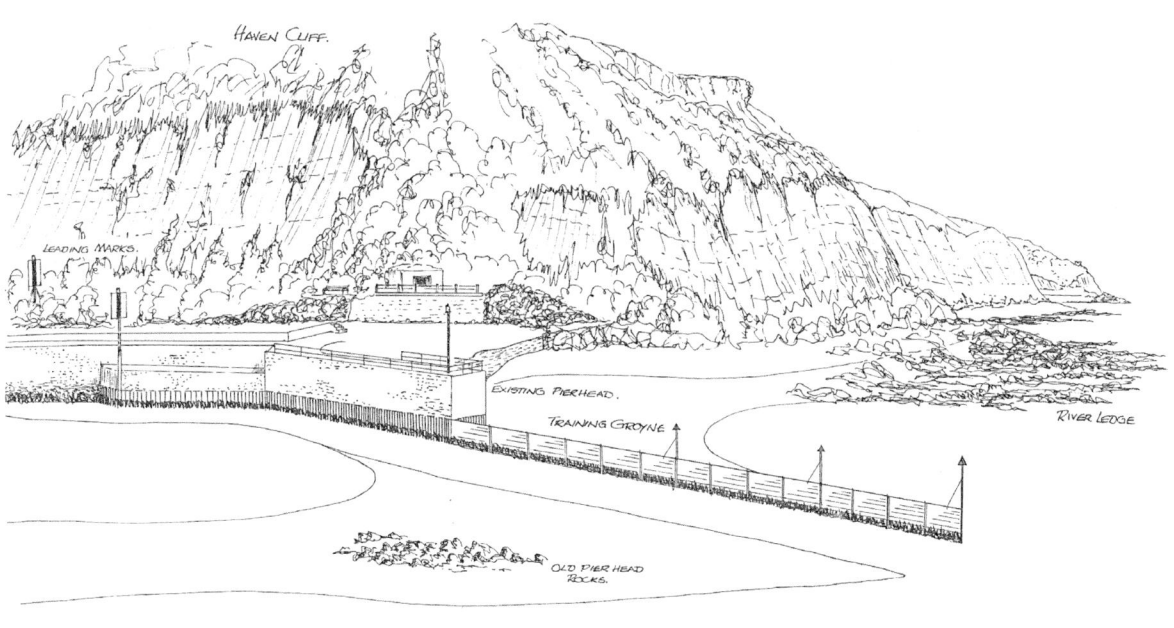

AYC proposal for harbour mouth improvement – 1991. (Nigel Daniel).

Pier extension, almost complete – 2000.

preference to a marina basin and housing development – fortunately neither received the financial backing to proceed.

In order to facilitate a large marina type development, it would require the construction of substantial breakwaters extending seaward into deep water. Only then would it provide safe access at all states of the tide. However, the design would also have to take into consideration and mitigate the formation of the shingle bar, the effects of the strong tidal stream and the ability to allow periodically the discharge of greatly increased flood water generated under spate conditions. None of these were addressed, and the obstacles were conveniently over looked.

In a counter proposal, the AYC offered a more appropriate solution based on the Lewis & Duvivier plan. Through the AYC, Eric Gordon Commodore, Ron Harwood President and the author produced a paper advocating a design much more in keeping with the present harbour and within a realistic budget. A groyne-type structure was proposed, simply extending seawards from the pier head. This would have the effect of training the ebb flow to produce a scoured and stable channel, preventing the formation of the shingle bar – adequately demonstrated during the previous century by Hallett's effective design.

After much consultation EDDC using its own funds finally decided to extend the existing pier head a further 25 metres seaward. The 'harbour arm extension' a more substantial groyne type structure, was constructed using sheet piling driven into the marl and then filled with concrete. The top surface of the concrete fill was cast using a granite aggregate to produce a high abrasion resistance to damage from the beach material. The structure was built approximately to half tide height, above which a heavy wooden groyne structure was added to aid navigation. The seaward end was marked by a starboard hand beacon from which a navigation light is displayed. The green flashing light has range of some two nautical miles, indicating the entrance to those intrepid sailors who navigate the harbour in the hours of darkness.

The old wall underpinned and encased – 1996.

The extension was built as a trial with the ultimate intention of extending to the low spring tide mark – a further 50 metres seaward. The trial extension was also a condition of English Nature in order to observe the effect upon the surrounding beach. Accumulation of shingle beneath Haven Cliff was deemed undesirable as it would provide greater protection to the cliff base and would be out of character with the eroding coastline further east!

Factors affecting the viability of the estuary

The Normal Tidal Limit is the point at which the level of a river or stream ceases to be affected by the tidal flow. In the case of the River Axe NTL is located at a point just above the Stedcombe Bend. During spring tides, the tidal limit reaches further inland, upstream of Axe Bridge. On exceptional springs the tide pushes further inland, some distance beyond Axe Bridge – in fact I have taken my lugger a few hundred yards above the bridge on such occasions. Within the upper tidal reaches of the estuary there has been a marked growth in the spread of reed beds – *phragmites australis*, introduced into the estuary some 100 years ago; early photographs of the upper estuary above Axmouth show no sign of them. On the east side of the estuary the reed beds became established in the area of Stedcombe Bend, and have since spread downstream into Gin Bottle Hole, where they have now completely choked the two back water channels which originally formed small islands. From this point the reeds have continued to spread south to the creek where the Stedcombe Stream enters the estuary (opposite Stafford Brook). Again, this is now almost totally blocked whereas thirty years ago one could take a rowing boat some quarter of a mile into the inlet. The reeds are now spreading from Axe Marsh into Axmouth Marsh, linking up and consuming the salt marsh islands. Similarly, on the west bank, the reed beds now occupy a sizeable portion of what was once a mud flat just downstream of where Stafford Brook enters the Axe.

Silting

The reed bed's presence is causing an artificial acceleration to the silting process of the estuary. The reeds are highly effective at slowing the rate of the stream and thus encouraging further silting. If the spread is not curtailed, the effect could quite radically accelerate the process of silting. Ultimately if unchecked their advance could totally choke the upper and mid-section of the estuary with all the implications of reduced tidal flow and scour of the entrance.

During the late 1980s drainage from Seaton Marsh was improved along with the new Seaton sewerage works based on the marsh, below Hillymead. A new east/west embankment was constructed between the Willoughby bank and the western shore line beneath Seaton's football ground. This effectively divided the area of reclaimed marsh, forming two distinct areas to the north and south of the new embankment. The bank was created by excavating a sizeable portion of the old grazing meadow named Great Ragged Jack. The excavated area conveniently called the Borrow Pit now forms a lagoon for wildfowl. Again, at the time of construction it was reported that what was thought to be old ship timbers were unearthed but no documentary evidence was recorded.

Top left: Seaton seafront flooded – 1974. (John Chandler).

Top right: Seawater flowing down Trevelyan Road – 1974. (John Chandler).

The purpose of the bank was to protect the southern half of the marsh from flooding. This included the new sewerage works, the old holiday camps and low-lying areas of Harbour Road. But it is still left the area vulnerable from extreme storms, when wave action overtops the beach and seafront. Under such conditions, the excess sea water naturally flows down the three escape routes, Beach, Burrow and Trevelyan Roads; filling Harbour Road.

A flood alleviation scheme was constructed as part of the marsh infill and development. A channel was formed to allow water to flow from Harbour Road to the east of the new residential development and exit into the estuary via a culvert beneath the Willoughby embankment south of the old Broad Sluice. The then South West Water Board insisted that a continuation pipeline extend eastwards from the embankment across the mudflats, to empty flood water directly into the river. The pipeline, subsequently covered with scalpings for protection, has now formed a low artificial bank higher than the surrounding mudflats.

This has resulted in significant silting in the channel downstream between Great Island saltings and the Willoughby embankment. In fact, the wreck of the *Patsy Ann* lies in this channel where at low tide a pool once surrounded it – always a good spot for peeler crabs; this has now completely silted up. Incidentally according to local sources, in the late 1950s the *Patsy Ann* was being craned from the railway into the river when it was dropped and broke its back on the concrete railway embankment; beyond repair it was abandoned to become a slowly decaying wreck.

The increased rate of silting within the estuary has in no small way resulted from modern farming practices. The run off from ploughed fields has greatly increased, aided by the destruction of many hedgerows, allowing rain water to run off the land unhindered carrying away the top soil. This is no new phenomena, Pulman voiced his own concerns regarding this very same matter nearly 150 years ago! He states:- *'As elsewhere the modern mania for the destruction of hedgerows and hedgerow timber is not without effect.'* He goes on to say that:- *'the indiscriminate draining of the land can be attributed to the decrease in volume of water in the Axe. Similarly, the influence of rainfall is naturally more direct and rapid.'* His astute observations remain highly relevant today, even with current conservation restrictions in place, the run off and resultant silting continues. Whilst the mid-stream channel remains relatively clear, it is the riverside mud flats, side channels and mooring basin that accumulate sediment more

The Present Day Harbour

Outfall pipe from Seaton Marsh.

readily. As a result, a programme of dredging is required to maintain the basin. Without this the basin would eventually revert back to the mud bank, resembling its previous form prior to the 1978 excavation, rendering a large proportion of the moorings unviable due to limited depth.

Flood defences

Sea levels are rising and look set to continue. Over the last century they are estimated to have risen 7 inches, or at a rate of just under 2mm per year. Predictions for future sea level rise vary enormously, but the rate of change appears to be increasing. Coupled with the subsidence of southern Britain, thought to be 5 centimetres over the next century, the resultant effect will have an undoubted consequence on the estuary. In a contrary way, this may actually help maintain the viability of the estuary, such that the volume of water entering and leaving the estuary will actually

The basin in 2021.

The Patsy Ann *lies stranded between the island and railway – early 1950s.*

increase, or at least compensate to a certain degree against the effects of silting. It is reported that the sea level has increased by 8cm since 2000. By rough calculation, this equates to an additional 20,000m³ of water entering the estuary during an average spring tide.

Although a rise in sea level will slowly start to impact on flood defences and the ecology of the area, the increased tidal prism will impact on the scouring effect at the entrance. The ability of sea defences to withstand ever increasing sea levels will be determined by how long the Willoughby embankment can act as an effective barrier in order to prevent inundation of Seaton Marshes.

With the construction of the railway line in 1868, the Willoughby embankment was raised again to prevent overtopping; even under the severest conditions it remained clear above the estuary flood water. However, on 14 February 2014, following a series of deep Atlantic depressions, extensive flooding was caused country wide. The combined effects of storm surge, low atmospheric pressure and heavy rain water backed up within the estuary resulted in extreme tidal heights. This caused the estuary to flood over the tramline embankment into Seaton Marshes, scouring the tram line ballast and leaving sections of line suspended. Where the flood water had broken through the ballast, it was swept onto the marsh. This may be an indication of things to come; managed retreat may eventually see Seaton Marshes given over to more regular inundation. Using the LiDAR data, the height of the embankment can be accurately measured and compared with predicted tidal heights.

The worst-case scenario occurs with a combination of high spring tides and severe southerly or, south-easterly gales (naturally accompanied by low pressure). The resultant storm surge raises the estuary level considerably, combined with prolonged heavy rain unable to escape, sea defences are severely tested. Under such conditions the estuary is unable to contain the volume of water and the marshes of Axmouth, Colyford Common and Axe Marsh quickly become inundated. Flood water also enters the low-lying area of marsh to the west of the old railway line beneath Stafford Brook Bridge.

The southern part of this area has recently been designated Black Hole Marsh, which now forms a brackish wetland nature reserve, into which the tidal flow is regulated by an ingenious float valve. This admits salt water of a designated salinity at certain states of the tide, maintaining the brackish lagoon. Incidentally the name Black Hole Marsh is a corruption of the adjacent River Axe feature, which was originally known as Black Pool. Black Hole Marsh is contained between a low embankment following the line of Stafford Brook to the north and the original east/west section of the Willoughby bank to the south. This old section of the embankment is lower than the raised railway and remains at the original seventeenth-century height. Under extreme conditions flood water can pass from the estuary via Stafford Brook, flood across Black Hole Marsh and over top the Willoughby embankment into the northern section of Seaton Marsh. If this occurs, the Borrow pit transverse embankment (which effectively splits the marsh in half, north/south), protects the southern area and the present-day sewerage plant. If the level rises further in the lower estuary, then the Willoughby embankment is breached.

In February 2014 the southern section of Seaton Marsh was flooded by both the estuary overtopping the embankment and by water entering through the flood alleviation channel from Harbour Road, fed by waves overtopping Seaton seafront and water entering from the harbour. As mentioned, drainage of Seaton Marsh is limited and only feasible at low water. Under spate conditions with the estuary remaining at a higher level, inundation of the marsh may persist for some time.

On the east side of the estuary, the Waterside Road to Axmouth was similarly constructed at such a height that it rarely floods, even with the combined effects of storm surge, high water and heavy rain. February 2014 proved to be one of those rare occasions. Previously the floods of July 2012 caused by a deluge of heavy rain almost reached the roadside, but this was primarily caused by rain water backing up within the estuary. The storm of February 2014 was worse in that it was accompanied by storm force winds creating a storm surge, preventing the escape of the swollen river water. The level in the estuary quickly rose and around the high-water period the road was flooded, more especially towards the village of Axmouth. Waves generated within the fetch of the estuary were breaking over Coronation Green to such an extent that a fishing vessel which had broken adrift ended up being stranded on the green. It was fortunate that the tidal height was only 3.6m (with an additional surge of 2.0m). Such an event combined with a high spring tide could have resulted in widespread inundation.

Other areas of the estuary that may be affected are concentrated closer to the harbour area. The height of the harbour walls is presently insufficient to prevent over topping during the combined effects of high tides and onshore gales. This leads to flooding of the harbourside lane and has led to flooding of the quayside properties

Seaton Marsh flooded – 2014.

in the past. On the west side of the harbour the low-lying area of the AYC compound also floods under similar conditions. More importantly flood water rises sufficiently to gain access to Harbour Road through the compound via the yacht club entrance gate (as observed in 2014). Having reached this level, flood water then flows downhill into Harbour Road, eventually spreading into the low-lying areas which were once occupied by two holiday camps – the original southern extent of Seaton Marsh.

The camps were subsequently demolished and a considerable area of the southern marsh adjacent to Harbour Road in-filled with imported spoil to accommodate a new supermarket and provide land for housing. Due to planning restrictions for development on flood plains the area was raised by over two metres, amounting to some 340,000 cubic metres of spoil. The infill material (sand) was dredged from the Bristol Channel and then pumped ashore via a pipeline from the dredger lying close to Seaton Beach. The original intention was to use heavier grade spoil from near the Isle of Wight but due to pumping difficulties and movement of the spoil on site it was quickly changed to finer grade sand. The infill of this area has unknown effects with regard to future flooding since the infill now displaces a large area that was once available to accommodate exceptional flood waters; it has yet to be seen if this will impact adversely on the remaining low-lying areas of Seaton. The change to finer grade infill may also eventually affect the estuary. In the course of natural drainage from the marsh area, spoil could migrate into the estuary, introducing additional silting. Only time will tell how these unknown effects will influence the estuary.

The protecting shingle bank, the *'mighty ridge of pebbles'* also becomes vulnerable in storm conditions. Large waves can overtop the ridge as seen in the freak conditions of 1979, severely lowering its protective height. This resulted in shingle being swept into the river, narrowing the harbour channel. It took many years for the combined effects of ebb tide and spate conditions for the channel to regain its original width. Having said this, the exceptionally heavy rain and flooding of July 2012 swept a considerable amount of shingle out of the channel in less than twelve hours! Re-building the shingle spit height is a much slower process. It depends on waves of the correct amplitude to cast shingle higher up the beach; too high and the ridge is flattened. As climate change takes effect, rising sea levels may bring about less certainty in this recovery process.

Ultimately the viability of the harbour rests in maintaining a clear entrance. This can only be achieved by the combined effects of the training wall and its ability to direct the tidal scour. Failure of the former and or reduction of the tidal volume would result in the demise of the harbour.

Fishing boat stranded on Coronation Green – 2014.

The harbour and entrance today

Since the building of the outer pier extension, it has afforded a degree of stability in the entrance channel from pier head to low water mark. Prior to this the foreshore channel was less stable, at times it could be deflected by the bar, causing the channel to run almost at right angles close to the beach. Deflection occurred either to the east or west, but on rare occasions the bar joined both banks enabling one to cross the entrance dry shod. The pier head extension has considerably reduced the frequency of this happening, although it has not completely stopped it. Under the right conditions the bar can still briefly block the entrance. This happens during neap tides with minimal scour, lasting only briefly before breaking through to re-establish the channel. For the majority of the time a bar of varying size forms to seaward of the pier head where the channel widens. So far, the channel alongside the pier which is deeper and narrower has not been blocked. Were this to happen it may take considerably more force to re-open the channel.

The bar formations are produced primarily during neap tides (less tidal flow) and with moderate to strong onshore winds where wave action develops the bar. Spring tides have the reverse effect; the increased ebb flow scours the foreshore and reduces the bar. Periods of heavy rain combined with spring tides have the greatest effect. The entrance channel is scoured considerably, both from the main shingle bank and the foreshore channel; under such conditions shingle is carried some distance beyond the low water mark. On the return to more stable conditions, wave action drives the shingle back onshore with a small bar forming to the east of the entrance. Predominantly the channel runs in a SSW'ly direction from the pierhead, and this is maintained by a combination of the ebb tide flowing from the estuary and the west setting coastal tidal stream. Once the ebb tide begins, the east-going coastal stream constrains the outflow, deflecting it to the east. But at half ebb the coastal stream reverses and flows west causing the outflow to deflect westwards. The period from half tide to low water is when the shingle is most dynamic in forming the bar, invariably forming on the east side of the channel.

The harbour's accessibility is determined by three factors: a vessel's draught in relation to the state of the tide, the sea state and finally the position of the bar. Shallow draught craft can operate from a period three and a half hours before high water to a similar period after, especially during neap tides where the low water depth is maintained at a higher level. During spring tides, the strength of the tidal stream has greater effect for lower powered craft, narrowing their window of accessibility. This, more especially for vessels returning to the harbour after high water where the strength of the

The rare occasion when the harbour is completely barred – 1990.

Entrance channel diverted following a strong run of easterlies – 2021.

ebb tide becomes the overriding factor in gaining access, and of course the harbour effectively dries out during springs.

All of the foregoing conditions are governed by the weather. Generally, with moderate onshore winds the harbour remains accessible. But with increased wind strength, seas start to break in the approaches and depending on the magnitude of the bar; the entrance is rendered dangerous except for the intrepid and experienced. Under such conditions the depth of water in the channel becomes more critical and usually dictates entry nearer to high water. Navigating the entrance always requires a healthy respect for prevailing conditions – even the most experienced are caught out now and again, and groundings on the bar are not infrequent.

At low water from the old bridge to a point just below the old warehouse the low water level remains impounded at a level of 1½ metres above chart datum. From this point downstream to the inner end of the pier the level drops by half a metre. Finally, from the pier head to low water springs the channel drops a further metre, passing over the shingle foreshore to reach the sea.

Entrance April 2020 from Haven Cliff.

At certain constriction points notable scour holes have formed. The first lies just downstream of the old bridge, and has a depth of 2 metres at low water. The constriction formed by the western approach embankment to the bridge accelerates the ebb flow, forming a hole in the river bed, where the old estuary channel existed. A second scour hole has formed just within the entrance at the base of the harbour wall. The depth at low water is some 2½ metres, a result of tidal scouring over the past one hundred and fifty years. The marl which is comparatively soft has been eroded away by the continual action of shingle movement within each ebb and flow cycle. The same action has caused erosion of steel piles supporting the entrance pier requiring remedial repairs in 2000.

Silt accumulates in the areas of weaker tidal stream, especially on the sides of the channel requiring periodic dredging both in the mooring basin and along the quayside. Silting above the bridges is more difficult to define. However, as discussed, the mud flats are slowly building and the channels behind the islands are slowly filling. The low water level above the bridges is further impounded by the line of steel piles and protecting boulders sunk into the river bed as part of the new bridge protection against erosion.

Present day activity

Today, the majority of craft use the harbour for leisure purposes. The harbour caters in the main for two aspects: the west side incorporates the yacht basin and the east side utilises the quay for fishing vessels. The AYC provides over 100 pontoon berths for yachts and motorboats. The Fish quay provides approximately 16 alongside berths and an additional 24 trot moorings which are laid between the quay and the bridge. The maximum size of craft is approximately 30 feet with a draught of 3 to 4 feet. The largest vessel to use the harbour in recent years (2002) was an historic Looe Lugger *Our Boys*, built in 1905. She measured 42 feet in length with a draught of almost 7 feet. This restricted her use to higher tides, but proved that larger vessels could still operate from the harbour; she berthed coincidentally outside the warehouse, where in the previous century trading vessels had once moored. Many smaller

Our Boys *between the bridges – 1997.*

craft use the yacht club slipway and are stored ashore within its compound. The yacht club has a smart new club house where once a prefabricated beach hut served the purpose, it now provides an excellent facility for all forms of marine recreational activities.

Fishing

Fishing consists mainly of potting for shellfish, long lining, netting and hand lines. Since the introduction of the Lyme Bay Marine Protection Area in 2008, the emphasis has changed away from trawling allowing the local inshore reefs to regenerate. Technology has provided development of faster craft able to cover much greater distances, fishing areas beyond the reach of the old traditional boats. Some of the local fleet will now head off on cross Channel excursions where bass fishing produces a lucrative income. Typically, these faster craft will travel some 60 miles to their fishing grounds. But not all are keen to embrace the 'advantages' of modern technology. Up until quite recently one fishing vessel of the old traditional clinker construction continued to fish inshore. She was typical of a class of beach boat that has almost disappeared from the shores of east Devon. *Sunbeam* owned by local fisherman Charlie Zeiman worked her pots and nets within the confines a few miles from the harbour entrance, a process that has gone on for centuries, Leland's quote from 1537 is still applicable – *'small fischar boats come in for succour'*. But time moves on, and *Sunbeam* has now been replaced by a more modern GRP vessel ending an association with wooden built working craft. The localised industry continues to see improvements, shellfish storage facilities have now been incorporated on the quayside helping to sustain the local fishermen. More recently with grant funding from the Blue Marine Foundation a lobster store has been constructed within the quay. Filtered storage tanks provide seawater that is regulated for temperature, light and salinity. This controlled environment permits longer term storage of lobsters, allowing Axmouth's fishermen to take advantage of market fluctuations.

Leisure activities

Axmouth-based yachts frequently ply the English Channel to the coast of Brittany and the Channel Islands. Some venture further afield to Ireland, Scotland, Spain and even to the Azores, but one voyage

Sunbeam - *the last traditional clinker fishing boat to work from Axmouth.*

The Present Day Harbour

clearly stands out. In 1993 local resident Tom Bridgman commenced building a 40-foot steel ketch in the yard of the Harbour Inn. When completed she was named *Axecalibre,* and was craned into the harbour from the Fish quay in the summer of 1996. After completing her fitting out alongside, Tom and his partner Dee set off on an adventure of a life time. *Axecalibre* quietly slipped her moorings one summer's morning and sailed away to circumnavigate the world. Navigating via the Caribbean, she transited the Panama Canal and then headed across the Pacific, visiting many of the remote islands, proudly displaying her home port of Axmouth on the transom. Coincidently I met up with *Axecalibre* in Auckland, New Zealand whilst aboard my ship – more than a few 'stiring tales of far voyages' were exchanged. She returned via the Indonesian archipelago, India and the Red Sea to Suez, completing her circumnavigation in Portugal, some nine years later!

The upper tidal estuary still remains navigable to vessels able to negotiate the bridges. The AYC holds a programme of dinghy races throughout the summer, using the fortnightly spring tides. There has been a resurgence of the Axe One Design fleet, following its near demise in the late 1970s. Just one boat remained in commission – No.1 *Whimbrel.* This was Jack Drew's own boat and was purchased by the author in 1983. However, in 2000 renewed interest in the class saw the building of a new AOD. for local resident Malcolm Gill. This rekindled interest in the class, and a further five new boats were been built and two originals restored from near dereliction. The class presently totals ten boats, the latest to join the fleet, No.26, was launched in 2022 and No.25 is presently under construction. The Axe is fortunate to have retained its indigenous class, as many such dinghies have now died out around the coastal estuaries of the South West.

Axecalibre *and* Our Boys *alongside –* 1996.

Launching AOD No.26 Avocet *– 2022. (Jane Calvert).*

Axmouth boat builders – Alex & Paul Mears – 2022. (H.J. Mears & Son).

Mears-built Branscombe Pearl II. *(H.J. Mears & Son).*

A more recent activity that now thrives within the harbour is the Axe Vale Canoe Club. From its humble beginnings using one of the Yacht Club's original huts back in 1979, it has now grown to form a base for nationally-recognised training, especially for its young members. Under the Royal Yachting Association, the Axe Yacht Club has for many years been a nationally accredited Training Centre, conducting dinghy instruction during the summer months and a series of navigation courses throughout the winter.

Axmouth boat building

And of course, Axmouth retains its traditional boat builders, H.J. Mears & Son. Paul Mears and his son Alex continue the custom of building both clinker- and carvel-built fishing boats. Over the years the yard has produced many fine vessels. Up until the late seventies Harold Mears and Paul mainly built fishing boats for the beach landings at Beer and Seaton.

These craft were typically in the region of 22 to 26 feet in length and of clinker construction, invariably planked with local elm, always with a 'tucked' garboard. A gradual change saw more of the fishermen favouring carvel construction and the use of mahogany became more popular especially with the demise of the elms. The carvel hulls still retained their traditional shape, with a broad beam and bluff bow making them excellent sea boats but equally well suited for working off of open beaches. A few larger vessels were built for customers further afield. The naturalist Tony Soper had a large launch built at Mears, whilst a South Devon fisherman from Salcombe had a large crabber built which worked its pots in mid Channel. Now times have changed and there is less call for the traditional style wooden boats so Mears now fit out more modern GRP fishing vessels, but the yard still retains the atmosphere of a small traditional boat yard. At the back of the shed there is invariably a small clinker-built boat under construction, sometimes on spec but always providing that link with the old traditions. Fortunately, there always seems to be a customer willing to purchase one of these fine boats which if well looked after provide years of faithful service. Interestingly Alex Mears became aware that the Salcombe crabber built by his father and grandfather in 1971 lay abandoned on the Isle of Mull. Knowing that the vessel had been well built, thoughts turned to recovering her. So, Alex arranged to have her piggy-backed on a local mussel dredger from Mull to Largs where she was hauled out and transported by road back to Axmouth for restoration. One of Mears typical working fishing boats still survives in its natural environment, *Branscombe Pearl II* continues to be fished by John Hughes from Branscombe Beach.

Another Mears boat that has been in service for over forty years is the Castle Ferry at Dartmouth, known to thousands of holiday visitors. *Achieve* still plies her trade between the Town Quay and Dartmouth Castle. She is very typical of a Mears beach boat, sweeping shear line, broad beam and heavily constructed.

Boat building at Axmouth represents the very last shore-based industry associated with the harbour's working heritage. Few records exist of previous boat building apart from during the eighteenth century when comparatively larger fishing vessels (30'- 35') were known to be built at Seaton. In 1825 records show that boat building was being carried out close to the harbour by

The Present Day Harbour

Top left: Achieve – Dartmouth. (H.J. Mears & Son).

Top right: Lugger beaching at Seaton – 1836, J.E. Fitzgerald. (Canterbury Museum NZ).

a certain Joseph Clarke (possible relation to the local ship owner George Clarke). At the time he was leasing a workshop from the Ackermans, built by Anthony Goodridge in what is described as the 'back' street in Seaton, probably one of the lanes leading off of Fore Street, down to the Underfleet.

Large three-masted luggers were clinker-built and represented the largest type of vessel capable of beach landing. Due to their size they would have probably been more suitable to Beer's more sheltered cove than Seaton's open beach. One would suspect that they were built on the western shore of the harbour for ease of launching and probably not far from where Mears operate today.

Harbour improvements continue

Harbour improvement work continues to this day. The yacht club's long serving Bosun/Assistant Harbour Master, Pete Poulson, now retired, led many improvement projects within the basin. During the winter of 2005 with volunteer members, the mooring basin perimeter was stabilised using stone filled gabions protecting the back slope of *'the mighty ridge of pebbles'*. Once in place the finished appearance is almost indistinguishable from the shingle bank. Further improvements continued with upgrading the moorings; the yacht club now provides pontoon berths in the mooring basin, quite an achievement for organization that relies on voluntary labour from within its membership. During the autumn of 2013 Pete led a project to install piles within the mooring basin to secure the pontoons; this has minimised maintenance and provides a more resilient mooring system.

Ironically the AYC basin now provides a level of mooring accommodation suggested by past developers but at a fraction of the cost, whilst at the same time retaining the unique character of this small West County port. Axmouth Harbour allows a diverse range of activities to be enjoyed, whether it is sailing, fishing, canoeing or just pottering up the estuary on a summer's evening. In all respects it continues to provide a safe haven.

The harbour's future

This coastline is of prime international, as well as national importance for its geological and geomorphological features. It was granted UNESCO World Landscape Heritage status in 2001 under the universally accepted title of the *Jurassic Coast*. This affords a measure of protection against uncontrolled coastal development, as does the national designation of Area of Outstanding Natural Beauty. Protection of the adjoining Haven Cliff comes within the Axmouth–Lyme Regis undercliff SSSI. These protection measures will hopefully help retain the character of the harbour whilst also determining the level and direction of future development. DEFRA have published a Shore Management Plan covering the English and Welsh coasts. The SMP provides a large-scale assessment of the risks associated with coastal evolution. It includes a policy framework to address these risks in a sustainable manner with respect to people and the developed, historic and natural environment. SMP2 (2011) – Durlston Head to Rame Head covers the local section of the coast, assessing the future coastal flooding risks and the associated management strategy defined in short, medium and long-term plans. In the case of the Axe estuary (Section 6a25 to 6a28), it proposes to maintain the harbour pier into the longer term, a case of 'hold the line', thus continuing to provide an open entrance for navigation and flood alleviation. However, management of the shingle spit – the *mighty ridge of shingle* – will have no intervention. Presently the spit is self-sustaining, the supply of shingle through longshore drift appears to be maintaining the feature without any intervention. Preservation of the shingle bank is imperative for the future existence of the harbour in its present form. The bank affords shelter not only to the harbour but to the lower estuary in general. Should the supply of shingle diminish then the harbour's future will be less certain.

The assessment also suggests that within the estuary a policy of 'hold the line' will exist along the eastern shore, whilst there may be a process of managed retreat along the western shoreline. This involves a possible re-alignment of the Willoughby embankment and thus the tram line. A partial re-alignment to the west would seem to serve little purpose since it is being moved 'inshore' on level ground that is not prone to erosion. The weakness is in the height of the embankment and the prospect of rising sea levels. In mitigation, the plan states that greater detailed consideration is required to investigate the future strategy.

Rather than re-alignment, a process of re-flooding the marshes may be preferable, allowing the estuary to work more closely to its original form, having the ability to absorb a greater volume of flood water whilst increasing the crucial tidal prism. The Otter estuary, which has many similarities to the Axe, is presently going through this very same process in allowing a previously reclaimed floodplain to revert to tidal saltmarsh.

This could be replicated within the Axe estuary. The section of Seaton Marsh contained between Black Hole Marsh and the transverse Borrow Pit embankment, the old Great Marsh and Great Ragged Jack, could revert to an inter tidal habitat. This represents a considerable area, some 25 hectares, equalling half the original 1660 reclaimed marsh. The network of abandoned creeks is clearly shown on recent LiDAR mapping. They are more prominent in the northern section, indicating their greater depth. Allowing this section of marsh to revert into an inter tidal zone would provide greater diversification to the already well-established wetlands, complementing the fresh water marsh to the south and the brackish Blackhole Marsh to the north. Additionally, this would enhance the

The Present Day Harbour

estuary's tidal prism – the all-important volume of water entering and leaving the estuary – whilst providing supplementary flood alleviation.

In 2019 the Axe estuary along with some other West Country sites was designated a Marine Conservation Zone. This recognises the diverse habits that exist within the tidal estuary and lends further protection to the harbour from future undesirable development.

The harbour's popularity continues to grow and within its present constraints is nearing full utilization. The mooring basin has been developed to take full advantage of the available space. The piled pontoon berths are fully utilized, to such a degree that a waiting list exists. Similarly, the alongside berths of the Fisherman's quay are fully occupied, supplemented with a number of trot moorings. Above the bridge additional trot and swinging moorings are available; added to this, a number of dry stored craft access the harbour from the main slipway.

Taking the facilities in their entirety it is difficult to see where further expansion could occur without changing the whole character of the harbour. Enlargement of the mooring basin is feasible but would be to the detriment of the existing shore side facilities. Any further development needs to be carefully weighed against over populating the harbour. The critical limiting factor is the harbour entrance. Restriction is twofold, the physical width and the tidal limitations, restricting the period available period for access. Presently the level of traffic can increase to a point where vessels are required to wait for a clear slot to navigate the entrance. This only occurs at peak periods and being more leisure-based it typically occurs at weekends. Overall, the harbour is presently working close to its natural limit. Perhaps the future should be a period of consolidation, retaining its unique character.

Axmouth Harbour today. (Jane Calvert).

Johanna Lucretia arrives off Axmouth – 2019. (Bruce Kenny).

Besides routine maintenance of the harbour wall, there is a long-term objective to complete the original pier extension as proposed by Lewis & Duvivier in 1974. Funding for this will inevitably be a challenge as will the planning process. The future plan could be viewed in two phases. Firstly the re-modelling of the current situation to ensure the desired effect. Whilst modelling the movement of shingle is notoriously difficult, it would provide a measure of confidence in the design. Historically there is a design basis to work from: Hallett's nineteenth-century pier was successful in stabilising the entrance, and in principle, the proposed extension would differ very little. Improvement of the harbour entrance would have many benefits, besides the more obvious navigational aspects. It would benefit the whole estuary ecosystem of mudflats, salt marshes and wetlands, especially now it has been designated a Marine Conservation Zone, with the implications of maintaining a *marine* connectivity. Importantly it would also ensure that flood alleviation is maintained, to avoid the historic condition of being *kept back like a three-quarter tide*.

The second phase of implementation would rely heavily on grant funding. Should this become available the present line of thought would be to extend the pier 20 metres seaward. In conjunction with this, an additional improvement could be achieved by 'fairing' the present hard angular bend in the entrance which resulted from the initial 1978 repair works. Producing a more even curve of the inner harbour wall would help smooth the tidal flow, both from a navigational perspective and enhancement of the essential scouring effect.

A schooner in the bay – 1836 – J.E. Fitzgerald. (Canterbury Museum NZ).

The days of commercial sail are long gone, as are commercial operations for Axmouth, but reminiscent of those times, on a summer's evening during 2019, a topsail schooner anchored off the harbour entrance and stayed for the night. The *Johanna Lucretia* typified the type of vessels which frequented the harbour during the 1800s (length on deck 65ft, LOA 96ft, beam 18ft and draught

8ft). In practical terms such a vessel could still enter the harbour, the depth is no shallower.

Under settled conditions on a spring tide, entry would still be feasible. Taking advantage of the brief period of slack tide around high water, a well fendered vessel of this size could negotiate the entrance. Berthing would still be possible alongside the old Warehouse quay and there is sufficient room to swing a vessel of her size (with assistance) for departure. Leaving would require similar benign conditions, but today the added advantages of manoeuvring a vessel under power would be comparatively easy when compared to the days of sail!

The painting at the bottom of the opposite page by J.E. Fitzgerald shows a similar topsail schooner setting sail from Seaton Bay – 185 years earlier!

To conclude

We have come a long way and seen many changes but I would like to think that Axmouth Harbour is no longer written off as so many commentators have suggested in the past. Once again it is a flourishing haven but with a change of scale and purpose, trade is no longer the driving force to maintain the harbour. Times have moved on and leisure activities have taken over where commercial interests once ruled.

But some things do not change, recalling Coxhead's comments:-

'The Harbour Inn at Axmouth is of great age and parts of it date back to the days when the haven was in a flourishing condition. In the cosy warmth of the tavern parlour travellers would have heard many stiring tales of far voyages, desperate sea-fights and wild storms as the hardy mariners thronging the room exchanged their experiences.'

If you wander into either the Harbour or Ship Inn today you are still likely to meet a few local *'mariners,'* for Axmouth still has a couple of sea captains, a few fishermen, a lifeboatman, a coastguard and more than a few villagers who just enjoy messing about in boats. I can assure you *'stiring tales of both near and far voyages'* are still told well into the night…

Nigel Daniel
Axmouth,
2023.

The Harbour Inn.

The Story of Axmouth Harbour

Appendix i
Axmouth Harbour – historical time line

Date	Event
10,000BC	Ice cap retreats – the river valleys of southern England are flooded – the Axe estuary becomes an established inlet.
2000BC	From 4000BC through to 2000BC Neolithic activity – the earliest users of the haven.
500BC	Establishment of the Iron Age Hillforts – Hawkesdown (Hochesdon).
400BC	Phoenician trading with the South West – possibly within the Axe estuary?
50AD	Roman influence – Attack on the Durotriges at Hawkesdown – Roman glandis found.
200	Axmouth is referred to as possibly being the Roman port of 'Uxelis'. A Roman road which may have been a spur of the Fosse Way leads to the eastern bank of the haven terminating at Axmouth. Establishment of Roman settlements, Honeyditches and Higher Holcombe.
340	Departure of the Romans – Danish and Viking raids. In Saxon times Fluta or Au Fleote becomes established as a port on the western bank of the haven.
881	Axmouth is bequeathed to Ethelweard, youngest son of King Alfred.
937	Anlaf the Danish King, lands at Axmouth – defeated by Athelstan King of Wessex further inland – a doubtful contender for the Battle of Brunnenburg, associations with Warlake and Axminster?
1049	Swey, son of Godwin, Earl of Wessex slays his nephew Bjorn at 'Axemouth'.
1066	King Edward the Confessor holds the manor of Axmouth just prior to the conquest.
1068	Domesday Book, the estate is called Alsemude – held by William the Conqueror – the first recorded naming of Axmouth. The manor becomes the property of the Norman baron Richard de Redvers.
1100	de Redvers grants the manor of Axmouth to the Abbey of St Mary, Montebourg, Normandy.
1107	de Redvers is buried in Montebourg Abbey having been granted its patronage by Henry I. Montebourg controls lands in England including Loders Priory and Axmouth.
1155	Control of Axmouth is granted to Loders Priory, Dorset.
1190	3rd Crusade departs from Dartmouth – Axmouth may have supplied shipping to assist.
1207	Tanneries in Axmouth return 20 shillings.
1215	Magna Carta – Axmouth retains certain privileges granted by either Henry I or II then under the ownership of Loders Priory. References to the privileged fishery later support eighteenth and nineteenth century prosecutions against local fisherman.
1256	Axmouth recorded as the first place in Devon to produce cider.
1285	The manor reverts to Montebourg.
1316	The manor reverts to Loders.
1320	Reference to the first identifiable ship, the *George*, with its home port in the haven.
1346	The Siege of Calais – the haven sends two ships and 25 mariners.
1377	Ramsden tenuously suggests that storms of that year caused a large slip at Haven Cliff with the unlikely result of blocking the estuary.
1380	William Umfraville grants 'Le Haven' at Axmouth to the Abbot of Newenham (a trust deed).
1399	Ten ships registered at Axmouth, six in Royal service.
1414	Loders Priory dissolved by Henry V (alien priory) and conferred upon the Abbey of Sion, Middlesex.

1450	Bishop Lacy grants forty days indulgence to improve the haven, the first indication of shingle barring the entrance.
1483	First mention of the Ship Inn, Axmouth.
1513	Henry VIII's wars with France press ships into service, 'Coleton Haven' mentioned, clearly referring to Axmouth Haven.
1536	Suppression of the monasteries – Axmouth returns to royal ownership.
1539	Axmouth is granted to Queen Catherine Parr, on her death it passes to Edward VI.
1542	Leland writes his account of the haven, describing 'the mighty ridge of pebbles where a small gut goeth into the sea'.
1552	The manor is granted to Walter Erle of Bindon by the dying Edward VI.
1557	Seaton Manor is acquired by John Willoughby.
1575	Collections made across the country for 'repairing' the haven.
1581	Axmouth and manor passes to Thomas Erle son of Walter Erle.
1583	Further collections made for the repair of the haven – second attempt to repair the haven
1597	Thomas Erle esq. dies, the manor transfers to his son Sir Walter Erle.
1614	An Act for the erection of a pier at Axmouth is proposed – third attempt to repair the haven.
1619	The Duke of Buckingham carries out a survey of ships and mariners of south Devon.
1623	Formation of the Dorchester Company by Sir Walter Erle, trading with New England.
1627	Sir Walter Yonge records in his diary the building of the Barrow.
1630	Risdon comments that Sir Walter Erle's efforts to repair the haven had some measure of success.
1638	Axmouth collier attacked by Turkish pirates.
1640	Sir William Pole writes the haven is once more a 'ruin'.
1643	Two prize ships taken into Axmouth.
1644	Stedcombe Manor is raised during an attack by the Royalist forces.
1660	John Willoughby (grandson) and Richard Mallock of Stepps commence reclamation of Seaton Marsh.
1679	Sir Walter Yonge acquires Stedcombe and Axmouth from the Erles.
1691	Richard Hallett of Lyme purchases the manor and harbour from Sir Walter Yonge.
1697	Hallett rebuilds Stedcombe House, but dies before occupying the new house. His nephew of the same name inherits the estate and the Barbados plantations.
1700	Local landowners and farmers attempt to reclaim the harbour – possibly the construction of Courd's pier based on the Erle's earlier works – fourth attempt to repair the haven.
1724	Stukely visits Axmouth and states that a stone pier 6 yards wide extends seaward at the entrance, constructed by Courd.
1747	Richard Hallett dies, the estate is inherited by his grandson Richard Hothersall Hallett.
1769	Rev. Francis Drake killed by smugglers at Bosshill Cross – (Tanyards Cross).
1800	The estuary is frequently blocked by shingle – at times held back like a '¾ tide'.
1806	The eminent Swiss geologist and scientist Jean Andre de Luc visits Axmouth and describes the harbour – prior to the building of the pier.
1806	John Hothersall Hallett proposes the construction of a new pier and quay – survey works carried out.
1806	Robert Searle completes the most detailed map to date of the lower Axe Valley, showing the river channel and embankment. Work starts on the construction of the new pier.
1807	The 'Rapids' and remains of Courd's works are cleared to deepen the channel within the harbour. Work commences on the construction of the pier.

The Story of Axmouth Harbour

1809	New pier and quay completed – first vessel of 70 tons enters with cargo of culm (fifth attempt).
1814	Richard Hothersall Hallett dies, John Hothersall Hallett takes over the estate and harbour.
1817	Renowned smuggler Jack Rattenbury sails stricken vessel into the harbour.
1824	The Great Storm – the harbour suffers little damage, unlike the Cobb, although Seaton Marshes are flooded.
1825	The schooner *Stedcombe* is taken by pirates off of Timor, Indonesia.
1826	The *Alexis*, 150 tons, the largest vessel to date to enter the harbour.
1830	8th April, Axmouth Harbour Act – to maintain and govern the harbour.
1838	The British Association for the advancement of Science conduct surveys to calculate mean sea level – Axmouth chosen along with two other ports.
1838	D.M. Stirling records the discovery of what is now known as the 'Axe Boat'.
1852	Capt. Sheringham RN surveys and produces a detailed chart of Axmouth Harbour.
1860	The first known photograph of the harbour showing trading vessels.
1864	At the age of eighty-eight J.H. Hallett dies, the estate is inherited by his nephew William Trelawney Hallett.
1867	The railway is constructed utilising the Willoughby embankment.
1869	Storm destroys the seaward section of the harbour pier.
1877	Axmouth Bridge is completed – a concrete structure, after hundreds of years the ferry ceases.
1879	The old Ship Inn is destroyed by fire.
1889	W.T. Hallett dies, the estate is left in debt to his wife.
1891	The manor and harbour sold to Samuel Sanders Stephens – then known as Stedcombe Estate, ending almost exactly 200 years of the Halletts' ownership.
1915	Storms sweep away the Customs House at the harbour entrance.
1924	Waterside Road replaces the old tidal lane to Axmouth
1931	Large slip occurs at Haven Cliff, just east of the harbour.
1936	Formation of the Seaton Sailing & Motorboat Club, fore runner of the Axe Yacht Club.
1939	Miss Maud Sanders Stephens uses ancient rights given before the Magna Carta to pursue a successful prosecution with regard to infringement of fishing rights within the tidal waters of the harbour, approaches and estuary.
1940	The Axmouth launch *Iolanthe* takes part in the evacuation of Dunkirk.
1940	The estuary is damned in two places as a defensive measure during WW2.
1940	Local fisherman Tom Newton guides a live mine out of harm's way – awarded OBE.
1948	Axe Yacht Club is formed, the SS&MBC continues but is eventually wound up with the membership absorbed into the AYC.
1952	A split in the AYC sees the formation of the Seaton Sailing Club.
1953	The first Axe One Design is launched.
1954	AYC secures a long-term lease from Stedcombe Estate.
1955	Deterioration of the harbour wall temporarily halted by concrete infill at the entrance.
1956	A concrete mooring jetty is built by the AYC downstream of Axmouth Bridge from the western bank.
1959	Maud Sanders Stephens dies ending the feudal ownership of Stedcombe Estate.
1958	Boat building returns to Axmouth – H.J. Mears sets up base above the bridge, having moved from Beer.
1967	The harbour is sold out of the Stedcombe Estate to Axminster RDC.
1967	Harbour wall collapses at the entrance.
1967	The Sub Chaser *Mervic* enters the harbour, at 80' the largest vessel to berth since commercial operations ceased.
1969	The AYC excavates a small mooring basin just south of Axmouth Bridge.

1971	Local government reorganisation sees EDDC acquire Axmouth Harbour.
1978	EDDC completes repairs at the harbour entrance, constructing a short 20m pier. First major repair since 1809 (sixth attempt).
1978	The AYC excavates a second much larger mooring basin south of the first and constructs a short gabion pier to protect the downstream embankment.
1979	Inundation of the harbour caused by an exceptional ground swell generated by an Atlantic storm far out to sea – harbour channel almost blocked by shingle resulting from seas overtopping the spit.
1980	The AYC's old jetty is demolished thus linking the two basins to form one large expanse of protected water.
1985	The Fish quay is built replacing the old crumbling wall – originally Hallett's commercial quay.
1988	Axmouth Harbour Management Company incorporated as lease holder of Axmouth Harbour. The non-profit organisation formed to facilitate the sub leasing of the harbour between the Fishermen's Association and the AYC.
1990	New Axmouth Bridge constructed immediately upstream of the old bridge. Ancient Bronze Age sword found in the river bed (RAMM).
1991	The AYC constructs an interlocking concrete slipway, providing a much-needed facility for both locals and visitors alike.
2000	Harbour pier extension built, projecting a further 20m seaward.
2002	Re-discovery of the 'Axe Boat' – sixteenth-century wreck located 50m upstream from Axmouth Bridge.
2005	The AYC constructs a new club house on the site of the original.
2008	The area of marsh to the north and west of the Willoughby embankment is re-flooded on a controlled basis to form a shallow brackish lagoon for waders and water fowl. It is named Black Hole Marsh from the adjacent River Axe feature originally called Black Pool.
2009	The AYC up-grade berthing by providing pontoon moorings within the basin.
2011	Infill of the lower part of Seaton Marshes for residential development is achieved by pumping dredged spoil in the form of sand transported from the Bristol Channel.
2011	The AYC celebrates seventy-five years of existence.
2012	Exceptional rain causes floods in July with much flooding of the lower estuary.
2013	The Axe One design celebrates its 60th year with a Diamond Jubilee Regatta.
2013	Continuing upgrades see the AYC pile the mooring basin to provide stability for the pontoon moorings.
2014	Exceptional February gales cause flooding – overtopping the Willoughby embankment and inundating Seaton Marshes. Waterside Road sees water lapping across the carriageway.
2019	The Axe estuary is designated a Marine Conservation Zone.
2021	February storms temporarily divert the entrance channel uncovering the foundations of the 1809 pier.
2023	Residential development of 'Seaton Quay' (old railway station) commences.

Axmouth Harbour Masters

Years	Name	Years	Name
1857-1859	Robert Start	1965-1971	Harold Mears
1859-1863	J. Major	1971-2002	East District District Council (no official appointment)
1863-1877	Alfred Bridgett		
1877-1937	Walter Real	2002-2018	Mark Williams EDDC CEO
1947-1950	Arthur Baker	2018-	Peter Bylth EDDC Beach Safety Officer
1950-1964	Charlie Ware		

Appendix ii

Tidal Notes

Local tides

Ordnance Datum is calculated using the mean sea level derived at Newlyn, Cornwall, from which all terrestrial heights are calculated (such as Bench Marks). In relation to this Chart Datum is the datum from which predicted tidal heights and charted depths are based.

Chart Datum approximates to the Lowest Astronomical Tide (LAT), effectively the lowest tide experienced in any locality. This provides the mariner with the least charted depth to be expected when referencing a nautical chart. Chart Datum is calculated for the majority of ports around the coastline, it takes into account local topographical effects that may modify tidal ranges (the difference between HW and LW) from one area to another. The relationship between local Chart Datum and Ordnance Datum is defined for most major ports.

By interpolation Chart Datum at Axmouth Harbour is calculated at 2.37 metres below Ordnance Datum (-2.37 OD).

By applying the height of tide to Chart Datum at any given time, the actual depth of water can be calculated. The following represent the mean tidal heights for Axmouth Harbour in relation to local Chart Datum:-

Tide gauge.

Mean High Water Spring = 4.0 metres - 13ft 02"

Mean Low Water Spring = 0.2 metres - 0ft 08"

Mean High Water Neaps = 2.8 metres - 9ft 02"

Mean Low Water Neaps = 1.2 metres - 3ft 11"

Historically, Axmouth tides have been based on Exmouth Dock. This came about through Exmouth being the nearest port with tidal predictions. Today, interpolated predictions are accessible for a far greater range of ports, with Lyme being the nearest. But over the years, Axmouth tidal observations have compared well with those of Exmouth Dock predictions.

A constant of five minutes needs to be added to Exmouth high water times, whilst forty minutes needs to be subtracted from Exmouth low water times. This is more noticeable during springs, when low water can occur up fifty minutes before Exmouth predictions.

This earlier LW anomaly compares more favourably with Lyme's predicted times, but its tidal ranges are noticeably greater than those observed at Axmouth. A tide gauge has been set up close to Axmouth Bridge which shows the current height of tide and compares well with Exmouth Dock. An old tide gauge exists on the harbour wall, the Roman numerals show the channel depth just below the old warehouse.

The maximum normal predicted tidal range at Axmouth is currently 4.4m. This generally occurs during the equinoctial spring tides (HW 4.4m, LW 0.0m). The minimum predicted tidal range is just 1.0m resulting from very slack neaps tides (HW 2.5m, LW 1.5m).

On rare occasions exceptionally high spring tides may reach a predicted height of 4.5m, equally low water may drop below chart datum to -0.2m, producing a tidal range of 4.7m. Under storm conditions the heights are increased significantly. Fortunately, it is rare that an exceptionally high spring tide coincides with storm force conditions. Under such circumstances one would expect to observe greater levels through a combination of tidal surge (wind driven) and the effect of low atmospheric pressure and in the estuary, heavy rain.

The tidal curve towards the head of Lyme Bay, including Axmouth Harbour becomes modified, especially during spring tides. The tidal cycle from one high water (HW) to the next is a little over twelve hours, more during neaps and less during springs. Rather than equal periods from low water to high water and back to low, the period of flood (rising tide) from low to high water is considerably more than that of the ebb (falling tide) period. Local low water typically occurs five hours after HW, resulting in the flood period taking some seven hours. This should always be taken into account when prawning at Culverhole in order to take advantage of the low water period!

The harbour dries out at low water except for the residual waters of the out-flowing Axe. The area of the mooring basin immediately downstream of the bridge is effectively impounded at low water. This is due to The Rapids acting as form of cill. Therefore, the low water level within the harbour basin is retained at a level of 1.5m above chart datum. On the flood tide, the water level within the harbour starts to rise over The Rapids approximately three and a half hours before local high water. This varies between springs and neaps; on very low neaps the level remains sufficiently high that the harbour on occasions does not fully dry out. It is on these rare occasions that shallow-draughted boats may navigate the harbour throughout the full tidal cycle.

The coastal tidal streams are generally rectilinear, especially close inshore. The east-going stream starts two and a half hours before local high water and continues through to four hours after. At this time the stream turns and sets west through low water until two and half hours before the next high water. This results in the maximum tidal stream strength occurring at or near local high water which produces a strong set to the east across the entrance to the harbour. Slightly further offshore the tidal stream is less defined in that it becomes more rotary; this was demonstrated by Captain Sheringham's observations during his survey of 1852.

Local high-water anomaly

A local tidal effect peculiar to Axmouth is produced during particularly high spring tides, generally those in excess of 4.3 metres. These high spring tides cause a modification of the tidal stream within the harbour and estuary around the period of high water. The flood tide continues to flow into the estuary for as much as forty-five minutes after the time of local predicted high water. The effect is caused by a combination of the harbour entrance constriction and the overflowing of the marshes and water meadows upstream.

Under normal conditions the incoming tidal stream starts to slacken as it approaches the time of high water. There is then a very brief period of slack before it changes and the ebb starts to flow out.

However, during these high spring tides, the tidal height exceeds the level of the inland river banks. The flood tide then flows unconstrained across the saltmarshes and water meadows, inundating Axmouth and Axe Marshes to the east, and Colyford Common to the west.

This anomaly can be observed as the time of predicted HW is approached, rather than slowing, the inward flow starts to increase once more. This is due to the almost unlimited area presented once the tide has risen above the saltmarshes. The inward flow only starts to slow once the sea level outside the estuary has dropped below that of the height of the water meadows. As it drops further, the stream reverses, the ebb tide takes hold and flows out of the estuary.

Storm conditions affecting tides

Southerly and South Easterly storms produce the greatest tidal surge due to the topographical nature of Lyme Bay and more locally Seaton Bay. The surge is funnelled into the bays causing significantly greater tidal heights than predicted. Added to this storm driven swell in the harbour entrance may peak at an additional metre, therefore the effective height may achieve some 6.5m above Chart Datum.

The effects of such conditions combining could be potentially disastrous. Probably the last such instance occurred during the 1824 storm, when many south coast towns and villages were inundated. Locally, even under the severest conditions it is very rare that either the Riverside Road ('Waterside') or the tramline embankment are over-topped (last occurred Feb 2014), although this is not to say that it may happen more frequently in the future, as sea levels rise and climate change takes effect.

LiDAR mapping shows that Waterside is generally +3.5m O.D., with the tramline marginally lower; +3.5m O.D. equates to a tidal height of 5.87m. The 2014 flood occurred with a tide of just 3.6m, which represents a surge of 2.3m. Therefore, in the event of high spring tides coinciding with extreme storm conditions a tidal height of 6.8m is feasible. With rising sea levels set to continue and greater climatic variations predicted, such events may become more prevalent.

Appendix iii

Axmouth Harbour – pilotage

The following Pilotage notes have been compiled by the author for use of the Axe Yacht Club. They are provided through the AYC website as guidance for vessels unfamiliar with the port and local users. They have been included as a reference to present day navigation of Axmouth Harbour. It should be noted, for navigational purposes, the AYC website must be consulted for current, up to date guidance.

Harbour description

This is a small drying harbour situated at the mouth of the River Axe, formed behind a large protecting shingle bank. The harbour provides access to shallow draught yachts and craft at high water under settled conditions. The entrance is located beneath Haven Cliff and is open to the prevailing south westerlies. The harbour approach channel varies in direction due to the shifting shingle bar. The inner entrance is narrow (approx. 10m) and formed between the shingle spit to the west and a short stone/concrete/wooden piled pier to the east. Within the harbour a small yacht basin lies to the west and fisherman's quay to the east. There is a fixed bridge immediately upstream of the basin (1.5m headroom at MHW), the River Axe estuary extends some 2 miles inland and is navigable at high water by small craft. Moderate to strong onshore winds and any significant swell may render the entrance impassable. Such conditions produce dangerous overfalls on the bar and within the entrance channel, aggravated by the strength of the ebb tide.

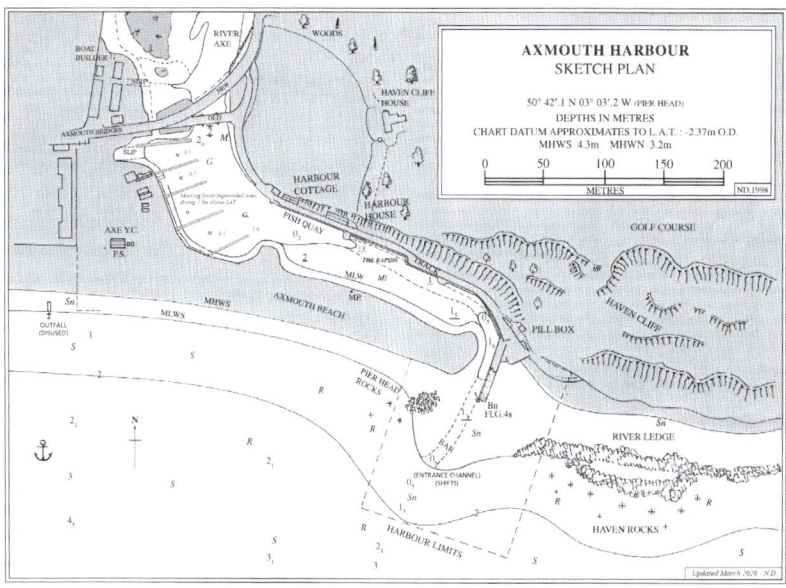

Axmouth Harbour chart. (Nigel Daniel).

The tidal streams run strongly in the entrance, especially during springs or when the river is in spate. The shingle bar is liable to frequent change, altering the direction of the entrance channel. Maintenance of the harbour entrance is totally dependent upon the water volume entering and leaving the estuary. This scouring effect, especially during the ebb flow helps clear shingle from the entrance. The effect is greatest during spring tides and less so during neaps. Similarly, the build-up of the shingle bar is more evident during neap tides due to the decreased flow, spring tides tend to scour the bar and widen the entrance channel.

Each vessel will have its own capabilities and limitations which need to be carefully considered in conjunction with these notes to ensure safe navigation. A prudent navigator will have taken into account all prevailing conditions to assess the safe execution of his intended passage before proceeding to sea.

Axmouth Harbour: pilotage notes – approaching from seaward

- Approach – The approach should be made only in daylight and in settled conditions. The entrance can be dangerous in anything more than a moderate onshore wind without local knowledge. Due to the strength of the tidal streams in the entrance, entry should be made within half an hour either side of local high water, so as to gain slack water. The entrance is located beneath Haven Cliff at the eastern extremity of Seaton Bay. There are no offshore dangers in the approach other than the shingle bar. At low water the old pier head rocks uncover approximately 20 metres to the west of the entrance and the River Ledge rocks uncover 30 metres to the east. It is advised that prior inspection of the approaches is made at low water to confirm the position of the bar and navigability of the entrance channel.

- Tides – Local tidal predictions (heights) are based on Exmouth Dock. HW Axmouth Harbour occurs five minutes after Exmouth Dock.

The harbour entrance taken under particularly favourable conditions; the entrance can be narrower.

- Tidal streams off the entrance and the adjacent coastline are rectilinear and generally weak, attaining 1.5 knots during springs and one knot during neaps. The east-going stream starts approximately four hours before HW Exmouth Dock, until two hours after, at which time it eases and turns to the west until two hours after local LW. Conversely the tidal streams in the entrance run strongly, requiring great caution.

    - Tidal streams in the entrance are usually stronger during the ebb, attaining 6 knots during springs, and increase considerably more after heavy rain, which can also greatly affect the strength of the neap ebb tide.
    - The flood tide can attain speeds of 5 knots. For this reason, it is necessary to enter as near to local high water as possible.
    - The ebb flow from the harbour entrance sets up overfalls on the bar and immediately seaward of it; this occurs from approximately one hour after HW through to LW.

- Anchorage – In settled conditions it is possible to anchor due south of the AYC club house (white building with grey slate roof and white mast) in approximately 5m of water, with a sand bottom and reasonably good holding. Avoid the old pier head rocks between the anchorage and the entrance. A more sheltered anchorage can be found off the village of Beer, although remains open to the South and East. Due to poor holding and limited room, there is no anchorage within the harbour.

- Approach and Entrance Channel – The entrance channel usually runs from the pier head in a SW'ly direction (but as stated is liable to change) with shingle drying each side extending approximately 75m. (LAT) seaward. The approximate line of approach is when the 'pillbox', situated beneath the cliff, is in transit with the pier head, providing a NE'ly heading. On making the approach due allowance should be made for the east going coastal tidal stream, setting a vessel to starboard at the time of local high water.

- In the close approach to the pier head beacon avoid being set onto the wall, aim to keep mid channel between the wall and shingle spit.

- Once inside the entrance there is a sharp turn to the west, following the line of the harbour wall. The AYC mooring basin with pontoons is situated just below the fixed bridge to port. Fishing vessels berth to starboard against the quay. The AYC landing pontoon is located to port immediately south of the bridge where a temporary berth can be found; but take care to avoid being swept onto the bridge. All berths in the harbour dry out.

- Depths – MHWS depths within the entrance channel are 3.3m decreasing to 2.5m within the harbour and 2.8m to 1.6m MHWN respectively. The shingle bar and entrance dry to 0.5m, shallowing further within the harbour. The mooring basin dries 1.5m, although there is approximately 0.3m impounded in the mooring basin at low water.

- Lights – A green beacon with a cone top mark and light is situated at the seaward end of the pier. The beacon displays a flashing green light every four seconds, at a height of 8 metres with a range of 2 miles – (Fl.G.4s.8m.2M) – 50°42.13'N 003°03.29'W.

Glossary of terms

Approaches	The area immediately offshore from the harbour entrance
Tidal Prism	The volume of water entering and leaving the estuary between high and low water
Flood tide	Incoming tide
Ebb tide	Outgoing tide
Neap tides	Lower than average tides
Spring tides	Higher than average tides
MHW	Mean High Water
MHWN	Mean High Water Neaps
MHWS	Mean High Water Springs
MLWN	Mean Low Water Neaps
MLWS	Mean Low Water Springs
Tidal Stream	The cyclical movement of water directly related to the times of high and low water
Spate	Outgoing tide enhanced by heavy rain – greatly accelerating the flow
Overfalls	Breaking waves caused by the tidal stream running against the wind/swell

References

Domesday Book – 1086
Leland's itinerary of c.1542
William Camden – antiquarian – 16c
Sir William Pole – *History of Devon* 16c
Sir Walter Yonge, diarist – local account – 1627
Tristram Risdon – *A Survey of Devonshire* – 1714
William Stukeley – *"Itinerarium Curiosum,"* published in 1724
Jean Andre du Luc – *Geological Travels*, Volume 3 - 1806 – translated 1811
Rev. Dr George Oliver – *Devon Monasteries* – 1820
Axmouth Harbour Act – 1830
British Association for the Advancement of Science – 1836
D.M. Stirling – *Guide to the Coast of South East Devon* – 1838
Peter Orlando Hutchinson – Sidmouth diarist and antiquarian – 1870s
T.C.Paris – *Handbook for Travellers in Devon* – 1863
G.P.R. Pulman – *Ramblings, Roaming & Recollections* – 1863
Francis Trevelyan Buckland – Logbook of a Fisherman and Zoologist – 1868
William Rogers – *Wanderings in Devon* – 1869
Francis Kilvert – *Kilvert's Diaries* 1871 – (reproduced by David Lockwood – *Kilvert, the Victorian*, 1994)
George P.R. Pulman – Pulman's *Book of the Axe* – 1875
Admiralty Sailing Directions – *Channel Pilot* – 1878
Francis Bickley – *Where Dorset meets Devon* – 1911
The Devon & Exeter Gazette April edition of 1931 – Report of Haven Cliff slip
Rev. O. J. Reichel – *Hundreds of Devon* – 1931
Western Morning News – Account of fisherman Tom Newton's bravery – 1941

Lieut. Col. J. V. Ramsden, Geologist – 'Axmouth Haven' – *Transactions of the Devon Association* – 1945
Axe Yacht Club – Archives – dating from 1951
Donald Payne/Vernon Boyle – *Devon's Harbours* – 1952. Publishers Christopher Johnson
J.W.R. Coxhead – 'East Devon's Lost Harbour' – *Transactions of the Devonshire Association* – 1974
Posford Duvivier Civil Engineers (formerly Lewis & Duvivier), Axmouth Harbour improvements – 1977
Margaret Parkinson – 'Axe Estuary & its Marshes' – *Transactions of the Devonshire Association* – 1985
Shiela Bird – *Seaton, Axmouth & Beer* Companion – 1988
Nigel Tattersfield – *The Forgotten Trade* – 1991
Maryanne Kowaleski – contributor to – *The New Maritime History of Devon* Vol 1 – 1992
Jon Adams & Kitty Brandon, Southampton University – *Axe Boat* – 2003
Fergus Cannan – 'Rediscovering a Medieval Mural in the Church of St Michael, Axmouth' – *Devon Archaeological Society Proceedings* – 2007
Winchester University – 2008, *Axe Estuary Wetlands – Geoarchaeological Survey* – Report No. 0708-14
Scopac: Standing Conference On Problems Associated with Coastlines Sediment Transport Study (*Beer Head to Lyme Regis*) – 2012
Devon Heritage Centre – various references, especially those relating to the Stedcombe Estate records
British Library – 2014, Robert Searle's 1806 map of S.E. Devon
National Library of Scotland – Nineteenth Century. OS maps